UNIVERSITY OF
CHESTER

Developmental Psychology in Action

This publication forms part of an Open University course ED209 *Child Development*. Details of this and other Open University courses can be obtained from the Student Registration and Enquiry Service, The Open University, PO Box 197, Milton Keynes, MK7 6BJ, United Kingdom: tel. +44 (0)870 333 4340, email general-enquiries@open.ac.uk

Alternatively, you may visit the Open University website at http://www.open.ac.uk where you can learn more about the wide range of courses and packs offered at all levels by The Open University.

To purchase a selection of Open University course materials visit http://www.ouw.co.uk, or contact Open University Worldwide, Michael Young Building, Walton Hall, Milton Keynes MK7 6AA, United Kingdom for a brochure. tel. +44 (0)1908 858785; fax +44 (0)1908 858787; email ouwenq@open.ac.uk

Developmental Psychology in Action

Clare Wood, Karen Littleton and
Kieron Sheehy

First published 2006 by Blackwell Publishing Ltd in association with The Open University

The Open University
Walton Hall, Milton Keynes
MK7 6AA

Blackwell Publishing Ltd:

350 Main Street, Malden, MA 02148-5020, USA
9600 Garsington Road, Oxford OX4 2DQ, UK
550 Swanston Street, Carlton, Victoria 3053, Australia

For further information on Blackwell Publishing please visit our website:
www.blackwellpublishing.com

Library of Congress Cataloguing in Publication Data has been applied for.
A catalogue record for this title is available from the British Library.

Edited, designed and typeset by The Open University.

Printed and bound in the United Kingdom by The Alden Group, Oxford.

ISBN 13: 978-1-4051-1695-4 (paperback)

ISBN 10: 1-4051-1695-1 (paperback)
1.1

Contents

Foreword 6

Introduction: developmental psychology in action 7
CLARE WOOD, KAREN LITTLETON AND KIERON SHEEHY

1 Understanding specific learning difficulties 9
CLARE WOOD, KIERON SHEEHY AND TERRI PASSENGER

2 Children and the legal system 53
HELEN WESTCOTT

3 Health psychology: children and development 99
TONY CASSIDY

4 Autism and developmental psychology 143
ANDREW GRAYSON

5 Psychology and education: understanding teaching
and learning 193
KAREN LITTLETON AND CLARE WOOD

Acknowledgements 230

Name index 232

Subject index 235

Foreword

We would like to acknowledge the significant contributions made by the many people involved in the production of this book.

First we would like to thank our editors, Julia Brennan, Bridgette Jones and Margaret Mellor, and the proofreader, Shereen Karmali. Their careful reading of the chapters and thoughtful comments regarding the development of the book have undoubtedly had a positive impact on its clarity and readability.

It was a privilege collaborating with our consultant authors and we have welcomed their flexibility in working with us to produce what we hope is interesting and effective learning material. We would also like to thank the critical readers Dr Koula Asimakopoulou, Professor Graham Davies, and Dr Alyson Davis for their constructive criticism of drafts.

Our academic colleagues Peter Barnes, Alan Carr, Tony Cassidy, Sharon Ding, Andrew Grayson, John Oates, Terri Passenger, Helen Westcott and Rob White deserve thanks for their contributions and for diligently commenting on drafts and revisions. We also wish to acknowledge the important contributions made by the book designers Sian Lewis and Jonathan Davies, the illustrators, Janis Gilbert, Victoria Eves and Jon Owen and the compositor Nikki Tolcher.

Finally, we would very much like to thank Iris Rowbotham and Maria Francis-Pitfield for their supportive management of this project and Stephanie Withers for her excellent secretarial support.

Clare Wood

Karen Littleton

Kieron Sheehy

Introduction: developmental psychology in action

Clare Wood, Karen Littleton and Kieron Sheehy

Developmental Psychology in Action looks at how psychologists contribute to the development and well-being of children in practical ways. The role of psychologists and psychological theory is considered with respect to specific topics which focus on child development in the context of social, educational and clinical issues. A recurring theme in the chapters concerns the role of psychologists as 'agents' of society who intervene to improve children's lives. Through their research and practice psychologists are also implicated in the construction of particular accounts and representations of the child and notions of competence. The chapters thus demonstrate that developmental psychologists do not exist in isolation from the social contexts that they study and that it is in these contexts that they actively create their subject.

Chapter 1 considers two specific learning difficulties (SpLD), dyslexia and dyspraxia, and begins with an exploration of what may cause them. Recognizing that 'cultural expectations regarding what are "fundamental" abilities play a role in determining a specific learning difficulty' (Chapter 1, Section 2.2), the focus of the chapter then shifts to the often contentious practices and processes of assessment. This concerns how some children come to be identified as experiencing either dyslexia or dyspraxia and the ways in which psychologists are involved in these processes. As the chapter makes clear, assessment is not just about identifying whether or not a child has a condition; it is about 'discovering the exact nature of the problems experienced by the child, thereby indicating ways in which he or she can be supported at home, school and elsewhere' (Chapter 1, Section 4). The consequences of living with an SpLD are thus highlighted, as are examples of intervention programmes designed to improve the attainment of people with SpLDs. While considering how research into the consequences of SpLD informs approaches to intervention, the chapter also stresses the importance of 'the need not to lose sight of the children as individuals with different experiences of what it is like to have an SpLD, which demand individualized as well as generic forms of support' (Chapter 1, Section 7).

The second chapter in the book presents an overview of children's involvement in the legal system and focuses on their competency as witnesses and culpability as offenders. The issue of children as witnesses is examined in some detail and it is in this context that research surrounding questioning techniques and children's understanding of truth and lies is considered. The discussion then moves on to consider children's culpability and whether they can be assumed to have criminal intent. Psychological theories of moral development and children's use of deception are also considered as part of this debate. Two underlying themes pervade the chapter: 'are children accurate and are children honest when they give evidence, either as witnesses or as defendants?' (Chapter 2,

Section 5.1). The research presented makes it clear that there are no simple answers to this question. Rather, the chapter highlights the inextricable interrelationships between children, adults and society, recognizing that 'children's performance in the legal system is a reflection of these complex relationships' (Chapter 2, Section 5.3). The chapter emphasizes the importance of not taking children 'out of context' and asserts that 'it is the responsibility of psychologists not to "theorize incompetent children" .... by contributing to legal or research environments which undermine their competence or compound their culpability' (Chapter 2, Section 5.3).

In Chapter 3, ways in which psychological research and theories have been used to promote healthy behaviours in children and support children with illness are discussed. The chapter also considers how health psychology relates to 'children at the level of the communities and cultures that they live in' and 'children as individuals and their experiences of illness and treatment' (Chapter 3, Section 1). The chapter suggests that while still a relatively new field of enquiry, health psychology 'offers the potential for a multilevel analysis of childhood health and illness, based on a conceptualization of child development that encompasses cultural, social and biological aspects' (Chapter 3, Section 8). The need for interdisciplinary research is also emphasized.

Chapter 4 addresses the topic of autism and developmental psychology. The opening sections present 'a view of autism constructed out of the first-hand accounts of people with autism (an account of autism "from the inside out")' and a 'description of autism from the point of view of non-autistic researchers and clinicians – a third-party perspective which has been constructed by "looking in" on autism, from the outside' (Chapter 4, Section 3). The chapter does not privilege one set of perspectives over another. Rather, it highlights the necessity of both insider and outsider accounts, if a 'grounded account of autism is to be achieved' (Chapter 4, Section 3.6). The chapter goes on to compare and contrast different psychological approaches to understanding autism and highlights how the theories and discourses developed by psychologists create particular views of autism. These views influence how research into autism is pursued and the image of autism projected in society as a whole.

The final chapter is concerned with 'the contributions that psychology and psychologists have made to the field of children's education; specifically, what psychological theory and research have to say about the nature of teaching and learning' (Chapter 5, Section 1). The chapter introduces three key theoretical traditions in the psychology of education that have influenced approaches to teaching and learning, both within the classroom and outside it: behaviourism, constructivism and socio-cultural approaches. Through discussing the details of theoretically informed educational interventions, the chapter illustrates how developmental theories and research shape the environments in which children develop and learn. It thereby echoes a recurrent theme in the book, highlighting the ways in which psychologists participate in the construction of contemporary reality.

Chapter 1
Understanding specific learning difficulties

Clare Wood, Kieron Sheehy and Terri Passenger

Contents

	Learning outcomes	11
1	Introduction	11
2	Specific learning difficulties	12
	2.1 Why '*specific* learning difficulties'?	12
	2.2 Two specific learning difficulties	12
3	The biological bases of SpLDs	18
	3.1 Comorbidity	19
	3.2 Heritability	19
	3.3 A neuropsychological explanation	20
4	Assessment	23
	4.1 Assessing dyslexia	24
	4.2 Assessing dyspraxia	31
5	Consequences	34
	5.1 Social exclusion	35
	5.2 Self-esteem	37
	5.3 Depression	38
	5.4 Academic achievement and motivation	39
6	Intervention	42
	6.1 What is targeted?	42
	6.2 When to intervene?	43
	6.3 School-based intervention strategies	44
7	Conclusion	48
	References	48

Learning outcomes

After you have studied this chapter you should be able to:

1 describe the nature of specific learning difficulties;
2 discuss the notion of comorbidity in relation to specific learning difficulties;
3 discuss issues relating to the assessment of specific learning difficulties;
4 discuss the consequences of experiencing a specific learning difficulty;
5 evaluate approaches to intervention.

1 Introduction

As a child I was slow to learn left from right and was easily confused by verbal instructions. I was, and still am, easily disorientated when I am out and about: I might walk one way up a street, but when I turn around to walk back, I see a completely different street and it is often years before I can instinctively recognize a street from any direction.

At school I was capable but slow. I hated reading and I despised reading aloud, usually totally misreading the text to the point where I seemed to be reading a different book. My initial attempts at writing were problematic – I wrote my letters and even complete words back to front. My handwriting was poor and it took me forever to write something down. Something I started on a Monday might not get finished until Tuesday. Rather than teachers picking up on my problems, I was punished for my shortcomings. One teacher put blackboard after blackboard of text up for us to copy down. I couldn't keep up. I was forever glancing at the board, not being able to remember more than a couple of words before forgetting what came next. Because of my inability to keep up, I was denied playtime, my lunch and made to stay late after school. I was separated from my classmates and made to sit at a table by myself in the hope I would work faster. Eventually, I was made to stand at the teacher's desk. During the time that person was my teacher I went home on time once.

(Simon, aged 34)

Most people can think of something that they cannot do well. In most cases the skill is unlikely to be something essential. For example, it may be some recreational activity, or something that computers, tools, or other people can do instead.

However, some people are unable to learn a basic skill that they need in order to gain employment or to function successfully at school, at work or in society. While they are competent in all other respects, they show a specific inability to acquire a fundamental skill, such as reading, writing, understanding basic mathematical concepts, co-ordinating their physical movements, controlling their attention or understanding subtle social and linguistic cues. These people experience a specific learning difficulty (SpLD). Simon experiences a specific learning difficulty in learning to read and write, known more commonly as dyslexia.

In this chapter you will read about two specific learning difficulties, dyslexia and dyspraxia, and consider what may cause them. The chapter discusses how such difficulties are identified, how psychologists are involved in this process, and some of the consequences of living with SpLDs. Finally, you will examine some intervention programmes designed to improve the attainment of people with SpLDs.

2   Specific learning difficulties

2.1 Why 'specific learning difficulties'?

Intelligence quotient (IQ)
This originally referred to the ratio of mental age to chronological age (multiplied by 100). It now represents a person's performance on a range of standardized tasks (intended to assess the full extent of cognitive skills and ability) relative to that of other people of the same age and background. A score of 100 is the mean score for any given age group, with a standard deviation of 15.

There is an important distinction to be made between people who experience SpLDs and 'learning difficulties' more generally. In the UK, learning difficulties (LDs) is a term used by psychologists to refer to general difficulties in acquiring new skills and knowledge, indicated by an intelligence quotient (IQ) of less than 70. That is, some professionals interpret IQ as indicative of not just a person's general cognitive ability, but also of a person's *potential* to learn. Therefore, a person with a low IQ will be seen as having a low learning potential and will be assessed as having learning difficulties, which might be 'mild', 'moderate' or 'severe'. Moreover, low scores will be apparent across the majority of the tasks in the IQ assessment battery. This contrasts with the term 'specific learning difficulties' where an IQ assessment will indicate a *variable profile* of ability, with good to high scores on many skills, but marked deficits in others. These deficits are treated as indicative of a specific difficulty, although the nature of the difficulties that accompany the main area of deficit can and does vary among individuals who have the same form of SpLD.

2.2 Two specific learning difficulties

This section will introduce two different forms of SpLD: dyslexia and dyspraxia. However, a range of other conditions are sometimes referred to as SpLDs because of the impact that their symptoms can have on educational attainment (see Figure 1).

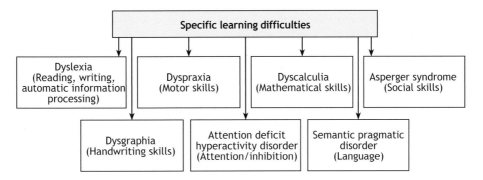

Figure 1   The range of conditions that has been associated with the term 'specific learning difficulties'.

Some people question whether 'recognized' specific learning difficulties are really any different from a specific difficulty in, say, singing in tune. Cultural expectations regarding what are 'fundamental' abilities play a role in determining a specific learning difficulty. For example, it is debatable whether the syndrome referred to as dyslexia (because of its impact on reading and writing) would have been identified if we lived in a non-literate society. Similarly, there has been resistance to seeing dyspraxia as problematic because clumsiness is more 'acceptable' than being unable to read or write, for example. However, the one thing that all the recognized specific deficits have in common is that they underpin a range of other skills, and so their impact is multiplied many times. This characteristic is not apparent in a specific deficit, say, in singing in tune.

Dyslexia

Dyslexia refers to a specific difficulty in learning to read and write. However, this is not the only difficulty that children with dyslexia experience (see Box 1) and there is variation in their symptoms.

The problems with written language appear to stem from more fundamental difficulties in rapid processing and sequencing of phonological information (speech sounds) in short-term memory (Mody *et al.*, 1997; Wolf and Bowers, 1999). Linked to this are difficulties in 'automatizing' behaviours, that is, learning a behaviour sufficiently well that it does not require conscious attention to perform it (Nicholson and Fawcett, 2001). Children with dyslexia also typically have particular difficulties with learning associations between verbal and visual information, such as the sounds associated with the letters of the alphabet. Because of the problems in rapid processing, sequencing and processing verbal information, mental arithmetic is also often difficult. Directional confusions are also common; children with dyslexia often have difficulty remembering left from right, and in co-ordinating their movements (Selikowitz, 1998). Some visual perception difficulties are also linked to the condition, such as unstable eye control during reading (Stein *et al.*, 2001).

Key behavioural characteristics of dyslexia

- A delay in learning to read
- Difficulty generating written language
- Poor spelling
- Poor short-term memory
- A delay or deficit in understanding letter–sound correspondences
- Some initial difficulty in recognizing rhyme
- Poor mental arithmetic
- Difficulty in learning labels (for example, names for new objects)
- Difficulty in naming objects and word finding
- Difficulty in learning sequences (such as the months of the year, the order of a sequence of tasks)
- Slowness in learning text or verbal information

Dyslexia is relatively common, with an estimated prevalence of between 5 and 10 per cent (Miles and Miles, 1999). Although the condition was first identified in 1896 and theories about its causes were proposed early in the twentieth century, it was not until the 1960s and 1970s that the first systematic attempts to investigate the condition began to emerge. Although historically more boys than girls have been identified as having dyslexia, to the ratio of around one girl to every four boys (Rutter and Yule, 1976), recent evidence suggests that dyslexia affects boys and girls equally (Everatt and Zabell, 2000).

Throughout the 1970s and 1980s there was a view that dyslexia was a label used by middle-class parents to excuse poor educational attainment or laziness in their children. This was largely due to the way that dyslexia was defined during this period. Early definitions were 'by exclusion', meaning that dyslexia was applied to any child who had reading difficulties that could not be attributed to any other 'reasonable cause' such as low intelligence, hearing difficulties, poor school attendance or behavioural difficulties. Such definitions said little about what dyslexia actually was and were problematic because they made assumptions about dyslexia being independent of other types of difficulty. For example, there is no logical reason why it might not co-occur with behavioural difficulties. Similarly, low intelligence is not a barrier to learning to read (Regan and Woods, 2000) and would therefore not explain why such a child might experience reading difficulties.

Contemporary definitions combine a discrepancy approach with evidence of positive indicators (reference to actual symptoms) of dyslexia. So-called 'discrepancy definitions' refer to a discrepancy between what a child might be *expected* to be able to read and write (given his or her age and performance on an IQ assessment) and what he or she actually *can* read and write. This discrepancy approach forms a key part of how dyslexia is identified by educational psychologists, but it is controversial and open to criticism, as you will see in Section 3. The British Dyslexia Association definition is widely recognized because, while still flagging the unexpected nature of dyslexia, it focuses on positive indicators which indicate the full range of dyslexic difficulties:

Dyslexia is best described as a combination of abilities and difficulties that affect the learning process in one or more of reading, spelling, writing. Accompanying weaknesses may be identified in speed of processing, short term memory, sequencing and organisation, auditory and/or visual perception, spoken language and motor skills. It is particularly related to mastering and using written language, which may include alphabetic, numeric and musical notation. ... Dyslexia can occur despite normal intellectual ability and teaching. It is independent of socio-economic or language background.

(Peer, 2002, p. 67)

This definition still suggests that any difficulties are unexpected (in the sense that they cannot be attributed to other factors which might offer a reasonable explanation).

Dyspraxia

Dyspraxia is used to describe the symptoms of people who experience problems in organizing their movements, and who also have problems with thought, perception and language (see Box 2). Formal definitions emphasize that attainment in fine and gross motor skills should be substantially below what might be expected given the chronological age and cognitive abilities of the person, and that those difficulties should interfere with daily activities. Dyspraxia is also known as developmental co-ordination disorder (DCD), the term that is increasingly used by researchers in the area both in the United Kingdom and especially abroad. As with dyslexia, people with dyspraxia experience a great variation in symptoms. Dyspraxia is estimated to affect 8 to 10 per cent of the population and males are more likely to be identified with the condition than females, to the ratio 4:1 (Kirby, 1999).

BOX 2

Key behavioural characteristics of dyspraxia

- Difficulty in producing co-ordinated, fluent action
- Poor sense of balance
- Difficulty in knowing what to do and judging what kind of response is acceptable
- Difficulty in retaining more than one piece of information, or sequences of information
- Weak muscle tone, impacting on the execution of movement patterns
- Poor body awareness (knowing where the body parts are in relation to one another)
- Poor kinaesthetic awareness (knowing where the body is in space), which affects spatial judgements – how far and in what direction
- Tendency to use the hand on its own side of the body only
- No clear preference for using one side of the body over the other
- Directional confusion (for example, reversal of letters and difficulty in asymmetrical movements such as tying laces).

Source: based on Macintyre, 2001, pp. 13–14.

At first, it can be hard to imagine how dyspraxia might impact on a child's academic attainment, given that it is primarily a condition that affects movement. Box 3 illustrates the way that it can affect a child in school.

BOX 3

Jack

Picture Jack, aged 9, coming into school on a wet day. The normal routine of waiting outside has been disrupted by bad weather and the cloakroom is noisy with children bustling around divesting themselves of a multitude of anoraks and wellies. Jack must find his own peg, but today it has disappeared beneath a pile of coats. He doesn't want to ask for help or he might be teased and the noise is confusing him even further.

Then, he must get out of his wellies and put on his trainers. While he tries to do this, his boots get kicked out of the way. Really agitated now, he chases after them in his socks which get soaked and so won't slip into his trainers. The struggle to get them on means that he has to balance on one foot and cross his hands over the midline of his body. This is impossibly difficult and he has to give up.

After that, lunch boxes have to be placed in the correct place – where's that again? – and notes from Mum have to be retrieved from his schoolbag and taken to the classroom. This means he must undo his schoolbag and because he clutches the bag tightly to his chest, all his books spill out onto the wet floor. Jack knows this will be discovered and he cries and so desperately wants to go home. The other children laugh and his books join the kicking game.

When Jack does get to the classroom, he discovers he hasn't left his coat in the cloakroom and he is sent back. By this time he is so unhappy that he is not sure whether the cloakroom is round that corner or the next one. He sits down for a rest and watches the infant children coming in, loses track of time and when the teacher sends someone to find him, he knows he will be scolded again – even though he's not sure why.

Source: Macintyre, 2001, pp. 9–10.

A more obvious source of academic difficulty for children with dyspraxia is the requirement to hand-write almost every piece of schoolwork; difficulties in co-ordination and planning mean that written work can be problematic.

Activity 1

Allow about 5 minutes

Visual feedback in handwriting

This activity will help you understand the importance of visual feedback during writing.

Write your name on a piece of paper using the hand you do not normally write with. Next, close your eyes and write your name, once again using the hand you do not normally use, keeping your eyes shut all the time. Compare the two attempts – what do you notice? What does this tell you about the role of constant visual feedback while writing?

Comment

When you wrote the letters with your eyes closed it is likely that your writing was severely affected. It might have drifted up or down the page; you may have written your letters too far apart or too close together. The spaces between the words may be irregular or the letters poorly formed. Writing with your opposite hand is something that you rarely do and it is therefore less 'automatic' – like the writing of a child who is still at primary school. It requires more conscious attention than normal writing, and you need visual feedback to monitor your performance during the task.

However, for children with dyspraxia, keeping their eyes open or closed seems to make no difference to the quality of their writing. It seems that part of their problem is that they do not use visual feedback to control the movement of their hand during writing. Figure 2 shows what happens when you ask a child with dyspraxia to write with their eyes open and closed.

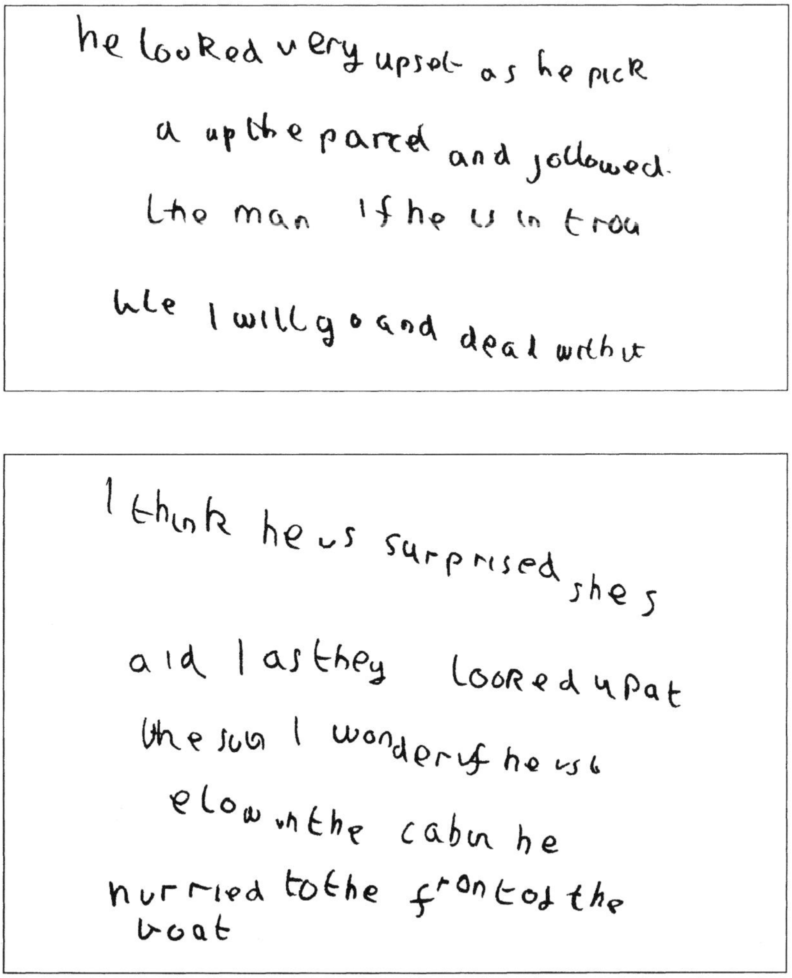

(a)

(b)

Figure 2   The handwriting of a child with dyspraxia (a) with eyes open and (b) with eyes closed (Portwood 1999, p. 156).

Research into dyspraxia really only began to develop during the 1990s. While the difficulties associated with dyspraxia are increasingly recognized, there is a lack of research into the best way of supporting children who show early signs of co-ordination difficulties, and intervention is often not attempted until the children reach school age.

Summary of Section 2

- 'Specific learning difficulties' refers to a range of conditions which are seen when a person experiences a specific difficulty in learning a fundamental skill.
- Dyslexia is an unexpected difficulty in learning to read and write, although difficulties in automatization of behaviour and information processing are apparent in other areas.
- Dyspraxia is an unexpected difficulty in balance, spatial and kinaesthetic awareness, and in planning and perceiving movement. Difficulties with language and social skills are also apparent.

3   The biological bases of SpLDs

In this section you will consider what is known about the biological bases of SpLDs. Before you engage in this discussion, however, you should first consider the idea of comorbidity, the presence of two different conditions simultaneously in the same person.

Activity 2

Allow about 10 minutes

Overlapping symptoms

This activity highlights the high degree of overlap that can be found between any two specific learning difficulties.

Review the material in Section 1, and make notes on any similarities that you notice in the accounts of dyslexia and dyspraxia.

Comment

You should notice that in both conditions boys tend to be over-represented (although, as has been hinted at already, this is a contentious point, for further discussion later in this chapter). Memory deficits are also apparent in both conditions, as are difficulties in organization and sequencing, albeit in different ways. Both groups are affected by difficulties in motor co-ordination, although to different degrees.

3.1 Comorbidity

Where two different conditions are present in one person, psychologists talk about the conditions being comorbid. As indicated by the results of Activity 2, there is considerable overlap in the symptoms associated with dyslexia and dyspraxia. In fact, there is significant co-occurrence of several different types of specific learning difficulty. For example, Kaplan *et al.* (2001) found that children with reading difficulties had a 51.6 per cent chance of having at least one other developmental difficulty.

One interpretation of this overlap is that all these conditions may have a common cause. If this is the case, then it is misleading to talk about 'comorbidity', because this term assumes that the co-occurring disorders have different causes. Kaplan *et al.* (2001) argue that most developmental disorders may be manifestations of atypical brain development (ABD). It is suggested that as the brain develops anomalies occur that result in different specific cognitive and behavioural difficulties. However, it is also possible that two people with a disorder of the same area of the brain may experience very different symptoms because of the environmental factors that can impact on development. As a consequence, it is difficult to identify a single biological cause that can 'explain' specific learning difficulties, either as a group or as individual conditions. What psychologists have been able to do is to explore a range of factors that appear to contribute in relatively small ways to our understanding of what causes an SpLD.

3.2 Heritability

There is evidence that there may be a genetic component to SpLDs. Dyslexia and dyspraxia appear to have a 'familial' form where the parents, siblings and children of people with these conditions also experience the same difficulties, or another form of SpLD. The extent of genetic inheritance can be estimated using twin studies. In such studies, identical (monozygotic) and non-identical (dizygotic) twins are assessed to see how often both siblings experience the same condition. Identical twins share 100 per cent of their genes and dizygotic twins share 50 per cent; consequently it is possible to infer the degree of genetic 'risk' by such comparisons. It is informative to look at the degree of heritability for specific aspects of a disability, rather than for the condition as a whole, since it appears that some aspects of a syndrome are more 'heritable' than others. For example, twin studies of reading difficulties suggest that the phonological difficulties associated with dyslexia are strongly genetically influenced, with the degree of heritability being between 46 and 74 per cent (Stevenson, 1999).

In terms of which gene or genes contribute, the picture is complex and associations between conditions and specific genes are difficult to replicate. However, some research into reading ability suggests that genes on one chromosome appear to be associated with phonological processing, and genes on another chromosome are associated with a general difficulty in word reading (Grigorenko *et al.*, 1997). Few genetic studies have been conducted into dyspraxia to date.

Other evidence in support of a genetic component to SpLDs such as dyspraxia comes from recurring evidence that more boys than girls are identified as having them. This suggests that there may be an association between SpLDs and the chromosomes that distinguish girls and boys. For example, in colour-blindness (another condition where more males are affected than females), the explanation has been found to lie in genes on the X chromosome. Most females have two X chromosomes (one inherited from each parent) while most males have an XY combination. If someone inherits an X-linked gene predisposing them to a particular condition, compensation for this will be more possible for a female than for a male, because her other X chromosome may have a 'normal' copy of the gene. However, as yet no X-linked genes have been identified in connection with SpLDs. What the evidence does suggest is that females may need a higher 'genetic loading' (in other words, a stronger 'family history') than males for these conditions to be expressed. Some protective factors therefore may be operating in females but we do not yet know what these are. It has also been suggested that boys are more likely to exhibit bad behaviour as a consequence of their SpLDs than girls, and, as a result, girls with SpLDs may go unnoticed. While it is unlikely that such an account can fully explain the apparent sex bias in SpLDs, it is likely that it may contribute to some extent.

The genetic explanation is not a complete account of what 'causes' SpLDs. If it were, then identical twins would expect to experience the same SpLD as each other 100 per cent of the time. Twin studies show that they do not, meaning that other factors must play a role in 'causing' the conditions, or in preventing them from developing. Moreover, Stevenson (1999) argues that SpLDs 'are produced not by the effects of single major genes but rather by the joint action of a number of genes and environmental influences' (p. 163). Research is therefore concerned with identifying the *range* of genes involved in each SpLD, how they interact with each other and with environmental influences, and how they impact on aspects of neurological development.

3.3 A neuropsychological explanation

Children with SpLDs show different neurological patterns from those of typically developing children (Grigorenko, 2001). There is evidence that the cerebellum may be implicated in many forms of SpLD (see Figure 3). The cerebellum is involved in a range of cognitive functions, including language, memory, attention, visuo-spatial awareness, sensorimotor tasks and emotional functioning (Fabbro, 2000). These areas map onto the various forms of SpLD outlined in Section 2 and underpin many of the characteristic deficits associated with them. The cerebellum includes 50 per cent of the brain's neurons and takes a long time to develop fully (much of its development being postnatal). This prolonged period of maturation means that it is more vulnerable to developing abnormalities than other areas of the brain that mature more quickly.

Current research into the causes of SpLDs suggests that children with dyslexia and dyspraxia show signs of atypical cerebellar structure and/or functioning compared to that of control groups. In typical readers, the amount of grey matter on the right side is greater than on the left. In the case of dyslexia, Rae *et al.* (2002) found that adults with dyslexia showed cerebellar symmetry, and that the degree of symmetry was correlated with phonological decoding ability – that is, participants with more symmetrical cerebella were worse on a non-word reading task. Lundy-Ekman *et al.* (1991) suggest that many children with dyspraxia also experience difficulties that are associated with cerebellar disorder. Tests of cerebellar functioning, such as balance and motor co-ordination (see Figure 4) have also been found to discriminate between children with dyslexia and children whose reading ability is consistent with their IQ (Fawcett *et al.*, 2001).

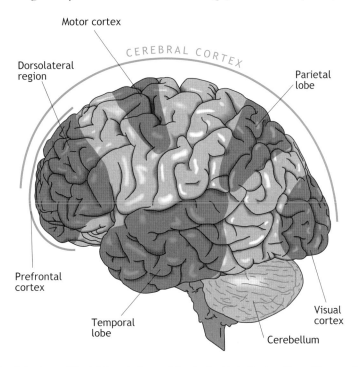

Figure 3   Side view of the left hemisphere of the brain. Note the location of the cerebellum.

It is worth reflecting on whether the differences in neurological profiles of children with SpLD are the cause of their difficulties, or a consequence of them. Different brain areas can adapt to take on the functions of damaged areas if that damage is acquired in early childhood – this is known as neuroplasticity. It is possible that some of the differences observed, to do with the lack of asymmetry in various brain regions, may be evidence of these areas adapting to take on new functions that cannot be carried out by other 'damaged' areas of the brain.

   As this discussion suggests, the causes of SpLDs are not clear, and there remains debate about whether they constitute a single condition or several distinctive conditions that reflect subtle differences in biological cause. The reason for briefly reviewing this evidence, and for highlighting the breadth of potential factors that may cause SpLDs, is that this lack of a simple cause means that the assessment and identification of the different forms of SpLD are varied and problematic. The next section deals specifically with the issue of how to identify children experiencing SpLDs.

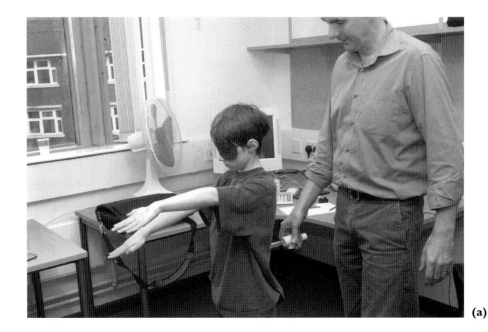

(a)

(b)

Figure 4   (a) Test of balance (postural stability) (b) test of motor co-ordination (bead threading).

Summary of Section 3

- There is a high degree of co-occurrence among the various forms of SpLD.
- This co-occurrence may be due to a common biological cause, or the conditions may simply be 'comorbid'.
- There is evidence of a genetic contribution to SpLDs, and this is likely to involve a number of genes.
- The brain development of children with dyslexia and dyspraxia differs from that of controls especially with respect to the functioning of the cerebellum.

4   Assessment

This section describes how children are identified as experiencing either dyslexia or dyspraxia, and the role of psychologists in this process. Assessment is not just concerned with identifying whether or not a child has a condition; it is about discovering the exact nature of the problems experienced by the child, thereby indicating ways in which he or she can be supported at home, school and elsewhere. There are important differences between the approaches taken to assess dyslexia and dyspraxia: one adopts an almost exclusively psychological approach and the other is more multidisciplinary. In this section you will read about the reasoning behind these approaches, as well the limitations of assessment practices.

You may have noticed that the terms 'assessment' and 'identification' have been used in relation to SpLDs, rather than 'diagnosis'. Diagnosis implies the identification of a medical syndrome or disease. Many children and adults with SpLDs feel that such a term is inappropriate, because although some aspects are problematic, other 'symptoms' are actually advantageous, and many of the skills they develop as a consequence of their difficulties are highly valued. Some people with dyslexia, for example, see their condition as a 'learning style', which has both advantages (such as strong visual skills) and disadvantages (weak auditory memory).

4.1 Assessing dyslexia

How a condition is defined influences how the psychologist goes about looking for it. You read in Section 2 that the early exclusionary definitions of dyslexia were replaced by a 'discrepancy' model, which is supplemented by the identification of positive indicators. To illustrate some of the issues to do with assessing children for dyslexia, you will now consider, stage by stage, the assessment of a fictional boy, Luther. Although Luther is fictional, the manner of his assessment is indicative of current approaches to assessing dyslexia, and if you have been assessed for dyslexia, or have children who have been assessed, you may recognize the approach that is outlined in this example.

Luther's assessment

Luther was 10 years 0 months when he was assessed because he did not appear to be reading and coping well with written language. It is still the case that many children experiencing dyslexia are not recognized as presenting a problem or put forward for assessment until relatively late in their school career (for example, at 10 to 13 years of age, sometimes older). This is often because of the difficulty in knowing whether the difficulties are simply a 'developmental lag' that will be recovered with time, or because of the financial implications of having an assessment, which parents are often expected to finance initially and can be quite expensive.

Luther's assessment consisted of an interview and a range of tests. Most children are assessed by an educational psychologist, but specially qualified teachers can also conduct assessments. First, an interview with his parents was conducted to provide background information regarding whether his early development was 'typical', whether there was any family incidence of dyslexia or other learning difficulties, and whether he had any emotional or social problems at school.

Luther was a good weight at birth, and achieved developmental milestones (for example, talking, crawling, walking) as expected. His health was generally good although he suffered from eczema. The early organization of Luther's physical skills was typical, with good hand–eye co-ordination and right hand dominance being established before he began school. Luther's parents are highly literate professionals who reported no difficulties with literacy themselves, and no incidence of dyslexia in their families.

Next, the assessment addressed whether Luther showed any signs of emotional or behavioural 'maladjustment'. Luther is a shy but polite child who does not appear to have any difficulties 'fitting in' at school and has good friendships. This part of the assessment can be seen as looking for evidence that Luther's difficulties are not caused by behavioural or emotional factors. The presence of emotional difficulties is an important 'positive indicator'. While emotional problems do not cause dyslexia, they sometimes result from it. Note, however, that the evidence for this in Luther's case came only from interviewing Luther and his parents.

The Wechsler Intelligence Scale for Children (WISC-III[UK]) was used to assess Luther's cognitive abilities. It consists of a battery of tests designed to assess the intellectual ability of children between the ages of 6 and 16 years. The thirteen individual sub-tests within the battery are organized into two groups: verbal tasks and performance tasks (see Box 4 and Figure 5).

The battery provides an estimate of the child's IQ, standardized on a scale where a score of 100 is the mean, and scores between 90–109 indicate the normal range of ability. Luther obtained an overall IQ of 122, a verbal IQ of 107 and a performance IQ of 133. Luther's scores for the individual sub-tests are illustrated in Figure 6 (10 indicates average performance).

The first thing to note is that Luther has a high IQ, and a discrepancy between his verbal and performance IQ scores. His high IQ is interpreted as evidence of his learning potential. Of key importance is Luther's profile of scores on the individual sub-tests. You will recall that SpLD is indicated by a profile with good to high scores on some measures, but very poor scores on others. Luther has difficulties with digit span (memory), coding and arithmetic.

A test that examined speed, accuracy and control for each hand was given. Luther's scores were 'normal', although his right hand seemed consistently faster. He is firmly right footed, eyed and eared with an accurate awareness of left and right. Tests which assess relative preference for and abilities with each side of the body are included because people with dyslexia sometimes have 'mixed laterality' – no clear dominance or preference for one side of their body. They are often observed to be ambidextrous.

Luther was given standard tests of word reading, story reading, reading comprehension and spelling ability. Luther obtained a score of 9 years 4 months on the single word reading task. On the contextual reading task and the spelling test, he performed at a level consistent with that of a child of 7 years 6 months. His reading comprehension score was age appropriate. His phonological awareness was also assessed using a standardized battery that assessed his sensitivity to, and ability to manipulate, sounds in words. This included an assessment of his ability to detect words that rhymed or started with the same sound, to read nonsense words such as 'mulp', and to make 'spoonerisms' (for example, saying 'cad bat' instead of 'bad cat'). On these tasks Luther performed at the level of a 7 year old.

BOX 4

Sub-tests of the WISC

Verbal

- Information sub-test (tests knowledge of common events, objects, places and people)

- Similarities sub-test (tests the ability to identify words which link pairs of verbal concepts)

- Arithmetic sub-test (tests the ability to perform mental arithmetic)

- Vocabulary sub-test (tests the ability to define words)

- Comprehension sub-test (tests the ability to solve everyday problems or understand social rules and concepts)

- Digit Span sub-test (tests immediate memory for strings of spoken digits)

Performance

- Picture Completion sub-test (tests the ability to identify parts missing from common objects)

- Coding sub-test (tests the ability to transcribe a simple code at speed)

- Picture Arrangement sub-test (tests the ability to rearrange line drawings in sequential order)

- Block Design sub-test (tests the ability to copy mosaics of increasing complexity using coloured tiles or blocks)

- Object Assembly sub-test (tets the ability to complete jigsaw puzzles)

- Symbol Search sub-test (tests the ability to search for target items in a series of shapes)

- Mazes sub-test (tests the ability to find the correct path through two-dimensional mazes)

(a)

(b)

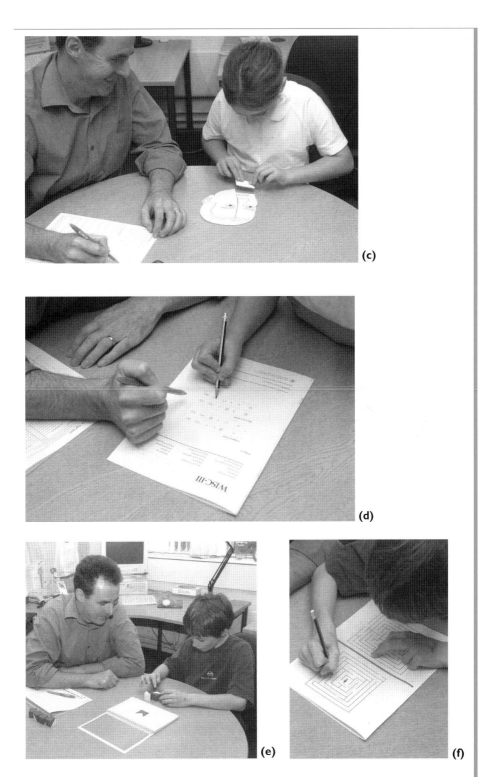

Figure 5   Some of the WISC sub-tests: (a) picture completion (b) picture arrangement (c) object assembly (d) symbol search (e) block design (f) mazes.

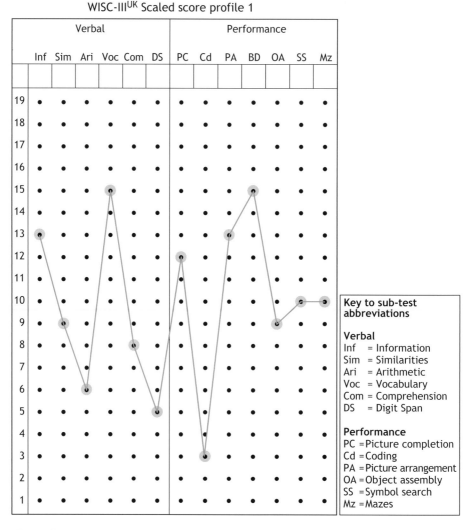

Figure 6   Luther's WISC profile.

Activity 3   *Evaluating the evidence*

Allow about
20 minutes

This activity will help you to reflect on the difficult nature of assessing dyslexia in practice.

In the light of what you have read so far, what evidence from the assessment do you think is of particular interest and what would your conclusion be? To help you to arrive at a decision, and also in order to think critically about assessment practice as illustrated by this example, Figure 7 illustrates the different types of 'evidence' that you know, from reading Sections 2 and 3, are associated with dyslexia. Re-read Luther's assessment and:

- place a tick in the areas of the chart where the psychologist has looked for evidence;

- shade in the segments where positive evidence of dyslexia was found.

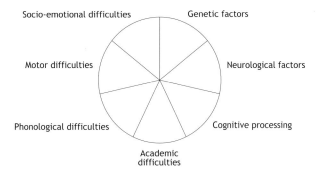

Figure 7   Evidence of developmental dyslexia (uncompleted).

Comment

Your diagram should look something like Figure 8.

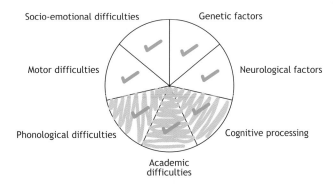

Figure 8   Evidence of developmental dyslexia (completed).

The assessment identified no evidence of a familial trait that might suggest a genetic cause, although this was assessed only indirectly, by interviewing Luther's parents. The questions to do with 'acquiring normal developmental milestones' and the laterality tasks were an attempt to identify some indication of neurological abnormalities. However, no problems were found in this area. Deficits were found with respect to cognitive processing (the variable profile on the WISC), academic difficulties (the problems with reading and spelling) and phonological difficulties. Motor difficulties were not formally assessed but the assessor noted no sign of 'clumsiness'. No socio-emotional difficulties were noted.

From this assessment Luther would be recognized as someone with dyslexia. Even though no evidence was found in many of the areas associated with dyslexia, specific difficulties in reading, phonological awareness and cognition were observed. These three areas of deficit are at the heart of the condition as it is currently defined. Because the condition is so heterogeneous (there is so much variation between individuals in terms of the combination of difficulties they will experience) the 'absence' of evidence with respect to the other sectors does not necessarily mean that dyslexia is not present. However, as you can see from this, the task of identifying the presence or absence of dyslexia can be problematic and in some cases controversial.

Issues with assessment

The assessment of Luther is indicative of current practices, and assumes that the discrepancy model is a valid one. This is not the necessarily the case. For example, there is evidence that children with very different IQ scores can achieve similar reading and spelling scores (Regan and Woods, 2000). Furthermore, the discrepancy view excludes children with general learning difficulties, and the validity of predicting 'potential' from IQ scores is debatable (British Psychological Society, 1999). In addition, any assessment is only ever a 'snapshot' that captures a child's performance at that time on that day, and as such is affected by any number of situational and motivational factors. Although psychologists can take this into account statistically, the idea of assessing 'learning potential' by measures of attainment at one point in time, rather than as a dynamic cognitive process over a period of time, is open to question.

The variable profile of cognitive test results can, however, help psychologists to understand children's strengths and weaknesses with particular aspects of cognitive performance. This can be useful in understanding a child's literacy difficulties and planning a subsequent teaching approach. The psychologist needs to use the profile information together with other data to understand the child's difficulties.

An alternative approach

For reasons such as those just described, an alternative approach to assessment that focuses on identifying 'severe and persistent problems' in learning to read and write, instead of using assessment merely to identify the presence of a 'syndrome', has been proposed by the British Psychological Society (1999). This approach is not yet practised widely. It suggests combining assessment with intervention, and places importance on how the child responds over time to teaching interventions. It assesses dyslexia by making a direct assessment of the child's learning. This forms part of a strategy in which assessment and teaching are interwoven. According to this model, the psychologist facilitates a cycle of 'clarification, consultation, observation, investigation, hypothesis generation, intervention, evaluation and further clarification' (British Psychological Society, 1999, p. 46). Box 5 shows the stages that make up this assessment model.

BOX 5

An alternative approach to assessing dyslexia

Assessing and evaluating word reading and spelling

Standardized reading and spelling tests may be used here, combined with observation of the strategies used by the child and an analysis of the types of errors made.

Assessing learning opportunities in the classroom

Key aspects include the degree to which the teaching strategies are appropriate for the particular child's strengths and weaknesses. For example, it might involve, in England and Wales, a consideration of the effects of the National Literacy Strategy, or whether children who are the youngest in their class are disadvantaged.

Assessing persistence

The child's rate of progress is monitored through regular assessments over a period of time. Progress charts make it possible to identify trends 'over relatively short time periods and make it possible to assess persistence without introducing delay into the process of assessment' (British Psychological Society, 1999, p. 53).

The focus of this approach is not on the identification of dyslexia as a specific syndrome (as in Luther's assessment), but on identifying children who are beginning to experience difficulties in such a way as to speed up intervention. Moreover, in seeing dyslexia as a persistent learning difficulty, it follows that the best way of identifying it is by assessing the child in his or her learning environment, and over a period of time.

4.2 Assessing dyspraxia

Many aspects of behaviour are associated with dyspraxia: visual–perceptual abilities, sequencing skills, learning, language development. This makes assessment difficult, and calls on the expertise of a range of professionals, including psychologists.

The following examples of parents' experiences of assessment illustrate both the emerging nature of knowledge in the field and its similarity to other specific learning difficulties.

> When Laura was about 3, our GP referred her to a paediatrician. She always had a blank face ... She [GP] thought it was a communication problem. We were upset when Asperger's was mentioned, but it wasn't. We were relieved when it was just to do with co-ordination. It took the speech therapist to sort it out.

> (William, quoted in Bolton, 2001, pp. 56–7)

> It stared off as attention deficit ... He was hyper ... up and down. Up and down, fidget, fidget, fidget. He was on and off Ritalin, but Dr [paediatrician] puts everybody on Ritalin, so that means nothin'. Then the special needs woman from the Board said it was dyslexia ... But the letter from the Board says special educational needs. Then the school doctor said it was dyspraxia and so did Dr [paediatrician]. That was after a lot of visits to the occupational therapist. She showed him how to smile. Before that he was always blank and cross looking and that puts people off. Dr [paediatrician] says it's hard to put your finger on just one name.

> (Valerie, quoted in Bolton, 2001, p. 57)

What these extracts illustrate is that dyspraxia is very difficult to identify initially, given the degree of overlap between it and other forms of SpLD. Moreover, you may have noted the symptoms of dyspraxia are treated as a matter for medical professionals rather than one for psychologists. This results in a very different process of referral and assessment compared to that of dyslexia, despite similarity in the ways that dyslexia and dyspraxia are defined, their symptoms and their impact on children's learning.

Why are the two conditions treated so differently? It is possible that this relates to the presence of unusual social behaviours in dyspraxia. Conditions like attention deficit hyperactivity disorder (ADHD), dyspraxia and Asperger Syndrome all involve medical experts in their identification and treatment. However, SpLDs that are socially less problematic, like dyslexia, are rarely subjected to medical intervention.

As the parents' accounts of assessment illustrate, assessment usually involves input from a range of professionals. Although most parents are aware of difficulties in development by the time their child is 3 years old, identification of the condition is usually made around the age of 6 ½ years (Bowens and Smith, 1999). Therefore the majority of assessments occur when the child has begun school and they often follow an assessment of special educational needs. This may involve a referral to an occupational therapist or a speech and language therapist.

Occupational therapists are health professionals who work collaboratively with their clients to facilitate independence in all aspects of their daily living, and they are often the first point of contact once it is suspected that a child may have dyspraxia. A child may have been referred for difficulties with handwriting, physical education, or dressing. Occupational therapists focus on developing the child's ability through activities that have a purpose, such as play, writing and tying laces. This approach encompasses psychological, physical and social aspects of the child's development and occupational therapists are uniquely placed to assess all aspects of the child's day-to-day activities: at home, school and play. They are able to identify the pervasive, persistent and severe signs that indicate dyspraxia.

A paediatrician will be asked to assess aspects of the child's physical development. A paediatrician is a consultant doctor who specializes in children's medicine, and who screens the child for medical conditions and neurological impairments that could be producing similar difficulties.

An educational psychologist assesses motor and perceptual development and skills such as sequencing and organization. As with the assessment of dyslexia, the psychologist's assessment will be multifaceted and may include:

- an interview with the child;
- individual cognitive and perceptual-motor tests;
- observations;
- consultation with parents and teachers to bring together a developmental history and current views of the child's experiences.

A test of visual and motor tasks capable of identifying specific motor difficulties will be used, such as the Developmental Test of Visual–Motor Integration (DVMI), or the Movement Assessment Battery for Children (the Movement ABC). To be considered 'dyspraxic', Geuze *et al.* (2001) recommend that children should have scores falling two standard deviations below the mean for their age group, which would put the child below the 5th percentile (that is, 95 children out of 100 would do better).

Similar to a dyslexia assessment, the WISC is used to indicate discrepant cognitive difficulties on specific sub-tests in children with dyspraxia. Children with dyspraxia perform relatively poorly in tests of Digit Span, Coding, Block Design and Arithmetic (Portwood, 2000). However, the assessor must bring together the full range of information – developmental history, cognitive assessment and perceptual–motor assessment – to make a decision regarding the presence of dyspraxia.

Activity 4   Multidisciplinary teams

Allow about 10 minutes

This activity will help you to reflect on the pros and cons of multidisciplinary teams.

Can you identify the advantages and disadvantages of having a range of professionals and a range of assessment tests? Consider these first from the perspective of the child and then from the perspective of one of the professionals involved.

Comment

For the child, being assessed on so many measures and by so many specialists can seem overwhelming, and the assessment process is lengthy. For the professionals involved, one of the difficulties can be in co-ordinating all the evidence. Moreover, there are issues to do with who makes the final 'diagnosis'. Psychologists provide evidence but do not make the final decision, because the assessment process is seen as co-ordinated by the health professionals involved, owing to the application of a 'medical' model of diagnosis for dyspraxia. Consequently, the typical pattern is that the occupational therapist makes a judgement, which is then endorsed by the paediatrician.

Summary of Section 4

- Assessment of dyslexia is typically conducted by an educational psychologist who administers a range of tests and interviews the family.
- Discrepancy-based assessment is problematic and alternative approaches have been proposed that assess learning as a dynamic process and combine assessment with intervention.
- Assessment of dyspraxia is conducted by multidisciplinary teams, which include psychologists who administer standardized assessments of cognitive and motor ability.

5 Consequences

This section will explore the consequences of experiencing an SpLD. As an introduction, Box 6 presents a case study by Madeleine Portwood (1999), an educational psychologist who was conducting research into the prevalence of SpLDs in Deerbolt, a young offender's institution in the United Kingdom catering for young people aged between 15 and 22 years.

BOX 6

Steven

Steven said that his early school days had been happy. He remembered with fondness particular teachers and the friends that he had made in the infant school. He felt that as the work became more difficult he was made to look foolish in front of other members of the class. He believed that he was being treated differently by the teachers and the other pupils. Nevertheless he had managed to survive until the end of primary school but felt that his inability to play football and other games skilfully excluded him from the group of boys with whom he would have liked to have been involved. On transfer to secondary school he found it was much easier to disguise his learning difficulties and discovered that insolence and verbal abuse towards teachers and peers achieved the desired outcome. He was removed from the classroom and allowed to spend the rest of the day in a room by himself.

By the age of 13, he had such a bad school record that he was given a number of fixed-term exclusions. In many ways this delighted him further because it meant that he did not have to go through the motions of attempting to do work and finding distractions to remove himself from it. He discovered that it was less stressful either staying at home or spending time with gangs of older youths, some of whom had left school and were unable to gain employment: at least they accepted him. He was the youngest member of the 'gang' and he was constantly being required to confirm his allegiance by doing as he was told.

By the age of 15, he had decided that he should no longer attend school and truanted every day. A variety of strategies had been employed to facilitate his return. None was successful.

By the age of 16, he had been convicted of a string of offences including taking cars without the owners' consent, and petty theft from large shops. It was his conviction for an aggravated burglary that resulted in his imprisonment in Deerbolt.

On assessment Steven performed all of the tasks to the best of his ability. He enjoyed being out of his cell and talking about himself. Although Steven had significant reading, handwriting and spelling problems with additional motor delays and perceptual difficulties, he achieved many average scores in the sub-tests of the Wechsler assessment.

Steven was asked about his future. He did not appear to have a great deal of hope. Any friends that he had had from his school days had long since gone. His mother had told him to leave home on numerous occasions prior to his custodial sentence. He held out no hope of returning home. He was due for release within two months but talked at length about the security he had found at Deerbolt. He was aware that he had lost his freedom and hence many of his privileges. He did not feel that there was a lot on offer outside. He thought he would not be able to afford any clothing. He did not know what sort of accommodation he would be offered and he just smiled and did not answer when I suggested that there might be the prospect of some training or job opportunities. His first statement was to attach some blame to his criminal record for his circumstances, but then he said, 'I can't get a job, I can't do anything, I can't even read properly.'

Source: Portwood, 1999, p. 86.

Activity 5   Consequences of SpLD

Allow about 5 minutes

This activity will encourage you to think about the various consequences of experiencing SpLD.

Re-read the case study of Steven and make notes on what the consequences of SpLD were in his case.

Comment

Steven's case study suggests that he experienced many consequences of having an SpLD, including exclusion – not just from school, but from his family and ultimately from society – low self-esteem, and a loss of academic motivation and achievement. His account of his future prospects suggests that he also had a negative view of himself and his situation. We will consider each of these issues in Sections 5.1–5.4 that follow.

5.1   Social exclusion

Exclusion often emerges as a theme in case studies of children with SpLDs. For example, Riddick (1996) conducted a qualitative study of children's and their parents' accounts of living with dyslexia. Twenty-two children from mainstream schools in the United Kingdom completed standardized, semi-structured interviews; the children's mothers also took part in the interviews. One of the themes that became apparent was the extent to which the children felt excluded from school activities because of their difficulties with written language. More striking is the way that the children's fear of social exclusion resulted in a form of self-imposed isolation: Riddick found that most of the children in her sample either did not tell other children that they had dyslexia or told only their closest friends. Some avoided close contact with other children to avoid being 'found out'. The children's fears of how other children might react to their dyslexia appear to be justified as Riddick also found that 50 per cent of the children were teased at school about their difficulties. Perhaps as a consequence of such experiences, the majority of children valued the friendships that they had with other children who also had dyslexia.

The results of 'self-report' studies of the kind conducted by Riddick need to be treated with caution because respondents can be selective in what they remember and report. As a result, 'triangulation' is important: the researcher should present evidence from several different sources and demonstrate consistency in the evidence presented. Riddick does this by interviewing the mothers and the children separately. As a reader, you can evaluate the evidence by looking for consistency across the results of self-report studies and those of observational and experimental studies.

Children with 'visible' forms of SpLD such as dyspraxia also experience social exclusion. Smyth and Anderson (2000) noted in their observational study of children's playground activity that children with co-ordination disorders spent more time alone and were less likely to engage in some types of large-group activities. They concluded that:

> ... clumsy children may be less competent in activities which are both social and physical. Poor coordination makes physical activities more attention demanding and therefore reduces the child's capacity to deal with the social world, increasing the likelihood of perceived incompetence within that world.

(Smyth and Anderson, 2000, p. 411)

There has been interest in the fact that SpLDs appear to be linked to antisocial behaviour and may be over-represented in prison populations and young offender units. However, such claims have been disputed. For example, Rice (1998) has suggested that the reading 'difficulties' observed in prison populations are more likely to result from poor instructional methods and motivational factors. Rice (1998) conducted a study of 323 prisoners in England and Wales and found no evidence of a higher prevalence of dyslexia in prison populations when strict criteria related to reading performance were used. However, Rice's study has been criticized by Reid and Kirk (2001), who suggest that Rice used a very narrow definition of 'dyslexia as reading disability' that ignored the other ways in which dyslexia can manifest itself. They conducted their own study into the prevalence of dyslexia in young offenders; it is described in Research summary 1.

RESEARCH SUMMARY 1

The Young Offender Study

From the largest young offender unit in Scotland, Kirk and Reid (2001) recruited 50 young offenders who volunteered for dyslexia screening using a computerized screening test known as Quickscan. Quickscan is not a full assessment of the kind described in Section 4, but is a checklist of behaviours, which includes those that people with dyslexia find difficult. The person simply has to respond 'yes' or 'no' to the questions on the screen, such as:

- When making phone calls do you sometimes forget or confuse the numbers?
- Do you often find it difficult to learn facts?
- Do you know of anyone in your family who has dyslexia?
- Is it usually easy for you to find the key points in an article or a piece of text?

- Are you a fairly confident person?
- Do you usually find it difficult to concentrate?
- Do you sometimes confuse left and right?

Fifty per cent of those screened reported experiencing positive indicators of dyslexia: three people displayed most indicators, three displayed many indicators, 17 displayed some indicators and two people displayed borderline indicators. Self-esteem was found to be low for all these individuals. Time constraints meant that it was not possible to conduct a full assessment with all those identified as 'at risk' but six were identified at random for a full assessment with an educational psychologist using age-appropriate IQ and literacy tests. All six showed evidence of a dyslexic profile on these measures. Kirk and Reid suggest that the very high prevalence rate is partly the result of using volunteers rather than a randomly selected sample from the unit, but is sufficient evidence of higher prevalence of dyslexia among young offenders than in the normal population.

Reid and Kirk (2001) suggest that while it is unlikely that dyslexia 'causes' delinquency in some children, if it is not recognized and supported appropriately it can result in 'social disaffection'. It is possible that school presents some children with an impossible environment to cope with and their resulting frustration may lead to delinquent activities in some cases – as illustrated by the case of Steven.

5.2 Self-esteem

Self-esteem refers to the degree to which a person believes that their present self is consistent with their ideal self-image. There is evidence to support the idea that children with SpLDs experience low self-esteem and related anxiety. For example, Riddick (1996) found that 95 per cent of the mothers in her study believed that dyslexia had had an impact on their child and 75 per cent of the children went through a period of 'considerable distress', showing physical signs of anxiety including bed-wetting.

Larger-scale quantitative studies have shown mixed support for the view that children with SpLDs have low self-esteem in general. For example, Skinner and Piek (2001) found that children with dyspraxia reported significantly lower general self-worth than matched controls. The younger children (aged between 8 and 10 years) with dyspraxia in the study perceived their scholastic competence, athletic competence, physical appearance and self-worth to be significantly lower than the controls perceived their own abilities to be. The adolescents with dyspraxia were similar but also perceived themselves to be less socially accepted but not lower in scholastic competence. All the children with dyspraxia were significantly more anxious than their peers.

A review by Huntington and Bender (1993) suggests that it is more correct to say that children with dyslexia show self-esteem issues that are related to a poor *academic* self-concept. For example, Montgomery (1994) conducted a study in the United States of self-concept in children aged between 11 and 16 years, with and without dyslexia. The children completed the Multidimensional Self Concept

Scale, which measures self-concept separately for academic, social, family, competence, affect and physical domains. The children were found to have significantly worse self-concept only on the academic and competence domains. Their self-ratings were very similar to their parents' ratings of what they believed their children's self-esteem to be.

5.3 Depression

Depression is characterized by negative attitudes to oneself, one's environment and one's future (Beck, 1976), and such negativity is hinted at in Steven's case study in Box 6. The prevalence of depression in children with SpLDs is greater than in children generally. For example, Goldstein *et al.* (1985) used the Children's Depression Inventory to assess 85 children with dyslexia, and found that 26 per cent were severely depressed; the standard data based on a typical sample suggests that a rate of 10 per cent should have been expected. Similarly, Portwood (1999) conducted a survey of 27 adults with dyspraxia who were taking part in an intervention programme: 51 per cent of her participants (aged between 16 and 31 years) reported experiencing psychiatric illness, including depression.

Consistent with such statistics is the finding that children with SpLDs are over-represented in populations of children who have suicidal feelings. Hayes and Sloat (1988) surveyed 129 high-school counsellors and asked them to complete a questionnaire on any suicide-related incident that they had experienced. Fourteen per cent of the suicides, suicide attempts or related incidents that were reported involved adolescents with dyslexia. This is high, considering that the prevalence of dyslexia in school populations is around 5 per cent.

Children with SpLDs appear to show patterns of attribution that are similar to those identified in individuals with depression. Most people attribute success at a task to their own abilities, and attribute failure to external factors (factors other than themselves). By contrast, Jacobsen *et al.* (1986) found that this pattern of attribution was reversed in adolescents with dyslexia, who attributed failure to personal factors more frequently than children of typical ability did.

However, this 'depressed' attributional style also seems to be associated with academic *progress* for children with dyslexia. Kistner *et al.* (1988) conducted a 2-year longitudinal study of 34 students with dyslexia, where their attributional style was initially assessed and their academic progress then monitored, along with teacher ratings of academic progress and classroom behaviour. They found that the children who attributed failure to personal factors that were within their control made the most academic progress and were rated by their teachers as showing the most appropriate classroom behaviour.

Moreover, Riddick (1996) found that personal distress did not necessarily relate to the severity of dyslexia experienced, but appeared to be more closely associated with the degree of support that the child had received from their school prior to identification of their condition. It also appeared to be the case that the children's self-esteem improved as a result of having their difficulties labelled. Similarly, Skinner and Piek (2001) found that in their study of children with development co-ordination disorder (DCD), the degree of perceived social support also contributed to the children's perceived self-worth.

▼

Activity 6   *Evaluating the evidence*

Allow about
10 minutes

This activity will help you to reflect on the implications of research into depression and SPLD.

Would you say, from the evidence in this section, that depression is an inevitable outcome of SpLDs? What situational factors might prevent a child from developing depression?

Comment

It seems likely that while depression is a serious problem for some children with SpLDs, many more are not affected by this type of psychiatric difficulty. However, it is hard to get a sense of how widespread depression actually is in SpLD populations. For example, the Portwood (1999) study could be seen as offering a 'biased' picture, because all the respondents might be severe cases (given they are participating in an adult intervention study). Moreover, we do not know what the incidence rates are for 'psychiatric illness' in the general population, and what proportion of her cases had depression, so her data are difficult to interpret. In terms of support, the work of Riddick (1996) and Skinner and Piek (2001) suggests that good social support and the early identification of the condition should limit the potential for experiencing depression.

▲

5.4 Academic achievement and motivation

In the account of Steven, it was apparent that he failed to fulfil his educational potential at school and lost his motivation to learn. It is of little surprise, given the data on self-esteem and negative patterns of attribution, that children with SpLDs often do not fulfil their academic potential. For example, it seems that the negative experiences that children with dyslexia may have in school, and the relationships that they often have with some teachers, serve to de-motivate them to the point where they feel incapable of succeeding (Riddick, 1996).

This may seem like a strong claim but there is some experimental work that supports such a suggestion. Firstly, there is the classic – but controversial – study by Rosenthal and Jacobson (1968) where teachers were told that some of the children in their class were going to 'bloom' academically because of their IQ scores. In fact, the children identified had been selected at random and the teachers were given false information. The researchers claimed that the children selected showed a significant increase in IQ compared to those who were not identified, and this was explained by suggesting that the teachers had given the 'bloomers' more positive attention and treated them differently. Although this study was widely criticized on methodological grounds, Brophy and Good (1974) have suggested that there is clear evidence from subsequent studies that teachers' expectations of their students can impact on children's attainment. However, Hargreaves (1972) has suggested that for this to happen, the teacher must be seen as important by the child, and must also share the child's view of his or her own ability.

You will probably have noticed the ethical problems surrounding a study like that of Rosenthal and Jacobson (1968). The use of deception, although central to the aims of the study, meant that the teachers were unable to give informed consent to their participation. Also, the procedure meant that the children who were not in the 'bloomers' group may have been disadvantaged by the participation of their teachers in the study. At the time when this study was conducted, such ethical concerns were given less attention than they are in contemporary psychological research, and it is unlikely that such a study would receive ethical approval today. However, at the time, it provided a valuable demonstration of the potential impact that teacher expectations may have on children's performance.

The role of mood on academic achievement in children with learning difficulties has also been demonstrated in a series of studies by Tanis Bryan and colleagues in the United States, as described in Research summary 2.

RESEARCH SUMMARY 2

The effect of mood on performance in children with a learning disability

Bryan and Bryan (1991) examined the effect of inducing a positive mood on children at risk of dyslexia, and older children who had dyslexia. Children in both age groups were randomly allocated to either a positive mood or neutral mood condition. The positive mood children were asked to think of something wonderful that had happened to them and made them very happy. The neutral mood children were told to count silently from 1 to 50. The children were then asked to complete fifty mathematical problems in 5 minutes. Before they started the task, they were asked to estimate how many of the problems they thought they could successfully complete in the time allowed.

In both age groups the children in the positive mood groups correctly completed significantly more mathematical problems than the children in the neutral mood groups. The number of problems that the older children estimated they could successfully complete in the time was also significantly higher in the positive mood group than it was in the neutral group.

The implication of such research is that if a teacher can raise the spirits of children with dyslexia, the result is more likely to be positive, both in the children's perception of what they can achieve, and in the actual attainment of those children.

If a specific learning difficulty is not identified until after the person has left school, it does not mean that such a person is incapable of succeeding, or will follow a similar set of experiences to those of Steven. A good example of such a person is Simon, whose recollections of school you read about at the beginning of this chapter. Simon is severely dyslexic. During his dyslexia assessment his overall IQ performance was at the 91st percentile, but he had a reading ability score at the 36th percentile and a reading rate score at the 2nd percentile. His academic and professional success has centred on his finding coping strategies that enable him to maximize his potential without drawing attention to his difficulties (see Box 7).

Simon

I got into engineering college based on projected school results and my position was sponsored by my employer. I was doing well, but didn't have the minimum English qualification to be in college. I had 'ungraded' in English O level. I needed a C grade. The college insisted that I re-take English O level two more times, and each time I scored 'ungraded'. The college debated throwing me out, but as I hadn't failed a single class or test they let me stay. In my third year, my English teacher accused me of cheating. In class, I was very poor, just scraping by. But on the end of year research project I scored 80 per cent. The teacher wanted to know how I could almost double my score and he tested me to see if I knew my report. The reason why I scored so highly was because I had no time restraints and a proofreader to check everything.

At work, I've learned to look competent. My letter and faxes are form-based layouts with well-rehearsed and proofread passages that I can copy and paste together. If given a technical manual to read, I ask colleagues to read the manual as well for their opinion. They are my parity check to help me see if I've understood things correctly.

I have now become a fiction writer in my spare time. I have published several novels and I have over seventy short story credits to my name. Writing is relatively easy. Re-reading and making the stories readable is another thing, but writing has helped with my dyslexia. In the four years that I've been writing there has been a significant improvement. At first, I really suffered with poor grammar and construction, but I now have a better understanding of what and how I write. Unfortunately, my reading has not improved. I rely on a proofreader every step of the way. I still don't write what I'm thinking and if asked to read a passage, I won't read exactly what I've written, but my accuracy has improved. My first three short stories took three months to edit – now I can do the same amount in a matter of weeks.

I don't expect that my writing will cure my problem. I will never be able to read quickly or accurately. I will not be able to remember a telephone number said to me without asking four or five times. But it does prove that just because I have dyslexia doesn't mean I am not an intelligent and capable person.

When I was in my thirties I decided to finally have a formal assessment for dyslexia. The assessment was hard going. It was intensive and made worse by the fact that the tests are prodding at your weaknesses. By the end of the last test I was a wreck. My eyes ached and my head throbbed. I couldn't believe the reassessment was my idea.

I felt a lot of self-imposed pressure during the battery of tests. Unlike a normal test where you usually have an idea whether you are doing any good or not, with the assessment I wasn't sure whether I was doing the right thing. Actually I thought I was doing pretty well until the results came through. I had thought that through my writing I might have improved as a dyslexic, rewiring my childhood errors. Sadly, it seemed that the fundamental problems were still there. The assessment only showed that my coping skills had improved.

Summary of Section 5

- Qualitative and quantitative studies suggest that people with SpLDs experience emotional and educational consequences.
- Many children with an SpLD experience social exclusion.
- The self-esteem of children with SpLDs is low, especially with respect to academic self-concept.
- Children with SpLDs are over-represented in statistics on children with depression, although the degree of prevalence is not clear.
- Many children with SpLDs experience reduced academic motivation.

6   Intervention

So far, this chapter has considered the nature and potential causes of specific learning difficulties, how they are identified, and the social and educational consequences of experiencing these difficulties. Such discussions inform this final section, which considers how to best support people with SpLDs.

The topic of intervention raises the question, often asked by children who experience dyslexia or dyspraxia, of whether their condition is 'curable'. However, as noted earlier, SpLDs do not have 'simple' causes that would be susceptible to 'simple' intervention. Few developmental conditions are 'reversible' in that sense. Instead, intervention is aimed at reducing the impact of the symptoms at a behavioural level. Some of the symptoms, such as the observed reading deficit in children with dyslexia, respond well to appropriate intervention, because there are a number of different cognitive 'routes' to reading. However, other characteristics of the same condition are more directly dependent on a 'faulty' cognitive mechanism, such as weaknesses in memory. In these cases, intervention aims to teach children how to cope with and compensate for such difficulties.

6.1 What is targeted?

Interventions are most frequently aimed at 'correcting' the key behavioural symptoms of the condition that interfere with the child's educational attainment (as in the study by Bryan and Bryan (1991) described in Section 5). Psychologists are commonly interested in programmes that look at changing the underlying cognitive processes that mediate the behaviours that they wish to change. In the case of dyspraxia, non-psychological interventions aim to improve co-ordination via specially designed physical activities. However, there is also interest in the potential for cognitive interventions in improving the motor control of these children (see Research summary 3).

RESEARCH SUMMARY 3

A cognitive treatment for children with motor difficulties

Miller *et al.* (2001) developed an intervention known as Cognitive Orientation to daily Occupational Performance (CO-OP). It teaches children a problem-solving strategy for approaching motor tasks that they wish to master, and they are encouraged to guide themselves verbally through the task, by asking themselves the following questions:

Goal   What do I want to do?

Plan   How am I going to do it?

Do   Do it!

Check   How well did my plan work?

The therapist encourages the children to identify aspects of the task that present difficulties and to generate and reflect on possible solutions. The therapist also encourages them to make links between situations and recognize how strategies could be applied in other situations.

In this study, 20 children (aged about 9 years) were randomly allocated to one of two treatment groups. One group was trained to use the CO-OP approach. The other group was exposed to the Contemporary Treatment Approach (CTA), which represented current approaches to treating co-ordination difficulties. In both groups the children were asked to identify three behaviours that they wanted to improve. Each child then received ten treatment sessions, each lasting 50 minutes.

While both groups benefited and showed improved motor proficiency, the CO-OP group showed greater improvement in self-ratings and parental ratings of performance and self-ratings of satisfaction. Follow-up data collected more than 6 months later suggested that the CO-OP group had greater long-term maintenance of the goals they achieved and strategies they had learned than the CTA group had.

Although the most common forms of psychological intervention for children with SpLDs involve some form of cognitive training, there are interventions that aim to reduce the severity of symptoms by intervening at a biological level. The most common form of biological intervention is to prescribe drugs, but the use of drug treatments for children with SpLDs is rare. The difficulties in adopting this approach are highlighted by the debate that emerged around prescribing methylphenidate (also known by the brand name 'Ritalin') for children with ADHD (see Baldwin and Cooper (2000) for a discussion).

6.2 When to intervene?

The question of when to intervene is complicated by practical issues to do with the age at which children are recognized as experiencing an SpLD. That is, many types of SpLD do not become apparent until children fail to make progress at school. Moreover, the 'discrepancy' approach to diagnosing SpLDs means that the children must be significantly behind for their age, so they often experience several years of difficulty before they are 'sufficiently' behind. As a result, interventions are typically aimed at schoolchildren who are not only trying to cope with their SpLD, but also with the negative experiences that they may have had since entering school. As a consequence, the effectiveness of school-based interventions is not as strong as one might hope or expect.

> ### Comment
>
> Torgesen (2001) notes that many interventions aimed at improving children's reading skills do not 'remediate' reading failure (that is, they do not result in the children's reading ability becoming age appropriate). Instead, such interventions only stabilize the degree of failure: the child's reading ability may improve, but the gap between chronological age and reading age remains the same.

Early identification of children who are 'at risk' of SpLD, as identified by the early presence of positive indicators, followed by a programme of intervention to help them develop necessary skills, is believed to be the best approach to limiting the impact of SpLD on school attainment. An example of an early intervention programme is given in the next section.

6.3 School-based intervention strategies

In this section you will look in detail at some recent school-based intervention programmes that have been designed and evaluated by psychologists working with teachers. The examples discussed deal with attempts to improve children's reading attainment, since reading development frequently suffers as a result of SpLDs.

Most school-based interventions rely on a key resource to whom the children have access: a teacher. Interventions commonly rely on either one-to-one contact with the teacher, or teaching to groups of no more than four to six children, because of the need for highly personalized and responsive tuition.

One example of such a programme is the Interactive Assessment and Teaching (IA&T) reading programme developed by Reason and Boote (1994). These researchers developed a step-by-step approach to tailoring support to individual students, based on the stage they have reached in their reading development. With respect to reading and writing, Moss and Reason (1998) identified three main areas in which children can experience difficulty:

* meaning – referring to the understanding and enjoyment of content;
* phonics – understanding the relationship between sounds and letters;
* fluency – the effortless and automatic recognition and reproduction of words.

Phonics and fluency are especially difficult for children with dyslexia. Table 1 shows the four developmental stages identified by Reason and Boote (1994) in relation to each of these skills.

Having established which of the four stages a child or a group of children is at with respect to each skill, the teacher then devises activities that aim to develop competency of that stage. The children's progress is monitored and their activities are designed to reflect their respective stages, resulting in a structured set of aims and programme of activities.

Table 1   **Four stages in learning to read**

Stage	Meaning	Phonics	Fluency
Stage 1 Early development	Enjoys and joins in reading and discussion of stories. Understands vocabulary of reading and writing.	Recognizes rhymes and rhyming words. Blends sounds into words. Can play 'I-Spy'	Matches words by sight. Matches letters by sight. Identifies some words by sight.
Stage 2 Beginning to read and write independently	Expects own reading to make sense. Uses context and initial letters in working out meaning.	Can read and write single letter sounds and words such as it, at, hat, sun, dog, lid, net, cup, red, bus.	Reads some 100 words fluently from initial books.
Stage 3 Becoming competent	Uses context to understand and predict meaning and to help with more complex phonics.	Can read and write words with consonant blends, consonant digraphs, vowel digraphs and silent 'e'.	Extensive and increasing sight vocabulary from books read.
Stage 4 Basic competencies achieved	Context and phonological cues are used automatically in combination. Selects books suitable to interests and needs.	Reads and writes words with more advanced phonics: silent letters, longer word endings, polysyllabic words.	Reads and writes all commonly used words with ease.

Source: Reason and Boote, 1994, p. 32.

A formal evaluation of the effectiveness of the IA&T programme as an early intervention strategy for small groups of young children (aged approximately 6 years) who were identified as 'at risk' of reading failure is detailed in Research summary 4.

RESEARCH SUMMARY 4

Early reading intervention

In a study by Nicholson *et al.* (1999), 102 children aged 6 years were identified from four schools in the United Kingdom as at risk of reading failure, being the lowest-ranked readers in their class. Of these children, 62 were allocated to the experimental group who participated in the IA&T programme for 10 weeks (taking part in two half-hour sessions each week). The remaining 40 children acted as a control group during this period, participating in normal classroom activities in a different class in the same school or a similar school. The children in the experimental group improved their reading attainment, with their age-adjusted reading score (standardized score) increasing from a group average of 89 to 92.8. This shows that the gap between their reading ability and their chronological age had reduced during the intervention period. The control group's reading scores remained roughly the same (a change from 89.1 to 88.9). A significantly greater improvement in spelling scores was also found in the intervention group. The effect sizes for the children's improvement in reading age and spelling age were 1.71 and 1.24 respectively. An effect size of 1 is considered acceptable.

While the study found evidence that early intervention using the structured IA&T approach was effective overall, it was noted that 25 per cent of the children in the intervention group still had reading ages that were 6 months behind their chronological age after the intervention. Torgesen (2000) refers to such children as 'treatment resisters' and identifies the need to develop intervention approaches that are able to break the cycle of failure for these children. One solution that he suggests is to design 'intensive' programmes of intervention (Research summary 5).

RESEARCH SUMMARY 5

Intensive remediation

Torgesen *et al.* (2001) compared two different phonological awareness training programmes that were administered intensively to children aged between 8 and 10 years: 50 minutes of one-to-one instruction, twice a day, 5 days a week for 8 weeks. One programme, the Lindamood Phoneme Sequencing Program for Reading Spelling and Speech (LIPS), focused on practising the articulation of sounds, while the other (Embedded Phonics) taught phonological awareness in the context of reading large amounts of text.

There was little difference in effectiveness between the two forms of instruction, but the gains in ability were impressive, showing that during the intervention there were substantial gains in standardized reading ability, and the children continued to 'close the gap' after the intervention had finished. In the year after the intervention period, 40 per cent of the children were withdrawn from special education.

There were two problems with the results of the study described in Research summary 5. While reading accuracy was improved, fluency did not show the same degree of improvement. However, Torgesen (2001) reports that when intensive instruction is applied as a preventive programme of intervention instead of a remediation technique with older children, the children's fluency improves in the same way as their reading accuracy. Torgesen therefore suggests that the best approach to intervention in the case of reading ability is to identify children at risk of SpLD and invest in highly intensive programmes of intervention.

Computer-based intervention

While intensive schemes are effective, they are costly in terms of teacher time and difficult to resource in practice. As a result of these cost implications, psychologists have begun to focus on the potential of computers to assist children with specific learning difficulties. Nicholson *et al.* (2000) have developed the Reader's Interactive Teaching Assistant (RITA) – to act as a virtual teaching assistant. RITA has the same scope for producing a highly personalized teaching programme as traditional, teacher-led approaches (see Research summary 6).

RESEARCH SUMMARY 6

Computer-based intervention for children at risk of dyslexia

Nicholson *et al.* (2000) took the IA&T approach to teaching reading to children at risk of experiencing reading difficulties, and used this as the basis for a computer-based teaching assistant. The approach of initially assessing the student with respect to their reading development and deciding on a corresponding plan of activities was adopted and built into the computer system. For the purposes of the intervention the teacher determined which activities the child should complete, although it was also possible for the computer or the child to control this. RITA would first provide a series of suggested activities based on the child's progress within the four-step model from IA&T. The teachers were also shown how to develop their own, tailor-made computer-based activities for the system.

Two age groups of children who were showing signs of difficulty in learning to read participated in this study: 6 year olds and 8 year olds. Children who worked with RITA for two half-hour sessions a week (for ten weeks) were compared to a group who received the traditional IA&T intervention and a control group who received normal lessons. All three groups were matched for reading age and chronological age.

The children in the RITA group showed the same degree of improvement from pre-test to post-test as the children who received the IA&T intervention. Both intervention groups showed significantly greater improvement than the children in the control group did.

Given the issue of 'problem readers' in the study by Nicholson *et al.* (1999) described in Research summary 4, particular interest was paid to whether the children most at risk of reading failure would respond best to the computer or to the traditional form of the intervention. For the 6-year-old group no significant difference in improvement was found between the two methods, whereas the computer-based intervention was found to be more effective than the traditional intervention for the 8-year-old group. This group of children was also found to be significantly keener (based on teacher observation of their willingness to participate in the intervention sessions) than their counterparts in the traditional intervention.

Activity 7   *Interpreting results*

Allow about
10 minutes

This activity will give you practice in interpreting the results of a research study.

What reasons can you think of to explain why the 8 year olds responded to the computer intervention more positively than the younger children did?

Comment

It may be that the older children, who have had more opportunity for negative learning experiences with teachers, were keen to have access to a safe learning environment where they could make mistakes 'privately'. They might also have been more confident in using the computers than the younger children were.

Summary of Section 6

- Psychologists design and evaluate interventions that aim to improve the behavioural symptoms of SpLDs.
- Although intervention often occurs after identification, early intervention in the case of children 'at risk' of SpLD is the best approach.
- School-based interventions that aim to improve literacy attainment suggest that intervention needs to be highly personalized and structured if it is to be effective.
- In order to maximize the long-term impact of intervention, it is suggested that programmes also need to be intensive and preventive.
- Given the cost implications of personalized tuition in the classroom, psychologists are evaluating the potential of computers to act as 'teaching assistants' to support children with learning difficulties.

7   Conclusion

This chapter introduced you to some key issues in research into dyslexia and dyspraxia. The definition and assessment of SpLDs are highly contentious. Research into the consequences of SpLDs informs approaches to intervention, although more work is needed in both areas. Of central importance is the need not to lose sight of the children as individuals with different experiences of what it is like to have an SpLD, which demand individualized as well as generic forms of support.

References

Baldwin, S. and Cooper, P. (2000) 'Head to Head: how should ADHD be treated?' *The Psychologist*, vol. 13, pp. 598–602, British Psychological Society.

Beck, A. T. (1976) *Cognitive Therapy and the Emotional Disorders*, New York, NY, International Universities Press.

Bolton, S. (2001) 'When dyspraxia meets dyslexia at 11+.' EdD thesis, Open University.

Bowens, A. and Smith, I. (1999) *Childhood dyspraxia: some issues for the NHS*, Leeds, Nuffield Institute for Health.

British Psychological Society (1999) *Dyslexia, Literacy and Psychological Assessment*, Leicester, British Psychological Society.

Brophy, J. E. and Good, T. L. (1974) *Teacher–Student Relationships: causes and consequences*, New York, NY, Holt, Rinehart and Winston.

Bryan, T. and Bryan, J. (1991) 'Positive mood and math performance', *Journal of Learning Disabilities*, vol. 24, pp. 490–4.

Everatt, J. and Zabell, C. (2000) 'Gender differences in dyslexia', in Smythe, I. (ed.) *The Dyslexia Handbook*, Reading, British Dyslexia Association.

Fabbro, F. (2000) 'Introduction to language and cerebellum', *Journal of Neurolinguistics*, vol. 13, pp. 83–94.

Fawcett, A. J., Nicolson, R. I. and Maclagan, F. (2001) 'Cerebellar tests differentiate between groups of poor readers with and without IQ discrepancy', *Journal of Learning Disabilities*, vol. 34, pp. 119–33.

Geuze, R. H., Jongmans, M. J., Schoemaker, M. M. and Smits-Engelsman, B. C. M. (2001) 'Clinical and research diagnostic criteria for developmental coordination disorder: a review and discussion', *Human Movement Science*, vol. 20, pp. 7–47.

Goldstein, P., Paul, G. G. and Sanfilippo-Cohen, S. (1985) 'Depression and achievement in subgroups of children with learning disabilities', *Journal of Applied Developmental Psychology*, vol. 6, pp. 263–75.

Grigorenko, E. L. (2001) 'Developmental dyslexia: an update on genes, brains and environments', *Journal of Child Psychology and Psychiatry*, vol. 42, pp. 91–125.

Grigorenko, E. L., Wood, F. B., Meyer, M. S. *et al.* (1997) 'Susceptibility loci for distinct components of developmental dyslexia on Chromosomes 6 and 15', *American Journal of Human Genetics*, vol. 60, pp. 27–39.

Hargreaves, D. H. (1972) *Interpersonal Relations and Education*, London, Routledge and Kegan Paul.

Hayes, M. L. and Sloat, R. S. (1988) 'Preventing suicide in learning disabled children and adolescents', *Academic Therapy*, vol. 24, pp. 221–30.

Huntington, D. D. and Bender, W. N. (1993) 'Adolescents with learning disabilities at risk? Emotional well-being, depression, suicide', *Journal of Learning Disabilities*, vol. 26, pp. 159–66.

Jacobsen, B., Lowery, B. and DuCette, J. (1986) 'Attributions of learning disabled children', *Journal of Educational Psychology*, vol. 78, pp. 59–64.

Kaplan, B. J., Dewey, D. M., Crawford, S. G. and Wilson, B. N. (2001) 'The term *comorbidity* is of questionable value in reference to developmental disorders: data and theory', *Journal of Learning Disabilities*, vol. 34, pp. 555–65.

Kirby, A. (1999) *Dyspraxia: the hidden handicap*. London, Souvenir Press.

Kirk, J. and Reid, G. (2001) 'An examination of the relationship between dyslexia and offending in young people and the implications for the training system', *Dyslexia*, vol. 7, pp. 77–84.

Kistner, J. A., Osbourne, M. and Laverrier, L. (1988) 'Causal attributions of learning disabled children: developmental patterns and relation to academic progress', *Journal of Educational Psychology*, vol. 80, pp. 82–3.

Lundy-Ekman, L., Ivry, R. B., Keele, S. and Woollacott, M. (1991) 'Timing and force control deficits in clumsy children', *Journal of Cognitive Neuroscience*, vol. 3, 367–76.

Macintyre, C. (2001) *Dyspraxia 5–11*, London, David Fulton.

Miles, T. R. and Miles, E. (1999, 2nd edn) *Dyslexia: A Hundred Years On*, Buckingham, Open University Press.

Miller, L. T., Polatajko, H. J., Missiuna, C. *et al.* (2001) 'A pilot trial of a cognitive treatment for children with developmental co-ordination disorder', *Human Movement Science*, vol. 20, pp. 183–210.

Mody, M., Studdert-Kennedy, M. and Brady, S. (1997) 'Speech perception deficits in poor readers: auditory processing or phonological coding?', *Journal of Experimental Child Psychology*, vol. 64, pp. 199–231.

Montgomery, M. S. (1994) 'Self-concept and children with learning disabilities: observer–child concordance across six context-dependent domains', *Journal of Learning Disabilities*, vol. 27, pp. 254–62.

Moss, H. and Reason, R. (1998) 'Interactive group work with young children needing additional help in learning to read', *Support for Learning*, vol. 13, pp. 32–8.

Nicholson, R. I. and Fawcett, A. J. (2001) 'Dyslexia as learning disability', in Fawcett, A. (ed.) *Dyslexia: theory and good practice*, London, Whurr.

Nicholson, R. I., Fawcett, A. J., Moss, H. *et al.* (1999) 'Early reading intervention can be effective and cost effective', *British Journal of Educational Psychology*, vol. 69, pp. 47–62.

Nicholson, R. I. Fawcett A. J. and Nicholson M. K. (2000) 'Evaluation of a computer-based reading intervention in infant and junior school', *Journal of Research in Reading*, vol. 23, pp. 194–209.

Peer, L. (2002) 'What is dyslexia?', in Johnson, M. and Peer, L. (eds) *The Dyslexia Handbook 2002*. London, British Dyslexia Association.

Portwood, M. (1999, 2nd edn) *Developmental Dyspraxia: identification and intervention*, London, David Fulton.

Portwood, M. (2000) *Understanding Developmental Dyspraxia*, London, David Fulton.

Rae, C., Harasty, J. A., Dzendrowskyj, T. E. *et al.* (2002) 'Cerebellar morphology in developmental dyslexia', *Neuropsychologica*, vol. 40, 1285–1292.

Reason, R. and Boote, R. (1994) *Helping Children with Reading and Spelling: a special needs manual*, London, Routledge.

Regan, T. and Woods, W. (2000) 'Teachers' understandings of dyslexia: implications for educational psychology', *Educational Psychology in Practice*, vol. 16, pp. 333–46.

Reid, G. and Kirk, J. (2001) *Dyslexia in Adults: education and employment*, Chichester, Wiley.

Rice, M. (1998) *Dyslexia and Crime: some notes on the Dyspel claim*, Cambridge, University of Cambridge, Institute of Criminology.

Riddick, B. (1996) *Living with Dyslexia*, London, Routledge.

Rosenthal, R. and Jacobson, L. (1968) *Pygmalion in the Classroom*, New York, NY, Holt, Rinehart & Winston.

Rutter, M. and Yule, W. (1976) 'The concept of specific reading retardation', *Journal of Child Psychology and Psychiatry*, vol. 16, pp. 181–7.

Selikowitz, M. (1998, 2nd edn) *Dyslexia and Other Learning Difficulties: the facts*, Oxford, Oxford University Press.

Skinner, R. A. and Piek, J. P. (2001) 'Psychosocial implications of poor motor coordination in children and adolescents', *Human Movement Science*, vol. 20, pp. 73–94.

Smyth, M. M. and Anderson, H. I. (2000) 'Coping with clumsiness in the school playground: social and physical play in children with coordination impairments', *British Journal of Developmental Psychology*, vol. 18, pp. 389–413.

Stein, J., Talcott, J. and Witton, C. (2001) 'The sensorimotor basis of developmental dyslexia', in Fawcett, A. (ed.) *Dyslexia: theory and good practice*, London, Whurr.

Stevenson, J. (1999) 'The genetics of specific learning disorders', in Whitmore, K., Hart, H. and Willems, G. (eds) *A Neurodevelopmental Approach to Specific Learning Disorder*, London, MacKeith Press.

Torgesen, J. K. (2000) 'Individual differences in response to early interventions in reading: the lingering problem of treatment resisters', *Learning Disabilities Research & Practice*, vol. 15, pp. 55–64.

Torgesen, J. K. (2001) 'The theory and practice of intervention: comparing outcomes from prevention and remediation studies', in Fawcett, A. (ed.), *Dyslexia: theory and good practice*, London, Whurr.

Torgesen, J. K., Alexander, A. W., Wagner, R. K. *et al.* (2001) 'Intensive remedial instruction for children with severe reading disabilities: immediate and long-term outcomes from two instructional approaches', *Journal of Learning Disabilities*, vol. 34, pp. 33–59.

Wolf, M. and Bowers, P. (1999) 'The "double-deficit hypothesis" for the developmental dyslexias', *Journal of Educational Psychology*, vol. 91, pp. 1–24.

Chapter 2
Children and the legal system

Helen Westcott

Contents

	Learning outcomes	55
1	**Introduction**	**55**
	1.1 Competency and culpability	56
2	**Children and the legal system**	**59**
	2.1 Images of child witnesses in the legal system	59
	2.2 The Thompson and Venables case	61
	2.3 Children's involvement in the legal system	63
	2.4 Adversarial and inquisitorial systems of law	66
3	**Children's competency as witnesses**	**70**
	3.1 The questioning of children and the *Memorandum of Good Practice*	70
	3.2 Children's understanding of truth and lies	75
4	**Children and criminal responsibility**	**80**
	4.1 Criminal responsibility and *doli incapax*	80
	4.2 Psychological theories of moral development	81
	4.3 Deception in children	84
5	**Conclusion**	**89**
	5.1 Children's accuracy and honesty	89
	5.2 Competency, culpability and credibility	90
	5.3 Final remarks	91
	References	**92**

Learning outcomes

After you have studied this chapter you should be able to:
1   describe some of the roles psychologists may occupy in relation to children in the legal system;
2   discuss ways in which children and young people may be involved as witnesses or defendants in the legal system;
3   explain some ways in which psychologists have contributed to legal and procedural reforms relating to child witnesses;
4   discuss psychological research and theory in relation to children's competency as witnesses and their culpability as young offenders, including some methodological issues and implications for practice.

1   Introduction

The field of forensic psychology is growing rapidly, and psychologists interested in issues relating to children in the legal system – both as witnesses and defendants – are to be found in universities and in institutions such as young offender institutes.

- *Legal psychologists* concern themselves with the courts, and are generally witness centred. For example, they may be concerned with the way in which a young girl is called upon to testify about an assault she saw perpetrated upon her older brother.

- *Criminological psychologists* – sometimes known as forensic psychologists – are much more concerned with offenders. For example, they may examine rates of re-offending in a group of adolescent boys following different types of intervention.

Psychologists regularly act as expert witnesses in civil proceedings, and may be called by either party. However, they rarely appear in criminal proceedings in England and Wales since *R. versus Turner* (1975), a ruling which casts doubt on the value of expert evidence, and which states that the jury must decide the 'ultimate issue' (the key issue which the court is required to determine). In civil proceedings, a psychologist may be asked to view a videotaped investigative interview with a child who is suspected of being abused, to evaluate the questions asked by the interviewer as well as the child's demeanour. Other psychological assessments of a child may be sought, for example, from a clinical psychologist in the case of a young offender. Psychologists often act as 'neutral' court experts in childcare cases in civil courts, and will prepare written reports for the court on a particular aspect of a case. They may also prepare reports for sentencing decisions in the criminal courts. Psychologists work alongside legal professionals in other ways too, such as planning and delivering training for judges and other professionals, and in clinical work with young offenders in penal institutes.

Both legal and criminological psychologists collaborate with professionals from within the legal system such as police, probation and prison officers, as well as with academic lawyers. These relationships are not always easy: psychologists and lawyers tend to hold different views on the value of particular perspectives, theories and methods and this can lead to scepticism about one another's position (King, 1986; Nijboer, 1995). The rapidly growing body of research and professional activity in forensic psychology has been accompanied by the appearance of dedicated international academic journals such as *Law and Human Behavior*, *Legal and Criminological Psychology*, *Psychology, Public Policy and Law*, and *Psychology, Crime & Law*. The findings of psychological research can inform decision making in policy and practice, such as the development of new laws, or changes in legal procedures, for example, changes to the competency requirement described later. Expert witnesses also rely on such research to bolster their opinions when they testify in court. As you read this chapter you will learn about both the position of children in the eyes of the law and the ways in which psychological research and understanding have a bearing on that position.

Thinking about children as victims, witnesses and perpetrators of both violent and sexual crimes can be a difficult and challenging task. Media reports of attacks on children are not uncommon, and coverage can be explicit and emotive. High profile cases, such as the murder of 2-year-old James Bulger by two 10-year-old boys in 1993, and the manslaughter of two small boys by 11-year old Mary Bell in 1968 (Sereny 1995), are reminders that children can themselves be perpetrators of crimes. Psychologists working within or alongside the legal system must balance the competing images and needs of victims and offenders, and contribute to the development of a legal system which can respond to children in both roles.

You may find that some of the material that follows makes for uncomfortable reading, particularly references to child sexual abuse and the discussion of the James Bulger case (referred to as the Thompson and Venables case, after the two defendants, from hereon) and its implications for young defendants in the legal system. While examining the issues raised, discussions of such examples must not lose sight of the suffering of the victims and their families, and of others, such as members of the jury. Psychologists and lawyers working with children in the legal system have to find ways of working with difficult situations in a manner that remains sensitive to all concerned, and which acknowledges their own personal reactions to the situations that they encounter.

1.1 Competency and culpability

This chapter will explore some of the complex issues surrounding children's involvement in the legal system – as witnesses and as defendants – with a particular focus on the issues of their *competency,* and their *culpability.*

Activity I   When are children considered to be competent?

Allow about 5 minutes

This activity asks you to identify the ages at which children are considered to be competent in different aspects of their lives.

In the grid below, note the age at which you think a child in England and Wales is legally able to do certain things.

Activity	Age	Activity	Age
Have their body pierced		Get a part-time job	
Open a bank account		Drink alcohol in private	
Buy a pet		Drive a moped	
Give evidence at court		Be convicted of a criminal offence (including sexual offences such as rape)	
Buy cigarettes		Buy a firearm	
Marry with parental consent		Consent to sex with a same-aged peer	
Have flying lessons		Buy a lottery ticket	
Have their name placed on the sex offenders register		Vote in a general election	

Source: Hamilton et al., 2004.

Comment

Turn to the completed version of this grid at the end of the chapter to find out the answers. Do any of them surprise you? Compare the ages at which children are deemed competent to buy a pet or to get married, with the age at which they are deemed competent to be convicted of a criminal offence. You may reflect that competency is, in practice, a construction affected by prevailing historical and cultural views of childhood (and adulthood), as well as by the weight attached to certain activities within society.

Against such a backdrop of children's legally constructed competencies, this chapter will concentrate on children's competency to be a witness and their culpability as offenders. Both of these topics draw on psychological understanding in related areas, such as memory for events, social factors in interacting with adult authority figures, and moral development. Notions of both competency and culpability also raise important questions about children's accuracy and honesty in reporting events they have experienced.

Under the criminal law, a competent adult is, typically, a person who is aged 18 years or over and who acts rationally; autonomously choosing to act illegally on the basis of their personal preferences and values (Bonnie *et al.*, 1997, cited in Woolard *et al.*, 2001). Consequently, adults are generally considered to be responsible and accountable for their (criminal) actions (examples of 'incompetent' adults include those who have severe mental illness or severe mental impairment). However, the perception that children are immature and lacking in judgement means that they are not treated equally with adults, and this raises questions about the extent to which they should be seen as competent, and as culpable (accountable or blameworthy), in legal contexts (Woolard, 2002). As Activity 1 identifies, the law in England and Wales holds that children are deemed culpable – responsible for their criminal behaviour – from the age of 10 years. This compares with culpability at the age of 13 in France, 14 in Germany, Austria and Italy, 15 in Scandinavia, and 16 in Spain and Portugal (Rivlin, 2002).

In legal terms, competency has been defined as a witness's ability to understand questions asked of him or her, and to give answers which can be understood. Linked to this, the competency requirement distinguished between children's sworn and unsworn testimony.

Competency requirement
Witnesses may give evidence in criminal proceedings if they are able to understand questions put to them, and give answers which can be understood.

Until relatively recently, in order to give sworn testimony, a child had to be able to understand the implications of the oath. In England and Wales, the Criminal Justice Act 1991, and subsequently the Criminal Justice and Public Order Act 1994, removed these requirements. The existence and subsequent abolition of the competency requirement is particularly pertinent to a discussion of child witnesses, because the cognitive skills required in listening to, comprehending, and responding to questions are likely to be less well developed in child witnesses than in adult witnesses (Saywitz, 2002). These developments in the law also reflect changes in the way children are perceived by the legal system and this is the focus of the following section.

Summary of Section 1

- Forensic psychology is a rapidly growing field. Legal psychologists are usually witness centred, and criminological psychologists are usually interested in offenders.
- In England and Wales, children are held culpable for their criminal activities from the age of 10 years.
- Children are viewed as competent witnesses to the extent that they can understand questions asked of them, and provide comprehensible answers.
- Psychologists have a number of interests and roles in relation to children within the legal system. They may conduct research, carry out assessments, or provide expert assistance to the court.

2   Children and the legal system

Society at large is characterized by differing conceptions and portrayals of children and childhood and these contrasting – and sometimes conflicting – images are found in the legal and psycho-legal literature, too (Ceci and Bruck, 1995; Goodman, 1984). A common technique in the media is to position stereotypes of children's 'goodness' and innocence, such as a cherub-faced image, alongside stereotypes of 'evil' such as molestation, sexual intrigue and violence – a mix guaranteed to evoke an emotional response (Myers, 1994). Contrasting themes of morality and responsibility, protection and empowerment, welfare and punishment, arise whenever children are considered as victims or perpetrators of crime. At different times, certain of these themes have received more attention than others, depending on the prevailing social and cultural context.

2.1   Images of child witnesses in the legal system

Psychologists have been evaluating children's competency as possible witnesses since the beginning of the twentieth century. The French psychologist Alfred Binet, a pioneer in the study of intelligence, was one of the first to research children's testimony in a systematic way, discussing their suggestibility to misinformation (Binet, 1900). William Stern, one of the earliest psychologists to testify as an expert witness, conducted a series of experiments on what was called 'incidental memory', where children were questioned about a picture they had seen (Stern, 1910). In a similar vein, a Belgian psychologist named Varendonck conducted several studies on children's testimony. These were prompted by his involvement as an expert witness in a murder trial, where the prosecution's case centred on the testimony of two young children. In one study, eighteen children aged 7 years were asked the colour of a teacher's beard: sixteen of them gave an answer despite the fact that the teacher did not have a beard (Varendonck, 1911). Findings like this suggested that children may not act competently as witnesses and, on the strength of his research, Varendonck is reported to have said, 'When are we going to give up, in all civilized nations, listening to children in courts of law?' (Goodman, 1984, p. 9).

The issues raised by early studies such as these are enduring ones: the effect of 'leading' questions on witnesses' testimony, the wish to please an adult authority figure, and the workings of children's memories. Nevertheless, the middle years of the twentieth century saw little interest by psychologists in children's testimony. In 1958, a landmark case (*R. versus. Wallwork*) concerning a man accused of incest with his 5-year-old daughter led to the virtual exclusion of child witnesses under the age of 8 years from the courtroom in England and Wales until decades later (Spencer and Flin, 1993). When the prosecution called the child as a witness they were unable to elicit any testimony from her in the witness box. The appeal court judge reviewing the case, Lord Goddard, commented, 'The jury could not attach any value to the evidence of a child of five; it is ridiculous to suppose that they could' (cited in Spencer and Flin, 1993, p. 53).

What were the particular concerns about children's testimony? Heydon, an English lawyer, has summarized them as follows:

> First, a child's powers of observation and memory are less reliable than an adult's. Secondly, children are prone to live in a make-believe world, so that they magnify incidents which happen to them or invent them completely. [...] Thirdly, they are also very egocentric, so that details seemingly unrelated to their own world are quickly forgotten by them. Fourthly, because of their immaturity they are very suggestible and can easily be influenced both by adults and other children. [...] A fifth danger is that children often have little notion of the duty to speak the truth, and they may fail to realize how important their evidence is in a case and how important it is for it to be accurate. Finally, children sometimes behave in a way evil beyond their years. They may consent to sexual offences against themselves and then deny consent. They may completely invent sexual offences.

(Heydon, 1984, p. 84)

Again, the underlying concerns are with children's accuracy and honesty as witnesses. Note that many of these characteristics could apply equally well to adults as to children, and most can be evaluated empirically. In the 1980s and beyond, psychologists became galvanized once more by issues connected to children's evidence, and a large psychological literature has accumulated that investigates – and often challenges – each of Heydon's concerns (Eisen *et al.*, 2002; Westcott *et al.*, 2002). Public awareness of child abuse in the 1970s, and especially sexual abuse in the 1980s, linked to concerns to protect children, was a particular motivator for psychologists to learn more about children's capabilities. There was also an increased openness in the courts, and among legal professionals, to the reception of psychological expert testimony. This led to a 'rehabilitation' of child witnesses in the 1980s, with many psychologists viewing children as competent witnesses, and campaigning with other professionals for legal reforms to promote children's welfare and empowerment (Spencer and Flin, 1993). The 1990s saw something of a 'backlash' again (Myers, 1994) with several leading psychologists publicly questioning the degree to which children could be relied upon as witnesses (Ceci and Bruck, 1995).

This conflicting portrayal of children in the legal system is dramatically illustrated in the high-profile case in which two 10-year-old boys were convicted of the murder of a toddler, James Bulger. In this case, the victim and defendants were all children, and competing images of 'innocence' and 'evil' were heavily relied upon by those involved with the case, or in writing about it (Morrison, 1997).

2.2 The Thompson and Venables case

In November 1993, Robert Thompson and Jon Venables became the youngest convicted murderers in Britain for almost 250 years. They had been tried in Preston Crown Court for the murder of James Bulger, a 2-year-old boy they had abducted from a shopping centre and later horrifically battered to death. Crucially, psychiatrists who interviewed the boys, and other expert witnesses such as their teachers, reported that they were capable of basic moral judgements (knowing right from wrong), and so it was possible for them to be tried for the murder. They were tried in an ordinary adult court, and were convicted and sentenced to be detained 'at Her Majesty's pleasure'.

Lawyers for the two boys did not appeal against their conviction in England, but later took their case to the European Commission of Human Rights (ECHR) in Strasbourg. They stated that it was wrong for children so young to be tried in an adult court with great publicity, and also that the trial had been unfair since it had been 'frightening, humiliating and intimidating'. Thus, they argued that the boys' trial was unlawful since it had amounted to 'inhumane and degrading treatment'.

In December 1999 the ECHR ruled that the boys had indeed been denied a fair trial, since, by being tried in an adult court, they were unable to participate in their trial. However, it also decided that the trial had not amounted to inhumane or degrading treatment. The Commission effectively ruled that the English system of trying young children, like Thompson and Venables, in adult courts was flawed (Rivlin, 2002). In February 2000, one of the first implications of these rulings was felt with respect to arrangements for the trial of young defendants in the Crown Court (Rivlin, 2002).

In order to prevent 'avoidable intimidation, humiliation or distress', and to promote the defendants' understanding and participation in the proceedings, several changes were required. At trial, Thompson and Venables had been seated on a raised platform; this was intended to make it easier for them to participate, but it had the effect of making them feel more exposed. Under the new arrangements all involved in the trial should reside at the same physical level, defendants should be allowed to sit with their parents, and there should be regular breaks. Robes and wigs should not be worn unless requested by the defendant, or ordered by the court 'for good reason'. Later in the chapter there will be an opportunity to compare these arrangements with those already existing in Youth Courts.

Arnon Bentovim, a psychiatrist who interviewed Venables in 1993, re-interviewed him in January 1995, more than 1 year after the trial. Bentovim reported:

> When the trial was mentioned, the applicant [Venables] had described his sense of shock when he had seen the public being let in and his considerable distress when his name and photograph were published. He had been terrified of being looked at in court and had frequently found himself worrying what people were thinking about him. Most of the time

Crown Court
The criminal court that tries individuals charged with offences that are too serious to be dealt with by the magistrates' court. The Crown Court also hears appeals against convictions or sentences imposed in the magistrates' courts, and from findings of guilt (and subsequent orders) made in the Youth Courts.

Youth Court
The court which deals with most young people (aged between 10 and 17 in England and Wales) who are prosecuted for criminal offences. Young people accused of homicide or rape are heard in the Crown Court.

Doli incapax
The rule by which child defendants under a specified age are deemed unable to have criminal intent, unless the prosecution can provide evidence to prove otherwise. In England and Wales *doli incapax* applied to children aged between 10 and 13 years, until it was abolished in the Crime and Disorder Act 1998.

Crown Prosecution Service (CPS)
The body responsible for most public prosecutions in England and Wales once a case has been started. The Crown Prosecutors place the evidence before the magistrates' court, or appoint barristers to appear in the Crown Court. The CPS will apply two tests to the evidence, both of which must be passed before it will proceed with a case: that of 'evidential sufficiency' and that of 'public interest'.

he had not been able to participate in the proceedings and had spent time counting in his head or making shapes with his shoes because he could not pay attention or process the whole proceedings. He did not follow when he heard his and T's [Thompson's] interviews with the police being played in court and he recalled crying at that time.

(Cited in Gillan, 1999)

In October 2000, ruling on the release of Thompson and Venables, Lord Chief Justice Woolf noted, 'However grave their crime, the fact remains that if that crime had been committed a few months earlier, when they were under 10, the boys could not have been tried or punished by the courts' (HMCS, 2000). Lord Chief Justice Woolf's comment speaks to the notion of children's criminal responsibility, and to the specific issue of *doli incapax* which will be discussed in Section 4. Vincent Moss, the jury foreman, interviewed 10 years after the case, commented:

A proper judgement would have been that they had behaved like confused, frightened and stupid children caught up in a situation they had created but could not deal with. The judge's pronouncement that they were 'evil' was just wrong – they didn't have the moral and intellectual capacity for this to be an accurate description.

(Moss, in Brooks, 2003, p. 4).

In a radio programme some time after the case, Moss had expressed his regret at the unanimous murder verdict, saying that 'guilty but with diminished responsibility' would have been more appropriate:

We should have gone back into court and said, yes, we do have a verdict: our verdict is that these young boys are in urgent need of social and psychiatric help.

(Morrison, 1997, p. 236).

How does this case relate to a discussion of children's competency and culpability? Morrison, a journalist who covered the case, argued that labelling Thompson and Venables as 'evil' deprived them of 'the right to be seen as children, or even as human' (2003, p. 3), and it certainly seems that a large number of people involved in the case did not ascribe the two boys particular consideration, or particular vulnerability, because of their young age. Commentators from some European countries were reportedly astounded that children so young would be dealt with by prosecution and incarceration.

In deciding to take the case forward, the Crown Prosecution Service (CPS) signalled its belief in the culpability of the defendants, reflecting the view of the Bulger family and a large proportion of the public at that time. This was bolstered by the conclusions of psychiatrists and other experts that the boys' moral development was sufficient for them to appreciate the implications of their actions in killing James (psychological theories of moral development will be discussed in Section 4). Yet, given that evidence about the boys' family backgrounds was ruled inadmissible, the jury were unable to evaluate whether violence the boys witnessed and experienced at home, or their personality characteristics, or educational factors (truancy and apparently low intelligence) could have had an impact on their ability sincerely to appreciate what they were doing – and hence their culpability. Morrison (1997) has suggested that Thompson's experiences of violence, for example, might have rendered him unable to distinguish between right and wrong, and unable to view violence as unacceptable. He also suggested (p. 168) that Venables was 'such a strange, explosive child' that at the time of the offence he was not responsible for his actions.

In what sense were the boys 'competent' at the time of their trial? Section 1 described how, in legal terms, competency is defined as a witness's ability to understand questions asked of him or her, and to give answers which can be understood. Thompson and Venables were defendants, not witnesses, but it is clear from Bentovim's report that Venables, at least, experienced some difficulties in understanding the processes surrounding him. Moss, the jury foreman, has commented that, for the boys, the trial was 'largely incomprehensible':

> They knew that they had done something terribly wrong and were to be punished for it but could not understand why they were in court for day after day with adults who were using language and concepts which had no reality for them.

(Moss, in Brooks, 2003, p. 5)

The ECHR ruling that the boys had been denied a fair trial would seem to support this interpretation. Finally, the resultant changes in Crown Court practice with regard to young defendants saw moves to arrangements more likely to enhance children's experiences, primarily through reducing stress, and thus to increase their competency to participate in proceedings.

2.3 Children's involvement in the legal system

In the Thompson and Venables case the child defendants appeared in an adult Crown Court due to the severity of the charges against them. Figure 1 (overleaf) summarizes the court service as it is structured in England and Wales; the Crown Court can be found within that structure. Figure 2 (page 65) gives an overview of children's possible involvement in both criminal and civil proceedings in England and Wales.

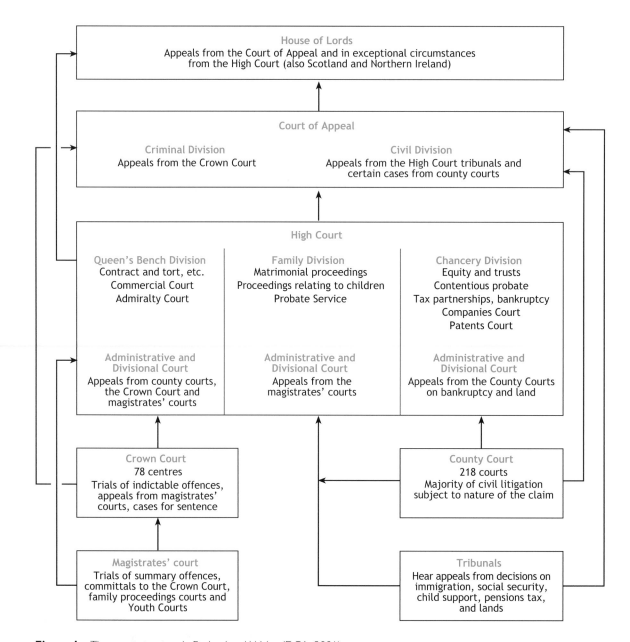

Figure 1   The court structure in England and Wales (DCA, 2001).

	Criminal proceedings		Civil proceedings			
	Summary trial	Trial on indictment	Emergency protection	Care proceedings (public law)	Disputes between carers (private law)	Wardship (now rare)
Which kind of court?	Youth Court/ magistrates' court	Crown Court	Magistrates' court	Magistrates' court/ County Court/ High Court	Magistrates' court/ County Court/ High Court	High Court
Key issues relating to children's involvement	Trials for less serious offences (e.g. theft); child may be a witness or the defendant	Trials for serious offences (e.g. murder or sexual assault); child may be a witness or the defendant	Child is in immediate and serious danger (e.g. from abuse)	Public authorities who wish to remove the child from the custody of their parents and put them into care, or put the child under local authority supervision	Parents are separating or divorcing and there are disputes about where the child shall live, access etc.	Wardship (the child becomes a 'ward' of the court and the court has ongoing jurisdiction until the child is 18)
Does the child appear at court?	Yes, if called as witness, or if appearing as defendant	Yes, if called as witness, or if appearing as defendant	No	Rarely	Rarely	Rarely
Who takes account of the child's interests, or presents their evidence to the court?	A Child Protection Service (CPS) lawyer if the child is a prosecution witness, a solicitor if the child is a defendant, or defence witness	Advocate appointed by the prosecution if the child is a witness, or advocate appointed by the defence if the child is a defendant or defence witness	Local authority (legal department on behalf of social services department) or NSPCC	Children's guardian	Children's guardian	Children's guardian

Figure 2   Children in the English legal system: an outline of their involvement.

Activity 2   *Children's involvement in the courts*

Allow about 5 minutes

This activity should help you to identify the ways in which children can become involved in different types of court proceedings.

Use the information in Figure 2 to identify the different ways in which children may become involved in court proceedings. Note the different roles that they may perform and the implications of these for whether or not they appear in court in person. Compare the involvement of children in criminal and civil proceedings. What differences do you notice?

Comment

There are some notable differences depending on whether the child's involvement is in criminal proceedings or in civil proceedings. For example, children rarely appear in civil courts, even if the case directly concerns them. Instead, a children's guardian will represent their interests. Conversely, children are increasingly testifying as witnesses in criminal courts. The degree to which children are heard about, and heard from, is something of a controversial issue, and is related to perceptions of their competency to participate in legal proceedings.

Cross-examination
The trial procedure whereby the lawyer representing the side which did not call the witness seeks to make its own case by questioning the other side's witness(es).

For example, it is debatable how well children are 'heard' in a criminal court, even when they do appear, as a consequence of legal constraints and practice during examination-in-chief and cross-examination (Esam, 2002; Henderson, 2002).

Lawyers' control of children's responses typically limits their answers to 'yes' or 'no', so they are unable to offer a full account. The use of legalistic jargon and complex language also restricts children's understanding of questioning, and thus limits the degree to which they can offer appropriate answers (Brennan and Brennan, 1988). By contrast, in civil courts it is possible to hear *about* children yet not *from* them, which also raises questions about their opportunity to participate fully in proceedings concerning their interests.

2.4 Adversarial and inquisitorial systems of law

Examination-in-chief
The trial procedure whereby the lawyer representing the side who has called the witness takes that person through his or her evidence.

The court service is structured to deal with the needs of different types of cases in separate courts (Figure 1). Burglary, murder and divorce, for example, vary along many dimensions, including whether they concern criminal or civil matters. The nature and severity of charges in criminal cases also determine whether a case can be heard by magistrates in lower-level courts (summary trial), or whether the case needs to be tried at a higher court, such as the Crown Court, with a professional judge presiding (trial on indictment).

The English system of law is adversarial (or accusatorial). That is 'each side presents a case before a court the function of which is limited to deciding who has won. The judges have nothing to do with the preliminary investigations, give no help to either side in presenting its case, and take no active steps to discover the truth, which emerges – or so the theory goes – from the clash of conflicting accounts' (Spencer and Flin, 1993, p. 75). Many legal systems in the world are founded on the adversarial system, and so are similar in major respects – for example, those in North America, Canada, and Australia.

Adversarial (accusatorial)
A trial system where both prosecution and defence present their case before a court which eventually decides who has won.

Key features of the adversarial system of justice – dependent on the individual case – include:

- the emphasis placed on live and oral eyewitness evidence at trial;
- frequent delays, for example between a crime taking place and being investigated and committed for trial, and between committal and trial;
- a formal court experience, including adversarial cross-examination;
- witnesses seeing (or 'confronting') the defendant in court;
- the trial taking place in open court, with press and public present.

Activity 3   Children's experiences of courts

Allow about 10 minutes

This activity invites you to reflect on how psychological factors have a bearing on children's experiences of courts.

Reflect on the features of an adversarial system listed above. What psychological considerations does each one raise, particularly for children? Note down any issues or implications that you consider might be important.

Comment

You may have thought about the stress involved in a live appearance in court, particularly in relation to being cross-examined, or to being near the defendant. Several researchers have recorded poignant illustrations of the stress child witnesses report experiencing (e.g. Plotnikoff and Woolfson, 2004). Children's lack of experience of formal settings and their limited knowledge of legal terminology are also significant. One study identified children's misunderstandings as to the nature of an oath (Lyon, 2002), and another reported common confusions, such as mistaking 'jury' for 'jewellery' (Warren-Leubecker et al., 1989). Delays before the trial starts negatively influence children's memories of an event, as the memory trace fades (Flin et al., 1992; Poole and White, 1993). While these issues may also apply to adult witnesses, they may cause particular problems due to children's relative lack of experience and knowledge. All these factors are likely to affect how competent children themselves feel, and how competent they are regarded by others to be, within the court setting.

Until recently, child witnesses called to appear in the Crown Court have received comparatively little consideration of their particular needs. By contrast, child defendants in most cases in England and Wales will appear in Youth Courts which have been specially designed to cater for their requirements (see Box 1). Thus, practice in the Youth Courts facilitates children's competence.

BOX 1

Youth Courts in England and Wales

Youth Courts were introduced in their current form in October 1992 and deal with children and young people aged between 10 and 17 years unless they are charged with homicide; aged 14 or above and charged with a 'grave crime' such as indecent assault or charged jointly with an adult. These exceptions are tried in the Crown Court, as in the Thompson and Venables case.

Some of the key features of the Youth Courts include:
- consideration for the welfare of the young person's welfare, including his or her long-term development;
- special pre-court procedures concerning the arrest, interview, detention and charging of children and young people and their cases;
- emphasis on parents' or guardians' involvement in the process and court proceedings;
- in-court procedures designed to make it easier for children and young people to follow the proceedings and participate more fully in them;
- specially trained magistrates;
- no person present unless authorized by the court;
- designated waiting areas, entrances and courtrooms where possible;
- a special form of the oath for all witnesses who 'promise' to tell the truth rather than 'swear' to do so;
- alternative terms for 'conviction' and 'sentence';
- limited media reporting and no identification of the young person in press reports.

Source: Gordon et al., 1999

Contrast the features of Youth Courts described in Box 1 with the experience in the criminal court, as described in Section 2.2. Following the Thompson and Venables case, practice in the Crown Court with respect to young defendants moved towards the type of practice already existing in the Youth Courts.

Scotland and Northern Ireland also follow the adversarial tradition, but Scotland in particular has some major differences. For example, all cases – not just those involving children – must have corroborating evidence (that is, a person cannot be convicted on the evidence of one witness alone) and there has never been an 'age limit' below which a child's evidence may not be received by the courts. Further, young defendants and young witnesses who have been offended against (sexually or otherwise abused); are subject to a system of Children's Hearings which share many of the features of Youth Courts.

Children's Hearings
A Scottish system of tribunals for considering cases where children under 16 years are thought to have committed offences, or to have been offended against, or to otherwise be beyond parental control.

Figure 3   Giving evidence at the Magistrates' court.

Many other European countries – for example, France and Germany – have an inquisitorial system of justice, which operates on somewhat different principles. In an inquisitorial system, 'the court is viewed as a public agency appointed to get to the bottom of the disputed matter. The court takes the initiative in gathering information as soon as it has notice of the dispute, builds up a file on the matter by questioning all those it thinks may have useful information to offer – including, in a criminal case, the defendant – and then applies its reasoning powers to the material it has collected in order to determine where truth lies' (Spencer and Flin, 1993, p. 75).

Inquisitorial
A trial system where the court is viewed as a public authority which takes an active role in investigating and adjudicating upon the disputed matter.

Children's experiences in the inquisitorial system can be very different to those in an adversarial system. In Germany, all decisions, including the verdict, are made by a panel of professional and lay judges (Köhnken, 2002). The child is questioned exclusively by the chairing judge, and the defendant is removed from the courtroom while the child witness testifies. No juries are involved in a criminal trial. If the defendant or victim is a child, the case is brought before a special juvenile court, and expert witnesses (usually psychologists) are often appointed by the court to aid it in judging the child's competency to testify, and the credibility of their statement (see Box 2).

BOX 2

Statement validity analysis and criteria-based content analysis

A system of 'statement validity analysis' (SVA) and 'criteria-based content analysis' (CBCA) was developed by German psychologists on the basis of their clinical experience (Steller and Köhnken, 1989; Undeutsch, 1989) in an attempt to evaluate the competency of the child witness – or, more specifically, the 'competency' of the child's *account*. Within CBCA, nineteen criteria are applied to children's statements. The more criteria that are present, the more the statement is regarded as credible and the greater the value placed on it. Many of the criteria relate to children's cognitive development, and include:

- general characteristics, such as the quantity of details provided, and whether they are produced in a child-like, disorganized way;
- specific contents, for example whether the child reports unexpected complications during the incident;
- peculiarities of content, such as accurately reported details misunderstood (e.g. when a child reports 'milky water' (semen) coming out of the perpetrator's penis during ejaculation);
- motivation-related content, for example admitting lack of memory;
- offence-specific elements, such as details characteristic of the offence.

Interestingly, the reliability and validity of SVA and CBCA itself have been hotly debated by other psychologists (usually those working from outside the tradition) in subsequent empirical studies (Vrij, 2005).

More recently the distinction between adversarial and inquisitorial systems has diminished as both systems 'borrow' from each other (Spencer and Flin, 1993; Köhnken, 2002). Some countries have further developed alternative approaches to dealing with cases involving children, particularly when they concern child protection matters (Spencer *et al.*, 1990; Bottoms and Goodman, 1996). The Netherlands, for example, has a 'confidential doctor' service to receive reports from anyone who suspects a child is being abused (Lamers-Winkelman and Buffing, 1996). Israel has 'youth interrogators' (David, 1990) who have the sole authority to interview children under 15 years of age who are the alleged victims, witnesses or perpetrators of sex crimes. The remainder of this chapter, however, concentrates on children's competency within adversarial systems of law.

Summary of Section 2

- Throughout history, images of children in the legal system have swung between negative and positive. Psychologists, too, have both publicly questioned and promoted children's competency as witnesses.
- The Thompson and Venables case raises many issues about the way society views and treats children as perpetrators and victims/witnesses of crime.

- Children's experiences of the legal system will differ depending on whether the proceedings are criminal or civil, and on whether the child is a defendant or a witness. Children rarely appear in person in civil courts.
- Systems of law may be adversarial or inquisitorial. The former in particular has a number of implications for children appearing as witnesses.

3 Children's competency as witnesses

Live (CCTV) links
A live television link which enables a witness not present in the courtroom itself to communicate with the court (e.g. from a room nearby). The witness sits in front of a television monitor and can see the faces of the people questioning him or her. At the same time, television pictures of the witness are relayed to the courtroom.

Videotaped evidence-in-chief
Usually a video recording of a previous interview with the witness (which may be edited). For example, it may be a video recording of an investigative interview of a child who is suspected of being sexually abused, carried out by a police officer or a social worker.

As already noted, the 1980s saw an increase in psychological interest in issues connected to children's testimony, and psychological research was to have a key role in facilitating reforms in legislation and procedure (Westcott *et al.*, 1999). England and Wales have perhaps gone furthest in accommodating the needs of child witnesses and highlighting the difficulties children face in adversarial criminal proceedings (Home Office, 1998), but many other countries have begun to adopt similar reforms too (Bottoms and Goodman, 1996; Spencer *et al.*, 1990).

In England and Wales, psychological research has been influential in two important respects: in the introduction and evaluation of video technology to assist children giving evidence (such as live closed circuit television (CCTV) links and videotaped evidence-in-chief; Davies and Noon, 1991; Davies *et al.*, 1995); and in the development of guidelines on how best to interview children including the *Memorandum of Good Practice on Video Recorded Interviews with Child Witnesses for Criminal Proceedings* (Home Office/DoH, 1992).

The *Memorandum of Good Practice,* in particular, is a good example of psycho-legal collaboration: it was drafted by a psychologist and a lawyer, and overseen by a steering group of interested professionals, policy makers and practitioners.

3.1 The questioning of children and the *Memorandum of Good Practice*

The *Memorandum of Good Practice* (Home Office/DoH, 1992) was published to accompany the video reforms of the 1991 Criminal Justice Act. It was intended to guide practitioners on the procedural and technical aspects of carrying out a videotaped investigative interview with a child. At the time it was published, the *Memorandum* represented a distillation of the best advice available for interviewers, based on the findings of psychological research and practical experience, as well as legal requirements. In 2002, to accompany the Youth Justice and Criminal Evidence Act, 1999, the *Memorandum* was revised following developments in law, practice and research, and incorporated into *Achieving Best Evidence in Criminal Proceedings: guidance for vulnerable or intimidated witnesses, including children* (Home Office, 2002). Before these documents are introduced, consider what psychological research has had to say about interviewing children in Research summary 1.

The effectiveness of different techniques of questioning child witnesses

Dent and Stephenson (1979) asked 40 children aged between 10 and 11 years to watch, on their own, a short film which showed a man stealing a parcel from a car, being apprehended, then escaping and being chased. Immediately after seeing the film (Session 1) each child was asked to recall as much about it as possible. They were then questioned in different ways according to three experimental conditions.

Condition 1: free report, where there were no questions but just a prompt to report all they could remember from the film;

Condition 2: general questions such as 'Tell me as much as you can about what the man in the white mac looked like and what he was wearing';

Condition 3: specific questions such as 'What colour hair did the man in the white mac have?'.

This procedure was repeated the next day (Session 2). On the third day (Session 3), 2 weeks later (Session 4) and 2 months later (Session 5), all of the children were interviewed again, using specific questions for all conditions. The amount of correct and incorrect information provided by the children was scored and is shown in Table 1.

Table I   **Children's recall of information according to different types of questions**

| | Questioning session | | | | |
| | Differentiated questioning | | Standard questioning (specific questions) | | |
Questioning condition	Session 1: Immediately after film	Session 2: Next day	Session 3: Third day	Session 4: 2 weeks later	Session 5: 2 months later
Mean correct points					
Condition 1: Free report	14.2	17.8	30.0	33.7	32.3
Condition 2: General questions	22.0	23.7	37.5	38.0	37.3
Condition 3: Specific questions	34.0	34.4	33.9	35.4	34.0
Mean incorrect points					
Condition 1: Free report	1.4	1.7	9.1	8.9	11.9
Condition 2: General questions	3.0	3.9	9.7	9.2	8.2
Condition 3: Specific questions	8.2	7.9	8.3	8.9	8.1

Source: Dent and Stephenson (1979).

Activity 4   *Children's performance under questioning*

Allow about
10 minutes

This activity further develops your ability to interpret numerical data.

Study the data in Table I and write down your interpretation of the results across the different conditions.

Comment

In the final three sessions (3 to 5), where all children were asked specific questions, there is no difference in the amount of correct or incorrect information recalled. In the first two sessions there are significant differences among conditions for both correct recall ($F = 19.4$, df = 2, $p < .001$) and for incorrect recall ($F = 24.4$, df = 2, $p < .001$). The children in the free report condition (Condition I) gave less correct and less incorrect information than children in either the general or specific questions conditions. The children answering general questions also provided less correct and less incorrect information than children answering specific questions. Answering specific questions brought about increases in the amount of both correct and incorrect details provided by children in the free report and general questions conditions, so that the performance of children in all three conditions was essentially the same.

To what extent does the experiment outlined in Research summary 1 mimic the actual experience of a child witnessing a real-life event and later being interviewed by a police officer about it? To be able to answer this question you have to consider how far the study represents the real-life event and thus how far the results may be generalized. This issue is a primary consideration for researchers and is called 'ecological validity'.

Although it may be easy to criticize the artificial nature of the study by Dent and Stephenson, in practice many psychologists use similar procedures today to investigate issues in relation to questioning children. Ethical and methodological constraints are particularly salient because most research in this area is carried out in the context of child sexual abuse investigations. In experimental studies, psychologists have typically staged an event, such as an argument between two actors or a magic show, which is witnessed by children who are later individually questioned about what happened (e.g. Ceci *et al.*, 2002). The event is usually recorded on video so that the researcher knows exactly what has happened and the accuracy and completeness of the child's account can be evaluated. Studies of this sort have been complemented by analyses of transcripts of interviews with children many of whom are suspected victims of sexual abuse (e.g. Sternberg *et al.*, 2001). Here accuracy and completeness cannot be verified, but actual questioning patterns can be examined. Both sources of information agree about the utility of different sorts of questions, and a 'typology' of questions has emerged (Lamb *et al.*, 2002).

Typology of questions

Experimental and applied research confirms the value of general (or open) questions, and raises concerns about the possible negative consequences of specific (or focused) questions. This contradicts some of the findings reported in Research summary 1, where Dent and Stephenson's early study (1979) found that general questions were less successful overall than specific questions.

Open questions require information to be recalled from memory, for example 'What happened yesterday?' They do not prescribe the witness's response in any specific way and, because of this, are most likely to get the most accurate information from the child's original memory. Most questions beginning with 'what', 'when', 'where' and 'who' – the so-called Wh- questions – are classified as open questions. *Facilitators*, such as 'OK' and 'hmm', encourage the child to continue his or her account. Since they, too, are non-leading and non-specific, they are effective at maintaining the witness's account without decreasing its accuracy. Although information elicited by open questions and facilitators is usually very accurate and thus of high quality, it is also usually limited in quantity. Interviewers are therefore likely to ask a child witness further questions.

Focused questions are specific but not leading. They require the witness to search their memory for details or aspects of the event that they have mentioned previously. They may be open-ended, or cued invitations to recall specific information such as 'What was he wearing?' Focused questions usually increase the number of correct details provided by witness because they offer cues or support for the child's memory. At the same time they often reduce the accuracy of the witness's account overall, because witnesses tend also to provide more inaccurate details, as is evident in Table 1 in Research summary 1. Such inaccuracies introduced by focused questions may be due to a failure to remember the specific item, or to social psychological factors, such as guessing in an effort to please the interviewer.

Option-posing questions, such as 'Was the door open or shut?', involve recognition memory. Such questions are sometimes referred to as 'closed' because they limit the answer the child can give, and they may also focus on aspects of the event that the witness has not already mentioned. In this way, they may also be considered 'leading', but the term *leading question* is usually reserved for questions which strongly suggest what response is required of the child (such as 'He was naughty, wasn't he?'), or assume details which the witness has not yet provided. Leading questions are the ones regarded as most problematic by both psychologists and lawyers in terms of the limited value they add – and the damage they can do – to a witness's account and its subsequent credibility. The possibility exists that the witness is not answering from memory at all, but rather is simply repeating or acquiescing to information contained in the question.

The *Memorandum of Good Practice* and its successor, *Achieving Best Evidence*, contain examples and explanations of these different types of questions and encourage interviewers to use open questions as much as possible. Both documents advocate a four-phase approach to investigative interviews, which is outlined in Box 3.

BOX 3

The Memorandum/Achieving Best Evidence phased interview

Phase 1: Rapport

The purpose of this phase is to establish a rapport or relationship between the interviewer and the child, so that the child is able to relax as much as possible. The interviewer should also reassure the child, refer to the video equipment, discuss 'ground rules' (for example, that it is acceptable for the child to answer 'I don't know') and convey the need for the child to tell the truth.

Phase 2: Free narrative

In this phase the child should be enabled to give an account of their experience, without questioning or interruptions from the interviewer. Only open-ended prompts or facilitators should be used to encourage the child.

Phase 3: Questioning

The interviewer uses questions to elicit further details, and missing information, from the child. Interviewers should make use of open questions as much as possible, with a progression through specific, closed and *exceptionally* leading questions, as necessary.

Phase 4: Closure

During this phase interviewers should check their understanding of the child's account (with each other, and possibly through further questioning of the child) and ensure that the child does not leave the interview distressed. They should thank the child, explain what will happen next and answer any questions the child may have.

Evaluations of *Memorandum* interviews show that interviewers have variable skills in incorporating the interview phases (Davies *et al.*, 1995; Westcott and Kynan, in press). In particular, free narrative and closure are often omitted or poorly conducted. Another major finding has been an over-reliance on specific questions, with too few open questions, and too many option-posing and leading questions being asked (Sternberg *et al.*, 2001). Coupled with the lack of a free narrative, these interviewer behaviours can result in the adult talking too much and taking control of the interview, rather than the child being enabled to give their account. However, the pressures on both interviewers and children in *Memorandum/Achieving Best Evidence* interviews are very great, and many other factors, including fear and embarrassment, make such interviews very difficult for all concerned (Westcott and Jones, 1997).

Although this typology of questions and this interviewing framework have developed in the context of investigative interviewing, they also raise important questions about the approach to interviewing children for research purposes (Westcott and Littleton, 2005). For example, it is very important to have a rapport phase which genuinely engages the child in the research activity. If children are given the opportunity to talk at length through the equivalent of a 'free narrative' phase, or through the use of open questions, the researcher is much more likely to gain the child's own perspective, and thus enhance their understanding. Researchers should also consider the types of questions that children encounter in their school environment, where they know that, in most circumstances, a teacher asking a question knows the answer already. How might that influence the responses that they give in a research interview where they may likewise assume the interviewer already knows the answer and try to guess what it is?

3.2   Children's understanding of truth and lies

In England and Wales, children giving evidence in *Memorandum* or *Achieving Best Evidence* interviews no longer have a formal assessment of their competency, or ability to tell the truth. Previously, the judge might ask the child questions (concerning truth-telling and telling lies, for example) in order to establish their competency, and whether or not their testimony should be given sworn or unsworn. Although there is no longer a formal assessment, interviewers conducting an investigative interview with a child on video will discuss with them the importance of telling the truth in the rapport phase (a gesture towards competency assessment). Psychologists have been interested in issues related to these developments, and have established that factors in three domains of children's development are likely to be relevant:

1   cognition, for example, their understanding of theory of mind (Perner, 1997);
2   language, as in their comprehension of abstract vocabulary such as 'truth', 'lies' and 'promise', and their understanding of the consequences of telling lies (Lyon, 2002);
3   their motivation to protect themselves or significant others (Lyon, 2002).

It is not clear that courts – or interviewers in videotaped interviews – have fully considered these different factors in their assessments of children's competency to take the oath, or their understanding of truth and lies (Bala *et al.*, 2001). Often quite young children are asked to show abstract understanding of relevant terms, something which can be difficult even for adults, as Activity 5 may demonstrate.

Activity 5   *Truth and lies*

Allow about
5 minutes

This activity highlights some of the problems of understanding and articulating abstract concepts.

Write down a definition of the terms 'truth' and 'lie'. Now explain the difference between the two.

Comment

You may have found this task harder than you expected – especially if you tried to avoid using circular reasoning (the truth is not telling lies, lying is the opposite of telling the truth, etc.).

▲

Lyon and his colleagues (Lyon, 2002) have highlighted some of the problems for children in traditional approaches to assessing their understanding of the oath. These principally concern the level of abstract reasoning required. As in Activity 5, such approaches usually involve asking a child either to define the terms 'truth' and 'lie' or to describe the difference between them. Lyon proposes that, instead, children are asked to identify statements as truth or lies, something which those as young as 4 years have been able to do in experimental studies (Bussey and Grimbeek, 2000). Research summary 2 summarizes one such study by Lyon and Saywitz (1999) which is an example of a collaboration between academics in the fields of law and psychology.

RESEARCH SUMMARY 2

Assessing children's understanding of truth and lies

Lyon and Saywitz (1999) identified 96 abused (physically, sexually and emotionally) and neglected children aged between 4 and 7 years who were awaiting judicial proceedings. They participated in a number of tasks designed to investigate their ability to identify truth and lies (identification task – A), distinguish between truth and lies (difference task – B), and define the terms (definition task – C).

In the identification task (A), children opened a 'door' on a picture to reveal an object, and were asked if it was the truth or a lie if 'somebody' either named the object as the child did, or named it incorrectly. For example, if the opened door revealed a picture of a lion, the experimenter would say, 'If somebody says that's a puppy, is that the truth or a lie?' This procedure was repeated four times.

In the difference task (B), children opened two doors and had to say if the pictures underneath each were the same (e.g. two pictures of identical cars), or different (e.g. a picture of a sock and a picture of a tree), and why. This procedure was repeated before the child was asked to say whether telling a lie and telling the truth were the same or different, and why.

In the definition task (C), the children were asked to define terms like cat and 'taking a nap' as if the experimenter was a baby and did not know what some words meant. Later the experimenter asked the child, 'How about telling a lie? Do you know what it means to tell a lie? What does it mean to tell a lie?' with the same procedure for the truth.

The results of this experiment are summarized in Figure 4.

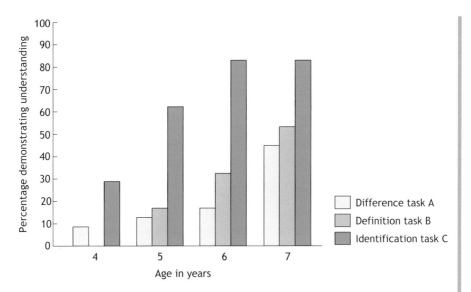

Figure 4 Percentage of participants demonstrating understanding as a function of age and task (Lyon and Saywitz, 1999).

Lyon and Saywitz concluded that most children were able to identify truthful statements and lies by the age of 5 years (task A), but that few children younger than 7 years could provide 'minimally sufficient' descriptions of either the difference between truth and lies (task B), or definitions of truth and lies (task C). Consequently, the difference and definition tasks underestimated children's actual understanding of the truth and lies.

You should note that it is unusual yet important for abused and neglected children to be participants in experimental studies. Abused and neglected children's performance might be adversely affected by psychological effects of abuse, such as clinical depression and low self-esteem, or by other factors associated with their abuse experience, such as problems with concentration or motivation. As a consequence, they may behave differently in such a study from children who have not been maltreated, and that in turn affects the degree to which the results can be generalized to the legal context.

Motivational factors have also been considered in this research programme (Lyon, 2002). Lyon and his colleagues suspected that children find discussing lies particularly difficult – for example because they fear that if they are seen to identify lies, then it might make the interviewer suspect that they would tell a lie. Similarly, children might find it unpleasant and possibly frightening to discuss the consequences of lying for themselves, or to call the interviewer a liar in test scenarios. Further studies have explored and confirmed these suppositions both by asking children to identify as lies statements made either by an adult interviewer or by a child in a story, and by asking them to discuss the consequences of lying for either themselves or for a child in a story. Children were more competent in identifying lies told by the story child, rather than by the interviewer, and when discussing the consequences for the story child rather than for themselves (Lyon, 2002).

From a legal perspective, it is important that motivational factors to tell the truth, or to lie, are addressed. Psychologists examining what interviewers actually do in investigative interviews (Huffman *et al.*, 1999; Westcott and Kynan, in press) have found that the following example is typical of an assessment of children's understanding of truth and lies:

Interviewer:	If I said that door was purple with pink spots [it is actually brown], would that be the truth or a lie?
Child:	A lie.
Interviewer:	If I said that the door was brown, would that be the truth or a lie?
Child:	The truth.

Although this child has demonstrated knowledge of the difference between true and false information (she knows what colour the door really is), the issues at stake in a court case involve more sophisticated cognitive, linguistic and moral factors (Perner, 1997). For example, does the child appreciate the possible consequences for the defendant if he or she is telling lies in a false allegation? Is there a reason why the child might be motivated to make a false allegation, for example in retaliation? *Achieving Best Evidence* (Home Office, 2002) includes examples of stories which can be used with children of different ages to initiate discussions of truth telling, including issues of intent and consequences, in investigative interviews (developed from work by psychologists, McCaron *et al.*, 2004).

Does asking a child to take an oath make them give more accurate evidence? Psychological research on this question is rather limited, and as yet there is no clear evidence to suggest that it does, although some studies have suggested that asking children to 'promise' to tell the truth may encourage truth telling (Lyon and Dorado, 1999; Talwar *et al.*, 2002). Research summary 3 describes an American study by Huffman *et al.* (1999) which investigated the relationship between discussing truth and lies, and children's subsequent accuracy in describing an event.

Assessing children's understanding of truth and lies

In the first part of their research, Huffman and her colleagues (1999) looked at discussions of truth and lies during interviews with children who were suspected of being sexually abused. They found that such 'standard' discussions were typically very basic (such as distinguishing between true and false information) and did not vary according to the age of the child being interviewed. Interviewers also relied on closed questions to elicit 'yes or no' answers from children when, as already noted, such questions are not the most desirable method for eliciting information. Huffman *et al.* went on to devise an experiment that built upon the descriptive knowledge they had obtained in their first analyses.

A 'standard' protocol was developed for discussing truth and lies (T&L). It contained one question asking if the child understood the difference between the truth and a lie, two questions requiring the child to make a truth–lie judgement (such as, 'If I said that you were a boy, would that be a truth or a lie?'), and one statement by the interviewer requesting the child to tell only the truth in the interview. By contrast, an 'elaborate' protocol included more open-ended questions, focused on examples and definitions of lies, included a question regarding the consequences of lying, and required children to make truth–lie judgements about three different scenarios. The researchers hypothesized that having children discuss truth and lying in a more elaborate or extended fashion would make them more accurate when asked to recall an event.

Sixty-seven children aged 4 to 6 years participated in a play event with a visitor to their pre-school. One week later, they were interviewed about the event, using a mixture of misleading and non-leading questions. After a further 2 days they were re-interviewed by a different interviewer in one of three conditions: no T&L (the control group), standard T&L, or elaborate T&L. Following the discussion of T&L (or no discussion of T&L for children in the control group), children were asked to recall the event and then were asked specific questions. Analyses showed that, at the time of the first interview, there were no differences in the accuracy of children's responses across conditions. However, after the second interview, there were differences. Specifically, children in the elaborate T&L condition were more accurate than children given the standard T&L or no T&L discussion, who did not differ from each other. The researchers went on to suggest that discussing T&L with young children is only effective if this discussion is more elaborate than that which typically takes place in investigative interviews.

Summary of Section 3

- There have been many innovations and reforms of legislation and legal procedure to encourage child witness evidence in England and Wales, such as the introduction of videotaped evidence, and the abolition of the competency requirement.
- Psychological research has informed the development of guidelines for interviewing child witnesses, notably the *Memorandum of Good Practice* (Home Office/DoH, 1992) and its successor, *Achieving Best Evidence* (Home Office, 2002).
- Psychologists have investigated children's competency to take the oath and their understanding of truth and lies. Researchers have suggested ways in which young children can be helped to demonstrate their understanding of truthful and untruthful statements, and subsequently to give more accurate reports.

4   Children and criminal responsibility

As noted at the start of this chapter, forensic psychologists are interested in many aspects of children's offending behaviour, such as family conflict and behavioural problems (Farrington, 1996). They are also interested in the treatment and rehabilitation of young offenders (Hollin and Howells, 1996). This section will focus on competency-related issues with respect to young offenders, and in doing so it maintains the link to the earlier consideration of the competency of witnesses.

4.1 Criminal responsibility and *doli incapax*

In the Thompson and Venables case, psychiatrists and teachers concluded that the boys were capable of certain moral judgements. This was necessary because of the *doli incapax* rule, which applied to young people aged between 10 and 13 years and presumed that they were unable to form criminal intent, *unless* the prosecution provided evidence that disproved this presumption. Children aged under 10 years in England and Wales cannot be charged with a criminal offence, because they are presumed by law (the Children and Young Persons Act 1933) not to be responsible for their actions. The presumption could therefore only be overcome if the court was convinced, beyond reasonable doubt, that the rule should be ignored. For *doli incapax* not to apply, prosecutors had to show (for example, through the assessments provided in the Thompson and Venables case) that the child defendant knew that what he or she was doing was seriously wrong, and was thus criminally responsible. *Doli incapax* was abolished in England and Wales by the Crime and Disorder Act 1998. A similar presumption, that a boy under the age of 14 was incapable of sexual intercourse, was abolished by the Sexual Offences Act 1993.

    The *doli incapax* rule was created by judges in the sixteenth and seventeenth centuries 'in an attempt to ameliorate an exceedingly harsh criminal law that mandated death for most offences' (Bedingfield, 1998, p. 481). In the later part of the twentieth century, however, this rule was seen by some judges as absurd and 'an affront to common sense' (*C (A Minor) versus Director of Public Prosecutions*, [1995]). Such statements implied that children, or rather society's view of children, had changed in some way, and they suggest perhaps that children today are – or are seen to be – more 'criminally culpable' than they were previously. Stephen Scarlett, the Senior Children's Magistrate in New South Wales, Australia, voiced such a view in 2000. He was advocating a drop in age at which *doli incapax* applied in Australia, from 14 to 12 years:

> It would seem obvious that children in the final stages of the 20th century are better educated and more sophisticated than their counterparts 200 years ago [...] A child of 12 in Australia has access to television, radio and the Internet, and has a far greater understanding of the world than a 12-year-old in rural Britain in 1769.

(cited in Urbas, 2000, p. 5).

However, Scarlett's contemporary, the president of the New South Wales Law Society counter-argued that 'Just because they are bombarded with electronic information [and] the Internet ... doesn't mean they have any greater intellectual development' (cited in Urbas, 2000, p. 5).

This is an illustration of competing constructions of children and their position as antagonists or victims, located in prevailing cultural conditions. Normally, three criteria have to be met if a person is to be held criminally responsible (Carson, 1995):

1   They knew the act was punishable or wrong when they were committing it.
2   They were aware of what they were doing, and were doing it voluntarily.
3   They were aware of short-term and long-term consequences of their behaviour.

Relevant questions in the context of this chapter therefore include: 'When do children know that an act is punishable or wrong?'; 'When are children aware of what they are doing?'; and 'When do children understand the consequences of their behaviour?' To what extent do psychological theories of moral development help to answer these questions? Applying such theories to the legal (or 'real-world') context is rarely straightforward.

4.2 Psychological theories of moral development

SG

According to Piaget, there is close correspondence between children's cognitive and moral development. In keeping with his stage theory of cognitive development, Piaget (1932) developed a similar model of moral development (see Box 4).

BOX 4

Key features of Piaget's theory of moral development

Age 0–5 years: Premoral

Little understanding of rules or morality.

Age 5–10 years: Moral realism

Rigid belief that rules must be obeyed and that actions are judged by their consequences. Children in this stage believe that the naughtier the behaviour, the greater should be the punishment, and also that naughty behaviour will always be punished.

Age 10+years: Moral relativism

Recognition that people have different moral standards, and greater flexibility in moral understanding, including individuals' intentions as well as consequences of behaviour. Children in this stage know that rules can be broken, and that wrong behaviour is not always punished. Further, they believe that punishment 'should fit the crime'.

Source: Piaget (1932).

He argued that games are important for children's moral development because through them children develop an understanding of how rules function and where they come from, as well as whether rules can be changed and, if so, with what consequences. Piaget argued that children generalize this experience and understanding of the use of rules to other contexts. He further distinguished between the *practice* of moral rules (moral *behaviour*) and the ability to *explain* those rules (moral *understanding*), with both developing separately and in parallel. According to this theory, by their early teens children have moved from a view of rules as constraints imposed by adults, to an understanding that rules are changeable, based on mutual co-operation and respect.

Kohlberg (1981) developed these ideas within his own theory of moral development, summarized in Figure 5. Like Piaget, Kohlberg assumed that all children follow a series of stages in moral development, but unlike Piaget he did not formally link the stages to specific ages, and he suggested that moral development continues through adolescence and adulthood.

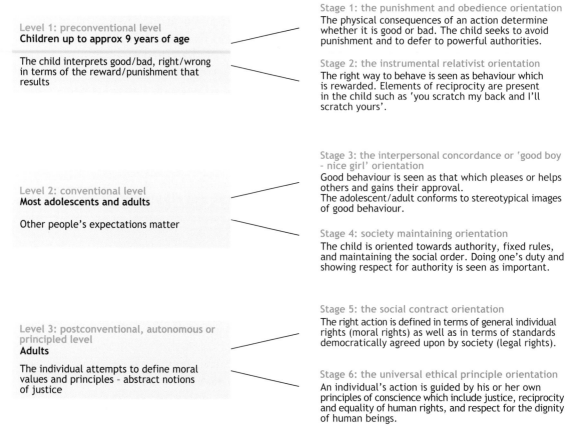

Level 1: preconventional level
Children up to approx 9 years of age

The child interprets good/bad, right/wrong in terms of the reward/punishment that results

Stage 1: the punishment and obedience orientation
The physical consequences of an action determine whether it is good or bad. The child seeks to avoid punishment and to defer to powerful authorities.

Stage 2: the instrumental relativist orientation
The right way to behave is seen as behaviour which is rewarded. Elements of reciprocity are present in the child such as 'you scratch my back and I'll scratch yours'.

Level 2: conventional level
Most adolescents and adults

Other people's expectations matter

Stage 3: the interpersonal concordance or 'good boy - nice girl' orientation
Good behaviour is seen as that which pleases or helps others and gains their approval.
The adolescent/adult conforms to stereotypical images of good behaviour.

Stage 4: society maintaining orientation
The child is oriented towards authority, fixed rules, and maintaining the social order. Doing one's duty and showing respect for authority is seen as important.

Level 3: postconventional, autonomous or principled level
Adults

The individual attempts to define moral values and principles - abstract notions of justice

Stage 5: the social contract orientation
The right action is defined in terms of general individual rights (moral rights) as well as in terms of standards democratically agreed upon by society (legal rights).

Stage 6: the universal ethical principle orientation
An individual's action is guided by his or her own principles of conscience which include justice, reciprocity and equality of human rights, and respect for the dignity of human beings.

Figure 5   Kohlberg's stages of moral development (adapted from Kohlberg, 1981, pp. 17–20).

Social learning theorists (e.g. Bandura, 1965) have approached the issue of moral development in a very different way from both Piaget and Kohlberg. Here, the emphasis is on social factors which influence moral behaviour, rather than moral understanding or reasoning (cognitive factors). Two types of learning are thought to be particularly influential on moral behaviour:

- direct learning – being rewarded (reinforced) for behaving in particular ways, and punished for behaving in certain other ways;
- observational learning – learning by observing other people being rewarded or punished for behaving in certain ways, and then behaving in the way that was rewarded.

According to social learning theory, moral behaviour – both children's and adults' – will show inconsistency across different situations, depending on the rewards or punishments applying in those situations, and will not be linked to particular ages as such.

Finally, Freud's psychodynamic model (1923) stressed the emotional component of moral development. Figure 6 shows Freud's representation of the relationships between the three forces in the psyche – the id, the ego and superego – and levels of consciousness. The id is focused on obtaining pleasure from satisfaction, whether in reality or in fantasy, or of biological needs. The ego is the reality-testing aspect of the self, concerned with integrating the different aspects of self. Finally, the superego is based on the introjection of moral attitudes through the child's identification with significant others, and so represents the conscience.

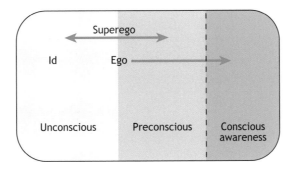

Figure 6   Relations between id, ego and superego and levels of consciousness (adapted from Freud, 1933).

The superego is thus concerned with moral issues and comprises the conscience and the ego-ideal. Within the superego, the conscience makes an individual feel guilty or ashamed of behaving badly, while the ego-ideal makes an individual feel proud of good behaviour. Freud believed that the superego developed at the age of 5 or 6 years as a result of the resolution of the Oedipus complex in boys and the Electra complex in girls. Children identify with the same-sex parent, and incorporate elements of their parents' moral standards within their superego.

As is often the case, applications of these psychological theories are not explicit. Piaget's findings imply that by the age of criminal responsibility in England – 10 years – children's moral development would have been completed, so that they should be held accountable for their actions. By contrast, Kohlberg's theory holds that at 10 years moral development is incomplete, so that it might seem harsh to hold children who are still developing morally criminally responsible. Freud's theory might suggest the need to consider family relationships and moral standards on a case-by-case basis. In the Thompson and Venables case, for example, the role of violent films was highlighted by the judge and media commentators. It seems likely that both the boys had watched such films and there was a discussion on whether this had led them to behave violently, an argument that draws support from the social learning theorists. Although psychological theories do not offer clear-cut and consistent guidance on the age of responsibility, they do, however, suggest issues that it may be helpful to consider.

A review of psychological theories and research related to children's criminal responsibility (Wilson, 2001), concludes that there is no evidence either for or against the viewpoint that children in the twenty-first century are more criminally culpable:

> [T]here are no known empirical studies that directly examine if children today have a better understanding of right and wrong than do children of previous generations. [...] It is now known that children's understanding of right and wrong is more complex than previously thought. It may be that children's thinking has developed greater complexity, but it is more likely that our understanding of children has merely improved. [...] More research is needed to establish exactly how children's understanding of right and wrong in different contexts develops.

> (Wilson, 2001, p. 22)

4.3 Deception in children

One factor which links back to questions around criminal responsibility and *doli incapax* is deception. For example, if the prosecution could prove that a child had acted deceptively it might be able to make a case that the presumption of innocence should be ignored. In the Thompson and Venables case, one of the issues the jury had to decide was 'whether the boys told lies out of panic, stupidity, confusion and fear – or because they knew what they'd done was wrong and were trying to hide it' (Morrison, 1997, p. 223). Children's awareness of what they are doing – and of the possible consequences – can be assessed in studies of children's deceptive behaviour. The ability to deceive draws on a number of cognitive skills such as theory of mind and is also related to the understanding of truth and lies discussed earlier. By taking the oath a witness is promising to tell the truth, and thus not to lie or deceive about their account of events. This final section will therefore consider some of what is known about children's deception.

Activity 6   *Deception in the early years*

Allow about
10 minutes

This activity explores your understanding of the nature of deception.

Spend a few minutes thinking about your own childhood, or that of children you know. Try to recall early incidents of intentional deception. What form did they take? How old were you, or the child you are thinking of? At what age do you think children are first able to deceive?

Comment

What factors have influenced your decision? Perhaps you have considered the type of lie – verbal or non-verbal – or the reason(s) why children might lie, such as to protect themselves or others.

Psychological research suggests that children are capable of simple deceptive behaviour, particularly to avoid punishment, by the age of about 3 years (Lewis, 1993). In its earliest form, such behaviour is likely to be non-verbal (for example, a boy shaking his head when asked if he has broken a toy) or one-word answers (for example, a girl answering 'no' when asked if she has eaten all the sweets). In a typical study, Lewis and colleagues (1989) instructed children aged between 33 and 37 months not to 'peek' at a toy while an experimenter left the room that they were in together. Most children did in fact look at the toy, but the great majority later denied that they had peeked, or would not answer the question. At around 5 years of age, children should be 'capable of telling plausible and convincing elaborate lies', but 'whether this is indeed the case needs to be investigated' (Vrij, 2002, p. 189).

In the context of this chapter, the motivation to tell lies is important. Would a child lie in court to detract from their own wrongdoing, or to obtain a conviction on false charges, or because they have been coached to do so? Vrij (2002) has suggested a developmental progression in the reasons why children lie:

- to avoid punishment;
- to obtain a reward;
- to protect their self-esteem;
- to maintain relationships (e.g. 'I didn't want to make him feel bad, that's why I didn't show my disappointment');
- to conform to norms and conventions.

Thus, younger children will tell the truth in order to avoid punishment, whereas older children will emphasize truth-telling in order to uphold the laws and rules of society; this is reminiscent of the later stages of moral development proposed by Kohlberg. Ruck (1996) showed children aged between 7 and 13 years various vignettes in which a child had witnessed or had been involved in a crime, and was subsequently required to testify in court. On the basis of his findings, Ruck developed a four-level scale to describe children's understanding of telling the truth in court:

Level 0: Irrelevant or no response;

Level 1: Concern with negative consequences to self;

Level 2: Concern with exhibiting good qualities and behaviour;

Level 3: Concern with the laws of society.

Ruck found that the younger children demonstrated reasoning at Level 1, whereas the oldest children were operating at Level 3.

Once again, it is important to note that Ruck's participants were 'typical' schoolchildren. Bearing in mind the earlier discussion on the involvement of abused and neglected children as participants in Lyon's research, you might speculate that involving young offenders as participants would give a different view of children's understanding of truth-telling and moral behaviour. For example, Palmer and Hollin (1998) investigated moral reasoning in young offenders and non-offenders, and found that the offenders had some specific and some global deficits in moral reasoning, particularly with respect to moral values related to delinquent behaviour.

Children may also lie for other reasons, such as to protect a loved one (Ceci and DeSimone Leichtman, 1992). This can be particularly relevant to a situation where a child is called as a witness in a case where the parent is accused of wrongdoing. Research summary 4 describes an experiment conducted by Talwar *et al.* (2004) where this type of lying was investigated. This is a further example of research stemming from interest in a subject which is shared by both psychologists and lawyers.

RESEARCH SUMMARY 4

Children's lie-telling behaviour

Talwar and her colleagues (Talwar *et al.*, 2004) arranged an experimental situation in which children aged between 3 and 11 years were coached by their parents not to report a transgression. The parents were acting as confederates of the experimenters and deliberately moved a puppet marked with a 'Do not touch' sign, which gave the appearance of the puppet breaking. The researchers were interested to see whether the children would tell the truth about who broke the puppet, and also whether a competency-type assessment involving a discussion of truth and lies (T&L) would promote truth-telling by the children.

Children were placed in one of three conditions:

1   The child witnessed the parent 'break' the puppet and was later questioned in the presence of the parent (parent present condition).
2   The child witnessed the parent 'break' the puppet and was later questioned without their parent present (parent absent condition).
3   The child did not witness the parent 'break' the puppet, but was coached by the parent not to tell the experimenter what had happened to the puppet before the child was later questioned in the absence of the parent (child absent condition).

All children were interviewed twice by two different interviewers about what had happened, using four questions (see Table 2). Between the first and second interview they underwent a discussion of T&L with the second interviewer as a type of competency assessment.

Table 2 Percentage of truthful responses to four questions in two interview conditions

Condition	First interview (%)			Second interview (%)		
	Parent absent	Parent present	Child absent	Parent absent	Parent present	Child absent
Question 1 What happened to the puppet? ('Mom broke it')	52	46	22	85	96	60
Question 2 Did you break the puppet? ('No')	100	98	100	100	100	100
Question 3 Did your mom (dad) break it? ('Yes')	80	67	51	89	96	69
Question 4 Did someone else break it? ('No')	98	96	76	91	91	78

Source: adapted from Talwar et al., 2004.

As shown in Table 2, regardless of whether the children were questioned in the presence or absence of the parent, most children told the truth. The researchers interpreted the 'child absent' condition to show that when the likelihood of the child being blamed for the transgression was reduced (the child was not present when the puppet got broken), significantly more children lied. Significantly more children told the truth in the second interview, after the T&L discussion when they had been asked to promise to tell the truth.

Other elements of this study are interesting in the context of the broader discussion. First, the parents explicitly attempted to coach their children to lie, although they were ultimately not that successful. The degree to which children's evidence may be tainted by coaching, such as in a disputed custody contest between parents, where one parent alleges that the child has reported abuse by the other parent, has been a frequent topic of concern. Note, too, the wording of Questions 2, 3 and 4. They are all closed questions, requiring one-word answers, which should make it easier for children to lie, because they do not have to provide a detailed response which elaborates their deception. Finally, this study speaks to the value of some kind of competency assessment or discussion of T&L in interviews with children (see Section 3).

Surprisingly, perhaps, psychological research on the nature of deceptive behaviour in children, and on the detection of deception in children, has been limited. Vrij (2002) suggests this may be because some people adhere to the maxim that 'children never lie', and indeed this has been a controversial issue in the field of child sexual abuse allegations. Would a child falsely accuse an adult of sexual abuse? Research suggests that the percentage of 'erroneous concerns' of sexual abuse that originate from children is small: in one study (Oates *et al.*, 2000) it amounted to 2.5 per cent of cases. By contrast, it is widely assumed that adults do lie, and research has instead concentrated mostly on differences in the behaviour of truth-tellers and liars, and on the extent to which people can detect deceit in adults (Vrij, 2000).

An interesting parallel is to be found in the field of suggestibility research. With children, psychologists have concentrated on whether or not they are suggestible, and the practical implications of this for interviewers. Adult suggestibility research has instead assumed that adults are suggestible, and has concentrated on theoretical mechanisms through which suggestibility effects might occur.

Vrij (2002) has summarized research findings on children's deception as follows:

children become better liars with increasing age;

parents are better detectors of lying than non-parents;

children's lies are easier to detect when listening to their voices than when looking at their faces;

lies are easier to detect by 'indirect methods' of lie detection;

introverted children and socially anxious children seem less likely to be believed by observers;

judges are better at detecting lies when analysing the content of children's speech than by paying attention to their non-verbal behaviour.

(Adapted from Vrij, 2002, pp. 189–90)

Vrij (2002) concludes that 'a clear picture about children's ability to lie (in court) and people's ability to detect such lies does not exist' (p. 190).

This may seem a surprising conclusion which challenges the conventional assumption of the adversarial tradition (Spencer and Flin, 1993), namely that the judge and jury will gain insight from seeing the behaviour of the witness 'live' on the stand, and that they will be able to 'read' non-verbal behaviour correctly to aid their decision making. This assumption has underpinned a great deal of resistance among the legal community to the introduction of videotaped evidence from children, and to the use of live links (CCTV) and screens by child witnesses appearing in court (Davies and Noon, 1991; Davies *et al.*, 1995). Lawyers prosecuting cases involving child witnesses fear that the technology lessens the impact of the child's evidence, whereas those acting for the defence believe the technology makes it easier for children to be deceptive. Vrij's conclusions suggest both sets of concerns are misplaced. His observation about introverted children is also interesting in the context of this chapter. Children appearing as witnesses or as defendants might well be expected to be socially anxious. Thus their credibility – or perceived competency – might have little to do with their honesty.

Summary of Section 4

- The age at which children can be held responsible for committing a criminal offence has been a source of debate; in England and Wales it is 10 years.
- The *doli incapax* rule in England and Wales presumed that children aged 10–13 years could not be charged with a criminal offence unless the prosecution proved criminal intent; this rule was abolished in England and Wales in 1998 (but still exists in some other countries).
- Four psychological theories of moral development have been proposed: by Piaget, Kohlberg, Freud and the social learning theorists (e.g. Bandura). They highlight factors it may be helpful to consider in individual cases concerning the culpability of young offenders.
- Children are able to behave deceptively from an early age, and by the age of 5 years should be capable of more elaborate verbal deceit. Psychological research on children's deceptive behaviour, especially as it relates to the courtroom, has been relatively limited to date.

5   Conclusion

At the beginning of this chapter Activity 1 highlighted that the way in which children, children's competency, and children's rights are viewed is a socially constructed phenomenon which changes over time and within societies. It is also important to acknowledge that simple dichotomies of children as either good or bad, passive victims or anti-social aggressors, gloss over complexities in their experiences and as a result are often unhelpful. Forensic psychologists must also avoid simplistic stereotypes of the role both of the law and of psychology in relation to children's competency and culpability.

5.1 Children's accuracy and honesty

Two underlying themes can be found throughout this chapter: are children accurate and are children honest when they give evidence, either as witnesses or as defendants? Inevitably, there are no simple answers to these questions, and psychological research can provide only pointers to consider. However, in addressing accuracy and honesty, this chapter has underlined the importance of considering: first, the physical and social context of the interaction with the child; secondly, factors stemming from adults who are interacting with the child; and, finally, factors associated with the children themselves.

The physical and social context

Activity 3 encouraged a consideration of the impact of the requirements of an adversarial system of justice upon children's evidence. Recall, for example, the effect of delays upon the accuracy of children's memory, or the influence of stress on their response to questioning. The Youth Courts (Box 1) have been developed specifically to create an environment that will promote children's accuracy and competency as far as possible.

The adult interviewer

Section 3.1 highlighted that the manner in which an adult questions a child can have a profound effect upon the accuracy of the child's account. To promote both accuracy and honesty, interviewers should ask children as many open-ended questions as possible. These promote reliance on the child's original memory (to enhance accuracy) and encourage detailed responses (thus making prolonged deception more difficult to maintain).

The children themselves

Psychologists have demonstrated that children are capable of simple deceptive behaviour from a relatively early age, and have also suggested a number of reasons why children might lie, both selfish (to protect themselves) and altruistically motivated (to protect loved ones). Current research on children's evidence has been returning to a theme first highlighted by William Stern and his wife Clara (1909, 1999) at the beginning of the twentieth century: the need to distinguish between outright lies and 'false beliefs' that children might have. Thus, it is thought that children may erroneously come to believe that they have experienced an event, for example because their original memory has been influenced by subsequent questioning (Ceci *et al.*, 1994). Thus, in the passing reference to research on false allegations of sexual abuse in Section 4, the term 'erroneous concerns' was used quite deliberately. 'Erroneous concerns' can include intentionally false allegations, as well as those arising from mistaken beliefs held by the child or by adult investigators, or from false beliefs caused by biased questioning that has affected the child's original memory for events (Westcott and Jones, 2003). In deciding whether an individual child is answering accurately or honestly, this chapter has suggested that a wide range of factors needs to be considered, including the child's cognitive, linguistic and moral development as well as their personal development and family background.

5.2 Competency, culpability and credibility

Vrij (2002) observed (Section 4) that children who are socially anxious are more likely to be judged as deceptive, irrespective of their honesty. It is important to note that accuracy and honesty are qualities which are quite separate from credibility, although there may be links between them. A girl may accurately report very few details about an event she has experienced, in a hesitant and unconvincing manner – she may be accurate and honest, but still lack credibility. Conversely, a boy may provide extensive and elaborate details about an event he has not experienced, relying either on his own imagination or on another source of information about the event, such as a friend's account. This boy may be acting deceptively, yet appear very credible. Forensic psychologists have researched perceptions of witness testimony, and found that confidence is a key factor in decision making about the credibility of a witness's evidence unrelated to the actual accuracy or honesty of the witness (Memon *et al.* 2003). For all sorts of reasons, however, children may lack this confidence when they appear in court. Poor interviewing practice may also damage the credibility of a child witness, for example, by failing to check ambiguities that emerge in the child's allegation or by the interviewer dominating an interview rather than enabling the child to give their own account (Westcott and Kynan, in press).

5.3 Final remarks

This chapter may have raised more questions than it has answered. How should decisions about children's competency and culpability be made? Are child witnesses and child defendants treated equally? Should the welfare principles behind the Youth Courts be extended to children who are witnesses in the Crown Court, and should young defendants be afforded the use of video provisions which apply to child witnesses there? If children can be convicted of criminal offences at 10 years, does this imply that they have reached levels of adult consciousness at that age? Such questions will continue to concern psychologists and lawyers for many years to come.

The relationships between children, adults and society are inextricably linked and children's performance in the legal system is a reflection of these complex relationships. To this extent it is important to consider children in context – many of the issues raised here apply also to adults: adults can be inaccurate, dishonest and lack credibility too. It is psychologists' responsibility not to 'theorize incompetent children' (Westcott and Littleton, 2005) by contributing to legal or research environments which undermine their competence or compound their culpability.

Answers to Activity 1

Activity	Age	Activity	Age
Have their body pierced	Any	Get a part-time job	14 years
Open a bank account	10 years	Drink alcohol in private	5 years
Buy a pet	12 years	Drive a moped	16 years
Give evidence at court	Any	Be convicted of a criminal offence (including sexual offences such as rape)	10 years
Buy cigarettes	16 years	Buy a firearm	17 years
Marry with parental consent	16 years	Consent to sex with a same-aged peer	16 years
Have flying lessons	Any	Buy a lottery ticket	16 years
Have name placed on the sex offenders register	10 years	Vote in a general election	18 years

Source: Hamilton et al., 2004

References

Bala, N., Lee, K., Lindsay, R. and Talwar, V. (2001) 'A legal and psychological critique of the present approach to the assessment of the competency of child witnesses', *Osgoode Hall Law Journal*, vol. 38, pp. 409–51.

Bandura, A. (1965) 'Influence of model's reinforcement contingencies on the acquisition of imitative responses', *Journal of Personality and Social Psychology*, vol. 1, pp. 589–95.

Bedingfield, D. (1998) *The Child in Need: Children, the state and the law*, Bristol, Family Law.

Binet, A. (1900) *La Suggestibilité*, Paris, Schleicher Frères.

Bonnie, R., Coughlin, A., Jeffries, J. and Low, P. (1997) *Criminal Law*, Westbury, NY, The Foundation Press.

Bottoms, B. L. and Goodman, G. S. (1996) *International Perspectives on Child Abuse and Children's Testimony: psychological research and law*, Thousand Oaks, CA, Sage.

Brennan, M. and Brennan, R. (1988, 2nd edn) *Strange Language*, Wagga Wagga, Riverina Murray Institute of Higher Education.

Brooks, L. (2003) 'I don't doubt they'd have been ripped to shreds', *The Guardian (G2)*, 6 February, pp. 4–5.

Bussey, K. and Grimbeek, E. J. (2000) 'Children's conceptions of lying and truth-telling: implications for child witnesses', *Legal and Criminological Psychology*, vol. 5, pp. 187–99.

C (A Minor) versus Director of Public Prosecutions, [1995] 2 WLR 383.

Carson, D. (1995) 'Criminal responsibility', in Bull, R. and Carson, D. (eds) *Handbook of Psychology in Legal Contexts*, pp. 277–89, Chichester, Wiley.

Ceci, S. J. and Bruck, M. (1995) *Jeopardy in the Courtroom: a scientific analysis of children's testimony*, Washington, American Psychological Association.

Ceci, S. J. and DeSimone Leichtman, M. (1992) '"I know that you know that I know that you broke the toy": a brief report of recursive awareness among 3-year-olds' in Ceci, S. J., DeSimone Leichtman, M. and Putnick, M. (eds) *Cognitive and Social Factors in Early Deception*, Hillsdale, NJ, Erlbaum.

Ceci, S. J., Huffmann, M. L., Smith, E. and Loftus, E. F. (1994) 'Repeatedly thinking about a non-event: source misattributions among preschoolers', *Consciousness and Cognition*, vol. 3, pp. 388–407.

Ceci, S. J., Crossman, A. M., Scullin, M. H., Gilstrap, L. and Huffman, M. L. (2002) 'Children's suggestibility research: implications for the courtroom and the forensic interview', in Westcott, H. L., Davies, G. M. and Bull, R. H. C. (eds) *Children's Testimony: a handbook of psychological research and forensic practice*, pp. 117–30, Chichester, Wiley.

David, H. (1990) 'The role of youth interrogator', in Spencer, J. R., Nicolson, R. G., Flin, R. and Bull, R. (eds) *Children's Evidence in Legal Proceedings: an international perspective*, Cambridge, University of Cambridge Faculty of Law.

Davies, G. M. and Noon, E. (1991) *An Evaluation of the Live Link for Child Witnesses*, London, Home Office.

Davies, G. M., Wilson, C., Mitchell, R. and Milsom, J. (1995) *Videotaping Children's Evidence: an evaluation*, London, Home Office.

Dent, H. R. and Stephenson, G. M. (1979) 'An experimental study of the effectiveness of different techniques of questioning child witnesses', *British Journal of Social and Clinical Psychology*, vol. 18, pp. 41–51.

DCA (2001) *Judicial Appointments Annual Report 2001–2002* [online] http://www.dca.gov.uk/judicial/ja_arep2002/annex_e.html (accessed 28 June 2005).

Eisen, M. L., Quas, J. A. and Goodman, G. S. (eds) (2002) *Memory and Suggestibility in the Forensic Interview*, Mahwah, NJ, Lawrence Erlbaum Associates.

Esam, B. (2002) 'Young witnesses: still no justice', in Westcott, H. L., Davies, G. M. and Bull, R. H. C. (eds) *Children's Testimony: a handbook of psychological research and forensic practice*, pp. 309–23, Chichester, Wiley.

Farrington, D. P. (1996) *Understanding and Preventing Youth Crime*, York, Joseph Rowntree Foundation.

Flin, R. H., Boon, J., Knox, A. and Bull, R. (1992) 'The effect of a five-month delay on children's and adults' eyewitness memory', *British Journal of Psychology*, vol. 83, pp. 323–35.

Freud, S. (1923) 'The ego and the id', in Strachey, J. (ed.) *Standard Edition: vol. 19*, pp. 1–66, London, The Hogarth Press.

Freud, S. (1933) 'New introductory lectures on psycho-analysis', in Strachey, J. (ed.) *Standard Edition: vol. 22*, pp. 1–182, London, The Hogarth Press.

Gillan, A. (1999) 'Fear and trauma in courtroom', *The Guardian*, December 17.

Goodman, G. S. (1984) 'Children's testimony in historical perspective', *Journal of Social Issues*, vol. 40, pp. 9–31.

Gordon, W., Cuddy, P. and Black, J. (1999) *Introduction to Youth Justice* (incorporating *Introduction to the Youth Court*), Winchester, Waterside Press.

Hamilton, C., Fiddy, A. and Paton, L. (2004) *At What Age Can I? A guide to age-based legislation*, Colchester, The Children's Legal Centre.

HMCS (2000) 'Thompson and Venables recommendation as to tariffs to the Secretary of State for Home Affairs' [online] http://www.hmcourts-service.gov.uk/legalprof/tariffs/tariff_t_v.htm (accessed 5 May 2005).

Henderson, E. (2002) 'Persuading and controlling: the theory of cross-examination in relation to children', in Westcott, H. L., Davies, G. M. and Bull, R. H. C. (eds) *Children's Testimony: a handbook of psychological research and forensic practice*, pp. 279–93, Chichester, Wiley.

Heydon, J. (1984) *Evidence. Cases and materials*, London, Butterworth.

Hollin, C. R. and Howells, K. (eds) (1996) *Clinical Approaches to Working with Young Offenders*, Chichester, Wiley.

Home Office (1998) *Speaking Up for Justice: Report of the Interdepartmental Working Group on the Treatment of Vulnerable or Intimidated Witnesses in the Criminal Justice System*, London, Home Office Procedures and Victims Unit.

Home Office (2002) *Achieving Best Evidence in Criminal Proceedings: guidance for vulnerable or intimidated witnesses, including children*, London, Home Office Communication Directorate.

Home Office/Department of Health (DoH) (1992) *Memorandum of Good Practice on Video Recorded Interviews with Child Witnesses for Criminal Proceedings*, London, HMSO.

Huffman, M. L., Warren, A. R. and Larson, S. M. (1999) 'Discussing truth and lies in interviews with children: whether, why and how?', *Applied Developmental Science*, vol. 3, pp. 6–15.

King, M. (1986) *Psychology In and Out of Court: a critical examination of legal psychology*, Oxford, Pergamon Press.

Kohlberg, L. (1981) *The Philosophy of Moral Development: moral stages and the idea of justice*, San Francisco, CA, Harper and Row.

Köhnken, G. (2002) 'A German perspective on children's testimony', in Westcott, H. L., Davies, G. M. and Bull, R. H. C. (eds) *Children's Testimony: a handbook of psychological research and forensic practice*, pp. 233–44, Chichester, Wiley.

Lamb, M.E., Orbach, Y., Sternberg, K.J., Esplin, P.W. and Hershkowitz, I. (2002) 'The effects of forensic interview practices on the quality of information provided by alleged victims of child abuse' in Westcott, H.L., Davies, G.M. and Bull, R.H.C. (eds), *Children's Testimony: A Handbook of Psychological Research and Forensic Practice*, pp. 131–45, Chichester, Wiley.

Lamers-Winkelman, F. and Buffing, F. (1996) 'Children's testimony in the Netherlands: a study of statement validity analysis' in Bottoms, B. L. and Goodman, G. S. (eds), *International Perspectives on Child Abuse and Children's Testimony: psychological research and law*, Thousand Oaks, CA, Sage.

Lewis, M. (1993) 'The development of deception', in Lewis, M. and Saarni, C. (eds) *Lying and Deception in Everyday Life*, New York, NY, The Guilford Press.

Lewis, M., Stanger, C. and Sullivan, M. W. (1989) 'Deception in three-year-olds', *Developmental Psychology*, vol. 25, pp. 439–43.

Lyon, T. D. (2002) 'Child witnesses and the oath', in Westcott, H. L., Davies, G. M. and Bull, R. H. C. (eds) *Children's Testimony: a handbook of psychological research and forensic practice*, pp. 245–60, Chichester, Wiley.

Lyon, T. D. and Dorado, J. S. (1999) 'Does the oath matter? Motivating maltreated children to tell the truth', paper presented at the Annual Meeting of the American Psychological Society, Denver, CO.

Lyon, T. D. and Saywitz, K. J. (1999) 'Young maltreated children's competence to take the oath', *Applied Developmental Science*, vol. 3, pp. 16–27.

McCaron, A. L., Ridgeway, S. and Williams, A. (2004) 'The truth and lie story: developing a tool for assessing child witnesses' ability to differentiate between truth and lies', *Child Abuse Review*, vol. 13, pp. 42–50.

Memon, A., Vrij, A. and Bull, R. (2003) *Psychology and Law: truthfulness, accuracy and credibility*, Chichester, Wiley.

Morrison, B. (1997) *As If*, London, Granta Books.

Morrison, B. (2003) 'Life after James' *The Guardian (G2)*, 6 February, pp. 2–4.

Myers, J. E. B. (1994) 'Definition and origins of the backlash against child protection', in Myers, J. E. B. (ed.) *The Backlash: child protection under fire*, Thousand Oaks, CA, Sage.

Nijboer, H. (1995) 'Expert evidence', in Bull, R. and Carson, D. (eds) *Handbook of Psychology in Legal Contexts*, Chichester, Wiley.

Oates, R. K., Jones, D. P. H., Denson, D., Sirotnak, A., Gary, N. and Krugman, R. D. (2000) 'Erroneous concerns about child sexual abuse', *Child Abuse & Neglect*, vol. 24, pp. 149–57.

Palmer, E. J. and Hollin, C. R. (1998) 'A comparison of patterns of moral development in young offenders and non-offenders', *Legal and Criminological Psychology*, vol. 3, pp. 225–35.

Perner, J. (1997) 'Children's competency in understanding the role of a witness: Truth, lies and moral ties', *Applied Cognitive Psychology*, vol. 11(S1), S21–S35.

Piaget, J. (1932) *The Moral Judgement of the Child*, London, Routledge and Kegan Paul.

Plotnikoff, J. and Woolfson, R. (2004) *In Their Own Words: the experiences of 50 young witnesses in criminal proceedings*, London, NSPCC.

Poole, D. and White, L. (1993) 'Two years later: effects of question repetition and retention interval on eyewitness testimony of children and adults', *Developmental Psychology*, vol. 29, pp. 844–53.

Rivlin, G. (2002, 2nd edn) *First Steps in the Law*, Oxford, Oxford University Press.

Ruck, M. D. (1996) 'Why children think they should tell the truth in court: developmental considerations for the assessment of competency', *Legal and Criminological Psychology*, vol. 1, pp. 103–16.

Saywitz, K. J. (2002) 'Developmental underpinnings of children's testimony', in Westcott, H. L., Davies, G. M. and Bull, R. H. C. (eds) *Children's Testimony: a handbook of psychological research and forensic practice*, Chichester, Wiley.

Sereny, G. (1995) *The Case of Mary Bell*, London, Pimlico.

Spencer, J. R. and Flin, R. (1993) *The Evidence of Children: the law and the psychology*, London, Blackstone.

Spencer, J. R., Nicolson, G., Flin, R. and Bull, R. (1990) *Children's Evidence in Legal Proceedings: an international perspective*, Cambridge, University of Cambridge Faculty of Law.

Steller, M. and Köhnken, G. (1989) 'Criteria-based content analysis', in Raskin, D. C. (ed.) *Psychological Methods in Criminal Investigation and Evidence*, pp. 217–45, New York, NY, Springer-Verlag.

Stern, C. and Stern, W. (1999, translated by J. T. Lamiell) *Recollection, Testimony and Lying in Early Childhood*, Washington, DC, American Psychological Association.

Stern, W. and Stern, C. (1990) *Erinnerung, Aussage und Lüge in der ersten Kindheit*, Leipzig, Barth.

Stern, W. (1910) 'Abstracts of lectures on the psychology of testimony and on the study of individuality', *American Journal of Psychology*, vol. 21, pp. 270–82.

Sternberg, K. J., Lamb, M. E., Davies, G. M., and Westcott, H. L. (2001) 'The Memorandum of Good Practice: theory versus application', *Child Abuse & Neglect*, vol. 25, pp. 669–81.

Talwar, V., Lee, K., Bala, N. and Lindsay, R. C. L. (2002) 'Children's conceptual knowledge of lying and its relation to their actual behaviours: implications for court competence examinations', *Law and Human Behavior*, vol. 26, pp. 395–415.

Talwar, V., Lee, K., Bala, N. and Lindsay, R. C. L. (2004) 'Children's lie-telling to conceal a parent's transgression: legal implications', *Law and Human Behavior*, vol. 28, pp. 411–35.

Undeutsch, U. (1989) 'The development of statement reality analysis', in Yuille, J. C. (ed.), *Credibility Assessment*, pp. 101–21, Dordrecht, Kluwer.

Urbas, G. (2000) *The Age of Criminal Responsibility*, Trends & Issues Paper 181 [online], Canberra, Australian Institute of Criminology, http://www.aic.gov.au/publications/tandi/ti181.pdf (accessed 5 May 2005).

Varendonck, J. (1911) 'Les témoignages d'enfants dans un procès retentissant', *Archives de Psychologie*, vol. 11, pp. 129–71.

Vrij, A. (2000) *Detecting Lies and Deceit. The psychology of lying and the implications for professional practice*, Chichester, Wiley.

Vrij, A. (2002) 'Deception in children: A literature review and implications for children's testimony' in Westcott, H. L., Davies, G. M. and Bull, R. H. C. (eds) *Children's Testimony: A handbook of psychological research and forensic practice*, pp. 175–94, Chichester, Wiley.

Vrij, A. (2005) 'Criteria-based content analysis: a qualitative review of the first 37 studies', *Psychology, Public Policy and Law*, vol. 11, pp. 3–41.

Warren-Leubecker, A., Tate, C. S., Hinton, I. D. and Ozbek, I. N. (1989) 'What do children know about the legal system and when do they know it? First steps down a less traveled path in child witness research', in Ceci, S. J., Toglia, M. P. and Ross, D. F. (eds) *Perspectives on Children's Testimony*, New York, NY, Springer Verlag.

Westcott, H. L. and Jones, D. P. H. (2003) 'Are children reliable witnesses to their experiences?', in Reder, P., Duncan, S. and Lucey, C. (eds) *Studies in the Assessment of Parenting*, London, Brunner-Routledge.

Westcott, H. L. and Jones, J. (1997) (eds) *Perspectives on the Memorandum: policy, practice and research in investigative interviewing*, Aldershot, Arena.

Westcott, H. L. and Kynan, S. (in press) 'Interviewer practice in investigative interviews for suspected child sexual abuse', *Psychology, Crime & Law*.

Westcott, H. L. and Littleton, K. S. (2005) 'Exploring meaning through interviews with children', in Greene, S. M. and Hogan, D. M. (eds) *Researching Children's Experiences: approaches and methods*, London, Sage.

Westcott, H. L., Davies, G. M. and Bull, R. H. C. (eds) (2002) *Children's Testimony: a handbook of psychological research and forensic practice*, Chichester, Wiley.

Westcott, H. L., Davies, G. M. and Spencer, J. R. (1999) 'Children, hearsay and the courts: a perspective from the United Kingdom', *Psychology, Public Policy and Law*, vol. 5, pp. 282–303.

Wilson, J. C. (2001) 'Are children today more criminally culpable than their earlier counterparts?', *Educational and Developmental Psychologist*, vol. 18, pp. 15–24.

Woolard, J. (2002) 'Capacity, competence, and the juvenile defendant: implications for research and policy', in Bottoms, B. L., Kovera, M. B. and McAuliff, B. D. (eds) *Children, Social Science, and the Law*, pp. 271–98, Edinburgh, Cambridge University Press.

Woolard, J. L., Fried, C. S. and Reppuci, N. D. (2001) 'Toward an expanded definition of adolescent competence in legal contexts', in Roesch, R., Corrado, R. R. and Dempster, R. (eds) *Psychology in the Courts: international advances in knowledge*, pp. 21–39, London, Routledge.

Chapter 3
Health psychology: children and development

Tony Cassidy

Contents

	Learning outcomes	101
1	Introduction: what is health psychology?	101
2	Understanding health-related behaviour	103
	2.1 Modelling health	104
3	The promotion and maintenance of health and healthy behaviour	106
	3.1 Influences on childhood eating behaviour	106
	3.2 Preventing skin cancer	109
	3.3 Sexual health, social influence and social cognition	111
4	Stress in childhood	114
	4.1 Sources of stress	115
	4.2 Coping styles	117
5	The prevention of illness	119
	5.1 Older childhood and adolescent drug misuse	119
	5.2 Social inoculation	120
	5.3 Theory of planned behaviour	121
6	Children's understanding and experiences of illness and medical treatment	124
	6.1 Cognitive development and understanding illness	124
	6.2 Children's experiences of pain and illness	126
	6.3 Improving children's experiences of hospitalization	129
7	Children's adherence to treatment	131
8	Conclusion	134
	References	135

After you have studied this chapter you should be able to:
1 define 'health psychology';
2 describe children's experiences of illness and medical treatment;
3 discuss, with examples, the ways in which psychology has been applied to issues relating to the health of children, and evaluate how successful these approaches have been.

1 Introduction: what is health psychology?

This chapter introduces you to an area of applied psychology known as health psychology. It aims to show you some of the ways in which psychological research and theories have been used to help promote healthy behaviours in children, and support children with illness. The chapter starts with a consideration of how health psychology relates to children at the level of the communities and cultures that they live in, and then moves on to a consideration of children as individuals and their experiences of illness and treatment. Before you read on, however, try Activity 1.

Activity 1

Allow about 12 minutes

Health and illness in childhood

This activity will help you to reflect on your own experiences of healthy behaviours and experience of illness and the role that psychology could play in promoting health and supporting children with illness.

Think back to your childhood and write down your recollections of what kinds of things adults asked you to do 'for the good of your health'. Beside each one, write down whether or not you did as you were instructed, and if not, why.

Next, think of a time when you were ill as a child. Who looked after you, and how did that make you feel? What other feelings do you associate with that time? What professionals, if any, were involved in your treatment?

Comment

You may remember your parents or other adults telling you to do things like eat your greens or not to run with a pair of scissors in your hand, or to wear a coat when you played outside in the spring or autumn, or to stop and look both ways before you crossed the road. When you look at the advice that you tended to follow, what was different about those instructions from the ones that you tended to ignore? It may have been that some types of advice made more sense, or that you felt you could get away with not obeying some of the others because the adult concerned was unable to monitor your behaviour. Given that information, think about how a psychologist could have encouraged you to do the things you did not want to as a child. How might they have encouraged you to adopt more of these 'healthy behaviours'?

When you were ill as a child you may have been looked after at home by a member of your family, or you may have needed to go to hospital for something more serious. The important thing to note is that these two contexts are likely to have evoked very different reactions: being at home and being looked after by a parent can be a comforting experience that children relish despite feeling unwell. In contrast, because hospital is a more unfamiliar environment with different smells and its own daily routine, it may evoke feelings of anxiety or disorientation, as can contact with some health professionals. However, this may not be true in the case of nurses or physiotherapists with whom you may have developed a relationship through repeated contact.

One area of research in health psychology is to consider children's health-related behaviours and reactions to being ill, theorize what psychological processes may underpin the behaviours and emotions experienced by children in these kinds of contexts, and then develop health initiatives based on these theories. In broad terms, then, health psychology is the application of psychology to health, illness and the healthcare process (BPS DHP, 2005). It is concerned with understanding how one can promote and maintain health, and also gain knowledge of the various factors that influence health and illness. Health psychologists develop models that attempt to describe the factors linked to health-related behaviours and explain the relationships between them. In this chapter you will be introduced to a range of these models and will consider the evidence that supports them. This often results in insights into the interactions between biological, social, emotional, cultural and behavioural factors and the ways in which they influence health and illness.

The stated aims of the British Psychological Society Division of Health Psychology (BPS DHP) indicate the breadth of the field of health psychology and its range of applications.

1   To study scientifically the psychological processes of health, illness and health care

2   To apply psychology to:

   (a)   the promotion and maintenance of health

   (b)   the analysis and improvement of the health care system and health policy formation

   (c)   the prevention of illness and disability and the enhancement of outcomes of those who are ill or disabled.

(BPS DHP, 2005, p. 1)

Health psychology can be applied to entire communities and be used to guide the development of healthcare and the formulation of health policy. It can also be applied to individuals, for example in preventive approaches to illness, and in the treatment and rehabilitation of physical and mental health.

Summary of Section 1

- Health psychology is the study of the psychological processes of health, illness and healthcare.
- Health and illness are understood by health psychologists through a consideration of the biological, social, emotional, cultural and behavioural factors that impact on them.

2   Understanding health-related behaviour

This section considers children as users of a healthcare system, for example, the National Health Service in the United Kingdom. The ways in which people use healthcare services have a significant impact on society both in terms of economics and a community's health. Health psychology has been applied to health service use and has facilitated understanding, and has been used to make recommendations for health service policy. Increasingly, psychologists note how issues of child development and health are influenced by social, economic and cultural diversity (Coscia *et al.*, 2001; Tucker, 2002). An example that illustrates this is research by Chen *et al.* (2003) on children with asthma. Asthma is one of the most common chronic illnesses in childhood, as well being as the most common reason for hospitalization in childhood (Mannino *et al.*, 1998). In their study, Chen and colleagues were interested in understanding the factors influencing rehospitalization and why a minority of children with asthma accounted for the majority of these hospitalizations (Adams *et al.*, 2000). Before you read about Chen *et al.*'s study in Research summary 1, try Activity 2 to reflect on your own ideas on this subject.

Activity 2   *Considering risk factors in asthma*

Allow about 25 minutes

This activity will help you think about the factors that might affect the rehospitalization of asthma patients.

I   Consider the definition of asthma given below.

[Asthma is] a respiratory disease characterized by an increased responsiveness of the trachea and bronchi to various stimuli, and manifested by widespread narrowing of the airways that changes in severity either spontaneously or as a result of treatment.

Symptoms: recurrent attacks of wheezing, shortness of breath, cough, and a feeling of tightness in the chest.

(Biology Dictionary: Hyperdictionary, 2005)

2   Consider which factors you would investigate in order to understand the likelihood of rehospitalization for treatment of asthma. Make a note of these and categorize them into biological, psychological, social and cultural factors.

3   Read Research summary 1 and compare your thoughts with the factors revealed by Chen *et al.*'s research.

RESEARCH SUMMARY 1

Hospitalization and childhood asthma

In 1999, between June and December, 206 children of 4–18 years of age were admitted to the St Louis Children's Hospital for treatment of asthma. From this group Chen and colleagues selected 115 children for whom asthma was their only chronic illness and who were hospitalized solely because of their asthma. The participants' families were asked to complete a variety of assessment scales. These were questionnaire-based measures which examined the social and financial impact of the children's illness on the family, the psychological impact of the children's illness on individual parents and the parents' beliefs about asthma and its treatment. The team also collected socio-economic data concerning the participants' neighbourhoods and data from medical records about the children's admissions to hospital during their life.

When these data were analysed it was found that the children's patterns of hospitalization were explained and predicted more by understanding the child's social and family situation and less so by the severity of their asthma, their medication or their age. For example, they concluded that the likelihood of children being rehospitalized in future was strongly dependent on caretaker characteristics such as being emotionally bothered by asthma. The children's lifetime history of hospitalizations was positively associated with factors such as family conflict and financial strain, as well as caretaker characteristics such as beliefs about being unable to manage their children's asthma.

Chen and her colleagues' results indicated that these associations were over and above the effects of the severity of the asthma symptoms, the medications being used, or the children's age. The team concluded that 'these findings could help guide future interventions targeted at the subgroup of children who represent a high proportion of acute asthma hospitalizations' (Chen *et al.*, 2003, p. 12).

Source: Chen et al., *2003.*

2.1 Modelling health

As you can see from Activity 2 and Research summary 1, in considering how to help children and their families, one may look towards theoretical and psychological factors rather than the medical factors alone. Indeed, various psychological theories have been used by health psychologists in examining people's use of healthcare systems. These range from behavioural approaches to more cognitive approaches such as the health belief model (Janz and Becker, 1984). Psychological models of health have been developed to indicate and explain how these factors relate to one another and interact.

The health belief model and the biopsychosocial model

The *health belief model* examines how the beliefs held by a person affect his or her use of the healthcare system, such as the time at which they contact the health service or seek advice from a doctor. However, as the example in Research summary 1 concerning asthma indicates, to focus on an individual's beliefs misses out on a range of significant factors that lie 'beyond the child'. Consequently the use and promotion of healthcare services have often been researched by health psychologists using a wider perspective, which includes:

- personal factors such as severity of illness, assessments of health, medical history, attitudes and beliefs about health and illness, coping strategies and health-related behaviours;
- social factors, such as demographic features and family relationships;
- access to the healthcare system, such as ease of availability and financial costs.

An important point for young children is how their patterns of access to health services are significantly influenced by their social and environmental situation, but also by the health-related beliefs of their carers.

As well as influencing how health services are accessed and used, this wide range of factors also has a significant impact in the development of health and illness in children. The *biopsychosocial model* of health and illness (Engel, 1977) is used to understand this. In contrast to the so-called traditional 'disease' model of health, the biopsychosocial model recognises the interplay between environment (particularly social factors), psychological processes and biological processes in explanations and interruptions in healthcare. The model implies that health is not merely the absence of organic disease (see Figure 1).

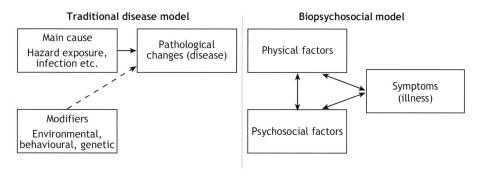

Figure 1   A comparison of the traditional 'disease' model of illness and the biopsychosocial model.

One area in which the biopsychosocial approach has been useful is in understanding 'lifestyle illnesses' and the consequences of lifestyle choices made by individuals in terms of diet, alcohol use, smoking, sexual behaviour and exercise. Thus, the psychological and environmental aspects of health and illness have become a major focus of improving children's health. Lifestyle behaviours and health risk-taking are a function of the attitudes, beliefs, emotional make-up and coping styles of individuals. However, understanding the developmental progression of these aspects is a relatively new area of investigation (Goreczny and Gage, 1999).

The next sections will illustrate various areas of child health psychology: as you read each one, consider how far the biopsychosocial model has been used to understand children's health-related behaviour.

Summary of Section 2

- The health belief model has been used by psychologists to understand how an individual person's beliefs will affect their health behaviours, such as the ways in which they will use healthcare services.
- An alternative model for understanding health-related behaviours is the biopsychosocial model, which recognizes the interplay between environmental, psychological and biological factors.

3   The promotion and maintenance of health and healthy behaviour

This section will look at several ways in which health psychologists have been involved in direct interventions with children, and how a broader perspective on health and a use of theoretical models can be helpful. You will see that the approaches to intervention outlined here are directed at investigating changes in cultural attitudes and behaviours, and are aimed at all children, not just children who are at heightened risk.

3.1   Influences on childhood eating behaviour

Surveys of childhood eating patterns indicate that children across socio-economic categories are at risk due to consuming over the recommended maximum of sugary and fatty foods and under the recommended minimum of vegetables, eggs, grains and other foods, particularly those with a high iron content (Nicklas *et al.*, 2001). Media portrayal of fast foods aimed at both children and parents makes it difficult to develop healthy food preferences in children. The consequence of unhealthy eating behaviours can be ill health or obesity, or both.

It is predicted that children born in the early twenty-first century will have a shorter life expectancy than their parents due to diet and obesity (Health Select Committee Report on Obesity, 2004). However, childhood obesity is the result of a complex interaction between many different factors including body type, cultural influences, activity level and attitudes to food. It is estimated that over 25 per cent of all American children are obese (Wang *et al.*, 2002) and the figure is growing (Ebbeling *et al.*, 2002).

Figure 2 It can be difficult to develop healthy food preferences in children.

Obese children are at risk from a range of disorders including diabetes, heart disease and stroke (Eveleth and Tanner, 1991). The ratio of a child's weight to their height (known as the Body Mass Index or BMI) at around age 10 is the best predictor of adult obesity; hence intervention in childhood can have a major impact on obesity. Children who have at least one obese parent but are not obese themselves at age 10 have a less than 15 per cent likelihood of becoming an obese adult. However, children who are obese at age 10, regardless of the BMI of parents, have a 65 per cent chance of becoming an obese adult (Whitaker *et al.*, 1997).

There is some evidence that heredity plays a part in weight problems as certain body types are more likely to store excess body fat (Woolston, 1987). However, a significant amount of evidence suggests that the family environment is the major source of influence over childhood eating behaviour (Vogt, 1999). Parents and siblings directly influence childhood eating patterns through the foods they provide or do not provide, and their responses to media and cultural influences. They also model eating patterns and choices, activity levels and recreational choices.

These concerns may lead some children to diet in an attempt to lose excess weight. However, several research studies have suggested that dieting in childhood is a major risk factor for 'Chronic body-image problems, weight cycling, obesity, eating disorders, exercise dependence, and the use of steroids in adolescence and adulthood' (McCabe and Ricciardelli, 2003, p. 40). Age, gender and BMI have been shown to be the most important factors influencing body dissatisfaction and body-change strategies in adolescence. There is also evidence that 7 and 8 year olds who identify themselves as dissatisfied with their bodies, and fear gaining weight, are likely to eat less and exercise to lose weight (see Ricciardelli and McCabe, 2001). McCabe and Ricciardelli (2003) carried out research on the use of these strategies by young pre-adolescent children. The research produced the following findings:

> Cognitions and strategies to lose weight (both dieting and exercise) had occurred at least sometimes for about 50% of both boys and girls in both age groups [...]
>
> Boys were more likely to be focused on both losing weight and increasing muscles, whereas girls were more focused on losing weight [...]
>
> However, there was a significant interaction between age and gender, with older girls being more likely to experience cognitions and weight-loss behaviors than younger girls, whereas there was no difference in weight-loss behaviors for older and younger boys.
>
> (McCabe and Riccardielli 2003, pp. 41–43)

Activity 3   Modelling children's problematic eating behaviours

Allow about 15 minutes

This activity will show you how you can summarize research evidence to develop a biopsychosocial model of children's problematic eating behaviours.

Re-read the material presented in this section on childhood eating behaviour, bearing in mind the biopsychosocial model described in Section 2. Make a note of what the problematic behaviours are, and then list the behaviours, symptoms, physical factors, and psychosocial factors that are described to you.

Comment

Your notes should look something like this.

> Behaviours: eating too many fatty or sugary foods, eating too few foods that are high in nutrients, too little exercise.
>
> Symptoms: ill health, obesity.
>
> Physical factors: whether or not you have an obese parent, body type (storing fat), age, gender, BMI.

Psychosocial factors: 'junk' foods portrayed as more appealing to children via the media, provision of food by the family, eating patterns modelled by family members, activity levels modelled by family members, whether or not the child is dissatisfied with his or her body and fears weight gain.

Having looked at why a poor diet in children can lead to problems, we now consider some initiatives developed to address these issues. One way in which psychologists have tried to influence children's food choices positively is through the application of social learning theory (see Research summary 1).

RESEARCH SUMMARY I

The Food Dudes

A group of psychologists at the University of Wales, Bangor, developed a novel approach to encouraging healthy eating in children that has been very successful (Tapper *et al.*, 2003). The programme identified key psychological factors influencing children's food choice. The approach is based on three basic psychological principles:

1   Repeated exposure to the taste of a food increases the liking for the food.
2   Social learning theory (Bandura, 1977), which would suggest that a child is more likely to imitate the behaviour of a person who is liked and admired by the child.
3   Rewards for behaviours that are desirable, achievable, contingent on performance, and for behaviours which is enjoyable and desired, are more likely to be effective in changing behaviour. This is consistent with a behaviourist approach.

The researchers developed a video of four older children called the 'Food Dudes' who appeared to gain super powers from eating fruit and vegetables, and then engaged in battle against the 'Junk Punks'. This was used as the source of modelling for the children and was combined with rewards, such as Food Dude stickers and pens, for eating the required amounts of fruit and vegetables. They also produced a video with animated characters called Jarvis and Jess for use with nursery age children. The programme has been tested in a number of schools and shown to be successful across the entire primary school age range.

The Food Dude scheme described in Research summary 1 provided opportunities for children to see positive behaviours being modelled and encouraged children to try out foods repeatedly, changing their views of themselves in relation to food preferences.

3.2 Preventing skin cancer

Skin cancer is the most common cancer in white populations, and it is increasing at a notable rate (Diepgen and Mahler, 2002). Children are exposed to sunshine more in primary than in secondary schools and overall childhood exposure 'accounts for an estimated 80% of the total lifetime exposure' (Preston and Stern, 1992, cited in Glanz *et al.*, 2002). Therefore, early intervention, in terms of increasing healthy behaviour, is essential. The behaviours required to minimize the risk of skin cancer are relatively straightforward, but getting children to engage in these behaviours is more complex. Research summary 2 provides details of an approach to address this problem.

RESEARCH SUMMARY 2

The Pool Cool Programme

Unlike the majority of sun safety programmes, which occur in schools, the Pool Cool Programme was run across 28 swimming pools in the United States. As with the 'Food Dudes' Programme the Pool Cool Programme was strongly influenced by Bandura's social learning theory. Glanz and colleagues (2002) identified the key behaviours they wished to influence. As might be expected, these are in line with standard sun-protection behaviour:

- using sunscreen;
- wearing hats and shirts;
- wearing sunglasses;
- seeking shade;
- avoiding sunburn.

They also identified outcomes in the pool environments, including:

- availability of sunscreen;
- shaded areas;
- widely visible sun-safety signage;
- pool policies favouring sun safety.

Figure 3   The incidence of skin cancer is increasing.

Consistent with social learning theory, Glanz *et al.* designed the programme to emphasize its social acceptability, ease, and the appeal of practising sun protection. The role models for the behaviour were the pool lifeguards. The programme began with a 1-hour training session for pool staff. Children took part in their usual swimming classes and received a series of eight Pool Cool sessions at the start of their swimming lesson. This was supported with rewarding interactive activities and access to laminated sheets outlining the goals of each session. Parents were given access to the materials and encountered Pool Cool signs at the pools they used. They also attended an orientation session with their children at the start of the programme. In addition to the training and materials the pool staff were given:

> a refillable pump sunscreen container, a portable shade structure or umbrellas (of their choosing), durable sun-safety signs modeled after traffic signs, and a sunscreen tips poster. A booklet entitled *Decision Maker's Guide for Sun Safe Swimming Pools*, along with informal consultations ... to guide pool managers toward more sun-safe pool environments and policies.

The effectiveness of the programme was evaluated using randomized control trials. The programme had a significant impact on the children's behaviours such as the maintenance and use of a sun-safe environment, but less so for the use of shirts, hats, and sunglasses.

Source: Glanz et al., 2002, p. 580.

The Pool Cool Programme included educational and environmental elements; it also considered the poolside environment, attempted to influence policy and addressed children, parents and staff. This type of approach, in which behaviours are influenced by the interaction of the physical and cultural environment as well as the social and intrapersonal issues, reflects an *ecological model* of health psychology (Stokols, 1992).

Ecological model
A multifaceted model of health psychology which encompasses behaviours, environmental factors and also policies that influence the health choices that people make. It differs from the biopsychosocial model due to its emphasis on the environment. This includes both the natural environment and the built environment.

3.3 Sexual health, social influence and social cognition

Since many health beliefs, attitudes and behaviours implicated in lifelong risk for chronic illness are part of the early developmental process, health psychologists place a great deal of emphasis on early intervention to develop positive health behaviours. Often such primary prevention provides the information needed to change the attitudes of both parents and children. However, the link between increased knowledge, changes in attitudes and behaviour is often weak (Bruvold and Rundall, 1988). While most parents and teachers applaud and support education programmes aimed at changing eating behaviours or preventing skin cancer, the issues surrounding safe sex and drug use are more controversial. Approaches to intervention based on increasing knowledge about the topic (referred to as 'rational' models of health promotion) have been found to be less effective than the social influence approach. The social influence approach recognizes the role of peers in the development of children's attitudes through social norms, particularly for older children and adolescents. It aims to help children to develop the skills to translate knowledge about health behaviours into health behaviours in a social context (Evans, 2001). One area where the social influence approach is used in conjunction with the rational model is in school health programmes, where health issues are part of the curriculum.

In adolescent sexual behaviour there has been an increase in the frequency of premarital sexual activity, the numbers of sexual partners and earlier sexual activity (Kost and Forrest, 1992; Abraham *et al.*, 2002). All of this coupled with the experimental nature of sexual activity at this age increases the risk of sexually transmitted diseases. In the recent past the attention of healthcare professionals has been focused on the increase in HIV and AIDS, however there is a range of other sexually transmitted diseases that can have a significant impact on young people (Cates and Berman, 1999).

There is considerable debate as to causes for earlier and increased sexual activity in boys and girls. Hofferth (1987) suggests that the major factors are mother's education, religious affiliation, age at menarche and family stability at age 14. Others tend to locate a major source of influence in increased commercialization of sexual behaviour in the media or in the availability of planning clinics and contraception (e.g. Abraham *et al.*, 2002). It is likely that such factors interact, and so a focus for health psychology has been to prevent risk-taking and increase positive health behaviours. There are two targets for primary prevention of sexual risk-taking: sexual abstinence, or engaging in what has been termed 'safe sex' (i.e. the use of condoms). Early interventions which aimed to reduce risk-taking through fear induction have not been very successful (Ross *et al.*, 1990).

An example of a research-informed and theory-driven approach is the SHARE programme (Sexual Health and Relationships: Safe, Happy and Responsible) (Abraham *et al.*, 2002). The programme draws on developmentally relevant theory as well as social cognition models that have been developed in adult populations.

RESEARCH SUMMARY 3

The SHARE programme

The SHARE Programme (Sexual Health and Relationships: Safe, Happy and Responsible) is a five-day teacher training programme plus a 20-session pack: 10 sessions in the third year of secondary school (at 13–14 years) and 10 in the fourth year (at 14–15 years). It is intended to reduce unsafe sexual behaviours, reduce unwanted pregnancies, and improve the quality of sexual relationships.

The programme combines active learning (for example, work in small groups and games), information leaflets on sexual health, and development of skills, primarily through the use of interactive video but also through role playing.

Source: Wight et al., *2002, pp. 1–12.*

Older children and adolescents are preoccupied with self-image and have been described by developmental theorists as being constantly like actors on a stage, the focus of attention. The SHARE approach sees young males and females as having different priorities which are much more driven by identity formation than sexual health concerns alone. Abraham and colleagues (2002) use the terms homosocial and heterosocial to distinguish between attitudes that develop in same-sex contexts as opposed to cross-sex contexts. They argue that masculine and feminine identities in older childhood and adolescence develop largely in separate social worlds. Boys develop sexual identities which are much more focused on reputation among peers and involve concerns with genital pleasure. Girls, on the other hand, develop identities where sexual interactions are more bound up in relationships. One target for sex education, therefore, is the development of understanding through awareness of their homosocial learning and discussion of sexual behaviours (e.g. condom use) with the opposite sex. The second area that the programme draws on is empowerment and social control in decision making. Young people have to assimilate a great deal of information about sex from peers, media and parents, and this information often conflicts. Lack of knowledge limits the vocabulary available to young people and the homosocial development of gendered identities includes elements of segregated sexual language. For example, boys are embarrassed to talk about feelings and love or caring in the context of a homosocial socialization process that reinforces a macho image. The idea is therefore to empower young people to make choices and considered decisions which enhance their understanding of the nature of relationships and also their skills in communicating effectively about sexual behaviour.

However, a random trial evaluation of the SHARE programme, compared with a standard school sex education programme across 25 schools, noted 'no differences in sexual activity or sexual risk taking by the age of 16 years' (Wight *et al.*, 2002, p. 1). Students rated the programme highly and their knowledge of sexual health did improve but this did not have a significant influence on self-reported measures of potential 'exposure to sexually transmitted disease, use of condoms and contraceptives at first and most recent sexual intercourse, and unwanted pregnancies' (Wight *et al.*, 2002, p. 1). Wight *et al.* note that while several quasi-experiments suggest sex education programmes are effective in producing behavioural changes, most randomized trial studies do not support this view.

Summary of Section 3

- Health psychologists are sometimes involved in the prevention of risky health behaviour in children and in the promotion of safe choices.
- Research into children's eating patterns suggests that environmental factors, and family influences in particular, appear to account for the eating patterns the children adopt, but other factors, including age, gender and genetic influences, may also play a role.

- Social learning theory has been used as the basis of the 'Food Dudes' approach to encouraging children to make healthy food choices.
- An ecological model of health psychology recognizes that behaviours are affected by the interaction of the physical and cultural environment, including social and intrapersonal factors.
- The 'Pool Cool' Programme draws on the principles of social learning theory to promote sun protection behaviour in children in the United States, and reflects an ecological model of health psychology.
- The social influence approach to health psychology recognizes the role of peers in the development of attitudes, especially in older children and adolescents.
- The SHARE programme, which promotes sexual health in children, draws on theories of identity formation and social cognition. Transferring classroom-based skills into 'real world behaviours' is an important issue for this type of programme.

4   Stress in childhood

In this section we move away from the topic of health promotion to consider the topic of stress which is a central theme in health psychology (Cassidy, 1997). Stress is defined as an interaction between (a) an event in a person's life which is perceived as placing considerable or unreasonable demands on them and (b) their response to coping with the event (Hanley, 2002). As we shall see, the outcomes of these interactions can have a significant negative impact on children's health. In looking at childhood stress we will consider the impact of a range of factors on stress and stress management through an exploration of two psychological models. These have been developed by psychologists to try to explain how and why we experience stress. Box 1 and Figure 4 outline a transactional model of stress.

The important element of the transactional model of stress is how the person responds to the event, and in this sense, any event is potentially stressful depending on how it is appraised by that individual. The transactional model of stress is useful to bear in mind when reading this section, as it highlights the importance of the interaction between the child and their environment.

BOX I

A transactional model of stress

When confronted with an event you make a primary appraisal; i.e. 'does this event present a threat to me at this time?' If you conclude that it does not then you will not experience stress. If it does, however, whether or not you will experience stress depends on your secondary appraisal; i.e. 'what resources do I have to cope with this situation?' For many people, the resources that they have available (e.g. personality characteristics, social support, financial resources) will be sufficient to allow them to cope effectively with the stressor. However, some people may not perceive themselves to have sufficient resources available to deal with the problem and as a result they experience a response that we would typically refer to as a stress response (Sheridan and Radmacher, 1992 quoted in Hanley, 2002).

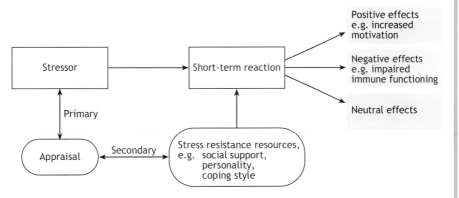

Figure 4   A transactional model of stress (Hanley, 2002, p. 6).

Source: Hanley, 2002.

4.1 Sources of stress

Sources of stress can be thought of in three groups: major events affecting large groups such as flooding or terrorist attacks; more personal stressors such as redundancy, or relationship break-up, and finally, background stressors or 'daily hassles' (Lazarus and Cohen, 1977, cited in Hanley, 2002). There are many factors which influence how we appraise and respond to stressors (Hanley, 2002; Cassidy, 1997). These include a person's perceived control over events, beliefs about one's own ability, personality characteristics and the level of social support available.

Children experience a wide range of events which are unpredictable and uncontrollable. Such events have the potential to produce negative health outcomes through stress (Cassidy, 1999). For example, psychological factors can produce susceptibility to illness through lowered immunity. Figure 5 presents a simplified model of this process.

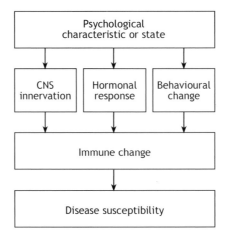

Figure 5 The relationship between psychological factors and disease and illness (adapted from Cohen and Herbert 1996, p. 118).

Figure 5 indicates that the effects of stress may impact directly on the central nervous system, or manifest themselves in consequential behaviours, such as poor eating or sleeping patterns.

Two principles underpin cognitive approaches to dealing with stress in childhood. The first is that an event is a stressor *because* of its appraisal by an individual. The second is that, due to this, any event has the potential to be a stressor (Lazarus and Folkman, 1984). In simple terms this means that if a child *perceives* an event as a threat then it has the potential to have health consequences.

Some of the events that impact on children's health relate to family relations (e.g. parental conflict – see Box 2), relationships with peers, and academic school experiences. However, researchers have focused on the negative impact of childhood events and have often ignored the positive. For example there is much more research on how negative peer relations (e.g. being bullied) impact on children, than on the benefits of developing strong and supportive friendships. Yet, the experience of positive relationships in childhood is important in the development of social skills and positive self-esteem (Asher and Coie, 1990). It therefore follows that if it is possible to identify the mechanisms that underpin good relationships, psychologists are likely to be better able to design preventive interventions.

BOX 2

Styles of coping with parental conflict

One way of looking at how children cope with parental conflict is to present them with filmed or live simulations of conflict and then ask them what they would do if the people in conflict were their parents. Using this approach Grych and Fincham (1993) identified four types of response: (1) direct intervention (e.g. interrupting them); (2) indirect intervention (e.g. trying to remove the cause of the conflict; (3) withdrawal (avoidance); and (4) do nothing. In a study which used observations of the children's behaviour during the simulation in addition to self-reports, Cummings (1987) identified three types of responses among 4–5 year olds. *Concerned emotional responders* were obviously distressed and expressed a desire to intervene; *ambivalent responders* seemed to experience both positive and negative affect and wanted to run away or hit the actors; *unresponsive children* showed no emotional or behavioural response although they said that they had been angry. They ignored the conflict and used avoidant strategies. These data suggest that children have difficulty in being unaffected by adult conflict, even when it is not apparent.

Box 2 shows one way in which children respond to stressful situations. Classification of children's response styles is also used in research into coping styles.

4.2 Coping styles

Children's coping responses are often categorized into *active coping* which involves positive problem-solving strategies, and *repressive coping* which involves emotional repression and denial. Some researchers further divide repressive coping into conscious and unconscious types (Phipps *et al.*, 1995). They use the term 'blunting' to describe a strategy that reduces emotional distress by actively limiting thoughts about the stressful situation. They found that those who blunt are able to change their coping styles whereas repressors are less flexible. In a meta-analysis of coping styles in children, Suls and Fletcher (1985) also found repressive styles were related to better outcomes where the stressor was short-term. The active coping approach worked better for long-term stressors. This corresponds to the finding that children with short-term illness prefer not to receive too much information whereas those with chronic illness prefer to have information (Siegel and Conte, 2001).

In Research summary 4 you will see that it appears that children, like adults, are more likely to use reactive or maladaptive coping responses themselves yet suggest proactive coping responses for their friends (Peterson *et al.*, 1999).

RESEARCH SUMMARY 4

Children's use of effective coping strategies

Three hundred and forty two 8-year-old children role-played a situation which involved either medical procedures or minor injuries. They had to say what they would do, and what they would recommend for a friend to do in the situation. The children's responses were then categorized into *proactive* strategies (e.g. take deep breaths), *reactive* strategies (e.g. pull away), and *neutral* strategies (i.e. passive acceptance). In choosing proactive responses for their friends, children demonstrated an awareness of more effective strategies. However they tended to choose less effective, reactive strategies for themselves. Peterson *et al.* (1999) argue that children may not choose the most effective strategy available to them when faced with a threatening situation, but there is scope for interventions to help children to adopt better coping responses.

Source: Peterson et al.*, 1999.*

The concept of resilience has also been used to examine the different ways in which children respond to stressful situations and has been used quite widely in the area of childhood stress and coping (Garmezy, 1991).

BOX 3

Resilience

Kobasa (1979) described a combination of factors including perceived control, level of commitment and tendency to see problems as challenges, which in some ways made the individual less vulnerable to stress (or more 'resilient'). Resilience appears to be partly heritable and interacts with a range of factors such as parental warmth in early childhood, temperament and environmental factors (Kim-Cohen *et al.*, 2004). In the childhood literature the concept of resilience is seen as a dynamic interactive process rather than a combination of relatively stable traits (Rutter, 1999). It is not seen as providing invulnerability to stress but is as defined by Fonagy *et al.* (1994) 'normal development under difficult conditions'.

Stress management programmes have been developed and used with children in a wide variety of situations. As we discuss later, the experience of hospitalization can provoke extreme anxiety in children (and their carers or parents) and stress management programmes have been used successfully in this context.

Summary of Section 4

- Stress is the interaction between a life event that is perceived to place considerable demands on a person and that person's response to coping with the event.
- Children's coping strategies can be thought of as either active or repressive, with active styles being better suited to long-term stressors, and repressive styles being better suited to short-term stressors.
- Children are likely to use reactive coping strategies if they are in a stressful situation, but recommend that their friends use proactive coping strategies. In this way, children show awareness of effective coping strategies but may not use them.
- Resilience refers to the child's ability to cope with stressful situations. A wide variety of factors contributes to this ability.

5 | The prevention of illness

This chapter began by considering health promotion, and health-related behaviours. We then examined some factors that are used to explain the way in which children react to factors that influence their health. In this section we examine preventive interventions in the context of drug use by children and adolescents. Prevention is usually categorized into three types, primary, secondary and tertiary (Caplan, 1964). *Primary prevention* involves an intervention before a problem occurs in order to prevent it from occurring at all and is probably closest to the lay view of prevention. It is the most difficult to enact since it means being able to predict who is likely to become ill, and it is the most difficult to demonstrate since if the problem does not occur it is difficult to prove that it was intervention that prevented it. Yet, arguably it is the most desirable and cost-effective in the long term. *Secondary prevention* refers to interventions that occur before the problem has fully developed, for example, before minor symptoms become a full blown chronic illness, and is probably the most common in healthcare. *Tertiary prevention* involves interventions at the stage when the problem has developed in order to prevent long-term damage or disability.

The focus on preventive intervention is a central theme of community-based psychology (Orford, 1992). Effective psychological prevention is multilevel, that is, it targets factors across individual, group and societal levels. This fits with the biopsychosocial model in health psychology where biological, psychological and social factors are implicated causally in both health and illness. Prevention of illness and enhancement of positive health cannot occur through focusing on single factors. Aspects of the person (e.g. communication skills), the family (e.g. parental warmth and encouragement), and the social environment (e.g. socio-economic status) have their impact through a combined and interactive effect (Olsson *et al.*, 2003). The next section begins by looking at the high priority and problematic area of drug misuse in child and adolescent health. You will then look at some models that have been applied to this type of issue.

5.1 Older childhood and adolescent drug misuse

Drug misuse in adolescence is a serious social and health issue in most parts of the industrialized world and is unfortunately also linked with other health issues such as AIDS and suicide. Eiser (1997) states that over 50 per cent of adolescent morbidity and mortality relates to preventable factors of lifestyle and risk-taking including suicide and unhealthy appetitive behaviours.

Three aspects of family background have been found to predict risk of drug use: parental involvement in crime, alcohol or drug misuse; poor relationship with parents; and affectionless and unsupportive parent–child interactions (Tapert *et al.*, 1999). Peers also play a major role in influencing drug use by adolescents, in terms of providing terms of reference for social identity, models of drug-related behaviours, and the source of information and the actual drugs used. As the number of drug users increases so too does the number of peers providing models or sources of influence. Having a poor relationship with one's parents may have a direct impact on drug use, or it may provide the source of stress which in turn influences the drug use.

The picture is further clouded by the prevalence of behaviour patterns such as rebelliousness, sensation-seeking, impulsivity, low self-esteem, and emotional problems such as aggression, depressed affect and suicidal ideation, among drug abusing adolescents (Tapert *et al.*, 1999). These factors interact with the family and stress factors to provide a complex pattern of potential causes for adolescent drug misuse. Older childhood is a time for experimentation, and experimentation is part of the typical development process. But experimentation can go wrong, and rather than being a staging post on the way to forming a healthy identity, it can become part of a destructive lifestyle. With substance misuse, treatments tend to combine detoxification and psychological therapy. However, the main focus for health psychologists is in prevention, and one of the approaches used with some success is based on the social psychology of persuasion.

McMurran (1994) suggests four levels of interventions in programmes designed to prevent drug misuse: changing the culture and context; controlling availability; strengthening individual resilience and minimizing the harm from drug use (McMurran, 1994). Changing the culture and strengthening resilience are areas of primary prevention since the intervention occurs before drug use begins to try to prevent it occurring. On the other hand, reducing the harm from drug use is secondary or tertiary prevention in Caplan's model outlined above. One example concerning controlling availability is that shop assistant behaviour (whether or not a shop assistant is willing to sell cigarettes) has been shown to be the strongest predictor of cigarette sales to under-age smokers (Klonoff and Landrine, 2004).

5.2 Social inoculation

The *social inoculation* theory of resistance to persuasion was developed by McGuire (1964). The basic premise is that decisions about behaviour, particularly in adolescence, are made in the context of social pressure which pushes and pulls young people in particular directions. If the social pressure is in the direction of a health-damaging behaviour such as drug use, to avoid becoming a user it is necessary to be able to resist the pressure. Social inoculation theory suggests that practising the skills necessary to avoid social pressure in a controlled environment will make children more resistant to social pressure. The typical approach is to use role-play situations in which children are supported in rehearsing what they would do when faced with pressure to engage in particular behaviours. Children are helped to explore a range of different responses and encouraged to use assertiveness as opposed to aggressiveness in resisting pressure. It is important that children do not just say no, they should also learn to develop arguments to support their resistance. In some cases, setting up focus groups to openly discuss peer pressure and behaviours such as drug use with an experienced individual as leader is sufficient to empower children in refusing negative peer pressure.

5.3 Theory of planned behaviour

In order to change behaviour we first need to be able to predict it, and in health psychology the major tools in this arena are the *social cognition models*. These were developed in social psychology to try to understand the discrepancy between attitude and behaviour. For example, most people who smoke do not hold positive attitudes towards smoking, in that they accept that smoking is harmful to health and they should give up smoking (Mullins, Borland and Hill, 1992). In order to understand this discrepancy theorists have posited a range of intervening variables, such as intention, and developed a range of models to be tested empirically. One of the best known models is the theory of planned behaviour (TPB) (Ajzen, 1985). The theory of planned behaviour considers the relationship between a person's behaviour and a set of measureable components. It is based on the idea that beliefs, attitudes and intentions are different components of the process leading to behaviour, and on the recognition that knowing someone's attitude does not mean that what they will do can be predicted. The 'gap' between one such component (attitudes) and behaviour is something that some health psychologists have been particularly interested in. Fishbein and Ajzen (1975) concluded that there was a number of factors that might intercede between attitude and behaviour. First of all there was the intention to perform the behaviour. So, if we do not like smoking and have formed an intention to stop, we are more likely to do so than if we have not formed that intention. Active engagement with planning how intentions are going to be carried out in specific circumstances is an important factor here (Gollwitzer, 1999). Second, there are factors that might make it more or less likely that an attitude will be translated into an intention. It might be that we dislike smoking but all our friends smoke and we would feel isolated if we stopped, hence we never make an intention to stop. This *subjective norm* has influenced our behaviour. It is an internal representation of the social and cultural context within which we exist and its informal rules. The other dimension is the person's *perceived behavioural control*. The TPB sees the subjective norm as intervening between attitude and intention and it may be related to broader group identity, beyond immediate friends and family.

Perceived control has a direct effect on both behaviour and intention. Hence a teenager is unlikely to develop an intention to stop smoking if they feel that they have no control over smoking, or have a perceived lack of control over their behaviour. Figure 6 illustrates an example of TPB in relation to dieting.

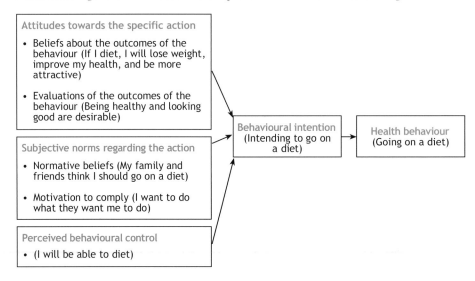

Figure 6   The theory of planned behaviour: the three key factors.

The TPB is a rational model of behaviour which assumes that we go through a range of processes involving thoughts, beliefs, feelings, and intentions before engaging in behaviour. However, the rationality assumption underpinning the model has attracted criticism.

BOX 4

Applying TPB to children's exercise behaviour

One example of the application of the TPB to child health behaviour is a study by Hagger *et al.* (2001) on children's intentions and behaviour regarding exercise. They measured the attitudes, subjective norms, perceived behavioural control, intentions and past behaviour of 585 children aged 12–14 across two studies. They also observed whether or not the children actually engaged in the exercise they said they intended to perform. They found that adding the measure of past behaviour (Connor and Armitage, 1998) increased the strength of the relationship between intention and behaviour. The application of the model is in identifying the factors that predict behaviour so that they can be targeted in health promotion.

Activity 4

Allow about
10 minutes

'Rational' behaviour?

This activity leads you to reflect on the nature of 'rational' choices in unhealthy behaviour.

Think about the last time you had too much to eat or drink, or engaged in some other unhealthy behaviour. Was your choice made through a rational process? Do you think that if you had thought rationally about it you would not have engaged in the behaviour?

Comment

Other people who carried out this activity made the following comments:

Person 1

It was at a friend's house and the social pressures, I suppose, led me to eat far more than I actually wanted to, but what can you do you can't be rude, everyone else is eating. It was a special occasion and they'd really gone to town.

Person 2

Definitely not rational *(concerning drink)* the reason doesn't matter, it's like a habit, you like and do it without thinking. So you change your reasoning like. You've had a hard day so you need a few drinks to unwind, or there's something to celebrate so you need a drink. The reasoning changes but the habit *(of drinking)* just carries on. It's a habit. Once you go out you're going to drink.

Person 3

I'm on a strict diet and so that's it for me. I keep to it. I choose to follow it. I do allow myself off, it's allowed, but I still feel guilty afterwards.
You own responses are likely to be different to the above, however you should be able to identify some interacting factors that influenced your behaviour. The comments above highlight particular aspects. The experience of Person 1 seems to suggest the importance of the *subjective norm*. The experience of Person 2 might indicate a lack of *perceived control*. The experience of Person 3 initially suggests someone with clearly identified *intentions* about their eating behaviour. However, even when they give themselves permission to change from a 'strict' diet they still feel guilty. This might imply that this change was not something that they wanted to do at a rational level, or that issues underpinning the 'strict' diet itself might be considered further.

Summary of Section 5

- Primary prevention is intervention before the occurrence of a problem.
- Secondary prevention is intervention before a problem has fully developed.
- Tertiary prevention is intervention after the problem has developed, with a view to preventing longer term damage.

- Preventive programmes have been used to address children's use of drugs, and have variously focused on cultural factors, availability of drugs, resilience to temptation and minimizing harm when drugs are used.
- Social inoculation is one approach to drug misuse prevention, in which role-play situations are used to enable children to rehearse how they would behave if they were put under pressure to take drugs.
- The theory of planned behaviour (TPB) is used in health psychology to understand how attitudes and intentions are affected by subjective norms and the degree of perceived control over a situation, which in turn can result in someone producing a behaviour that may be inconsistent with what they believe in.

6   Children's understanding and experiences of illness and medical treatment

We now consider children's developing understanding of illness and their experiences of receiving medical treatments. In doing so, you will notice a further focus on children as individuals (rather than as a group) in the literature on child health psychology.

6.1 Cognitive development and understanding illness

Early research linked children's beliefs about illness to Piaget's stages of cognitive development (Bibace and Walsh, 1980). In the *pre-operational* stage children are seen as having limited ability in logical reasoning and as being highly egocentric. This approach suggested that, at this stage, beliefs about illness are vague and fraught with fear, and often superstitious. They tend not to grasp the finality of death and sometimes feel they are to blame for sudden deaths. During the *concrete operational* stage children develop more specific logical reasoning abilities, and begin to grasp the idea that illness and death have biological causes. Children, certainly at younger ages, tend to be poor at generalizing knowledge about one illness to other illnesses (Eiser, 1997). By the end of the concrete operational stage they understand that death is final and recognize their own mortality. Thinking becomes further refined during the *formal operational* stage and children can then understand the link between biology and psychology, between feelings and symptoms. In particular they tend to be better able to comprehend more immediate and short-term risks, and less able to understand the longer-term consequences of their behaviours. Yet, Piaget's theory has been criticized by social constructivists for its underestimation of the role of social and cultural factors in knowledge development. The ideas proposed by Bibace and Walsh were also criticized in that apparent age and/or stage differences are related to levels of access to knowledge rather than developmental stage (Bird and Podmore, 1990).

However, children's understanding of illness does appear to develop with age. This is seen most clearly in comparisons of children's understanding of mental and physical illness (Buchanan-Barrow and Barrett, 2005). Younger children (5–7 years), do not clearly differentiate between the two categories, while older children (9–11 years) make a clear distinction (Buchanan-Barrow and Barrett, 2005). A recent study found that children did not show a developmental progression regarding their understanding of the causes or consequences of physical illness and suggests their 'representations of physical illnesses are established in early childhood' (Buchanan-Barrow and Barrett, 2005). For example, nearly all children, across the age range 5–11 years identified the cause of a cold as 'she caught it' and the subsequence as being either 'stay at home' or 'see a doctor'.

In contrast, significant differences are found in children's identification of the causes and consequences of mental illness. Young children (5–7 years) are significantly more likely than older children to believe that mental illness could be 'caught'(i.e. their understanding mirrored their beliefs about physical illness).

> The two older groups of children were more likely than the youngest children to respond to Depression with '*to do with how she thinks and feels*' (Young = 40%; Middle = 75%; Old = 79%) and to Dementia with '*something is wrong with her brain*' (Young = 38%; Middle = 90%; Old = 98%). With Anorexia, the Old group were more likely than the Young or Middle groups to respond that '*it's to do with how she thinks and feels*' (Young = 43%, Middle = 43%, Old = 76%).
> (Buchanan-Barrow and Barrett, 2005, p. 18)

Similarly, older children demonstrated a developing understanding of the different consequences of mental and physical illness. For example, regarding depression, the consequence of needing help and support from relatives was expressed by 50 per cent of the 7–9 and 9–11 year olds, but by only 13 per cent of the 5–7 year olds. Overall this evidence suggests that children are developing their understanding of mental illness as their own experience grows (Buchanan-Barrow and Barrett, 2005).

Researchers have also considered whether children pass through developmental stages in their understanding of pain. Ross and Ross (1984) used semi-structured interviews with approximately 1,000 children aged between 5 and 12 years, and found no age trends. Children generally related pain to specific and recent events and did not recognize the pain as a warning sign. Gafney and Dunne (1986), however, suggest that children's understanding of pain fits with the stages of development espoused by Piaget. They asked children to complete the sentence 'Pain is ...', and found three categories of response across 5–14-year-old children. These reflected concrete, semi-abstract and abstract definitions corresponding to pre-operational, concrete operational and formal operational stages. Later research suggests that older children have more complex and precise understandings of pain, and this supports the idea of a developmental continuum (Harbeck and Peterson, 1992) rather than discrete stages. Research in this area can be difficult to compare as evidence for particular 'Piagetian stages' has often been defined in different ways and the demands of the experimental conditions have not always been made explicit (Hergenrather and Rabinowitz, 1991). As with other studies this can lead to an underestimation of children's cognitive abilities. Hergenrather and Rabinowitz (1991) review this evidence and conclude:

> If one assumes young (preoperational and concrete operational) children lack certain inferential abilities, such as understanding cause and effect, then one might further assume education about causes and prevention is unnecessary for this age group. The extent of emotional and educational support provided for children with chronic diseases or experiencing acute health crises can be enhanced by the recognition that children can understand basic facts of disease processes.

(Hergenrather and Rabinowitz, 1991, p. 957)

Thus, there is an interaction between children's personal experience of illnesses and their cognitive level in determining their understanding of the nature of health and illness.

6.2 Children's experiences of pain and illness

In Section 6.1 we examined ideas about how children's level of cognitive development can affect their understanding of illness and disability. In this section we consider how children's understanding of illness impacts on their quality of life. Although definitions of quality of life remain imprecise there is a consensus as to the features that need to be considered in discussing it. The life conditions of a person are clearly important. However, a person's subjective experience, personal values and aspirations are a major part of their overall quality of life (QoL) (Felce, 1997). This is important as proxy measures offered by parents or carers correlate poorly with direct measures of children's perceptions (Jenney and Campbell, 1997). However, there are situations where this cannot be obtained. Health psychologists may seek to explore these subjective aspects when seeking to investigate quality of life. Much work in health-related quality of life with children has focused on the development of QoL measures and on specific disorders, particularly cancer, for which the Pediatric Cancer Quality of Life Inventory (PCQL), (Varni *et al.*, 1998) has been developed. There is a consensus that such measures are also useful more widely, to inform interventions, in areas such as pain management and general adjustment to chronic illness.

Very early experience of pain in infants is thought to have a long-term impact through its effect on the development of the neurological pathways of the pain system during this period of high brain plasticity (Anand and Carr, 1989). Methodologically and ethically it is a difficult area to research, but some studies suggest that early interventions to reduce pain have an impact on later pain responses (Taddio *et al.*, 1997). For example, boys who had been circumcized either using an anaesthetic cream or a placebo cream were video recorded later during routine vaccinations at 4 and 6 months. Taddio *et al.* (1997) found that 'placebo' circumcized infants did feel increased levels of pain in comparison to those receiving the anaesthetic or those not circumcized at all. Further, the circumsized infants gave stronger pain responses to subsequent vaccinations than uncircumsized infants. Various measures such as facial expression and cry duration were used as indices of pain. So it is likely that children's early experiences of pain can have long-term consequences. Furthermore, there is evidence to suggest that children are less likely than adults to receive adequate analgesia in some hospital interventions due to the influence of erroneous adult beliefs about children's experience of pain. Sahinler (2002) notes the following myths:

> Children do not feel pain.
> Children do not remember pain.
> Analgesics can do more harm than good.
> Addressing and treating pain takes too much time.
>
> Pain builds character.
> Children are at increased risk for addiction to narcotics.
>
> (Sahinler, 2002, p. 127)

The literature clearly shows that there is a complex relationship between pain and negative emotions (Robinson and Riley, 1999). It suggests that (a) negative emotions increase sensitivity to pain; (b) negative emotions increase the likelihood of disability and the development of chronic conditions related to pain; (c) chronic pain produces negative emotions; and (d) the relationship between pain and emotion can be mediated by factors that reduce stress such as social support, perceived control and coping style (Robinson and Riley, 1999). McGrath and McAlpine (1993) argue that fear plays an essential part in the child's experience of pain. In their developmental categorization of fear in childhood, Albano *et al.* (2001) suggest that the fear of death and serious illness emerges only in later childhood (13–18 years). However, for children who experience illness early in life, particularly chronic illness or illness requiring surgery, it is likely that this fear evolves earlier.

The influence of social support

The child's emotional experience of illness is mediated by many factors and perhaps most prominent of these are pain and fear. Pain and fear are interdependent in the experience of illness and both are strongly influenced by understanding and communication (Cohen, 2002). This extends to the non-verbal cues given off by the carer. It has been shown that levels of anxiety in a mother are often reflected in her child's experience of pain and fear and ultimately in delayed recovery following surgery (Chambers *et al.*, 2002).

   Social support from the family has been identified as a major factor in a child's response to chronic illness. The process is interactive in that children with chronic illness often withdraw from social interaction as a result of fear of being ostracized. However, support is not limited to the family and some research has shown that peer support from classmates has an even bigger impact than family support (Varni and Katz, 1997). Thus, it seems that it is not a matter of who is supportive, but that good quality support is perceived to be provided by someone. Cognitive-behavioural interventions have been used to increase the effective use of social support in children with chronic illness (Varni *et al.*, 1994), and these interventions have been shown to have a high level of success in improving the quality of life for the children involved (Kibby, *et al.*, 1998). This type of intervention would be classified as 'tertiary' in Caplan's scheme, as discussed in Section 5.

Children's responses to illness

Eiser (1990) identified three major factors in children's responses to illness. The first factor is related to the degree to which the illness is life-threatening and disruptive of daily routine. The disruption of daily routine can potentially have a greater influence on the child's response (Ditto *et al.*, 1996). The second factor is related to understanding and attributions of causality, with more realistic attributions being predictive of better adjustment. Children who make internal attributions exhibit poorer coping (Bearison *et al.*, 1993). A third factor is the supportiveness of the family as displayed in open communication and general expressiveness. This to a large extent mirrors the adult literature where attributional style, coping style and social support are major aspects of the psychological outcome of physical illness.

The role of biofeedback in pain management

There are several types of biofeedback machines that facilitate children's relaxation and, since the 1970s, these have been used to manage pain and stress. The common principle in all biofeedback machines is that they allow children to gain control over specific physiological responses.

There are several types of biofeedback machines. These include electromyograph (EMG) machines that measure muscular tension; temperature biofeedback machines that monitor skin temperature (when children are anxious their skin temperature decreases); and machines that monitor the galvanic skin response (GSR). In GSR biofeedback machines, sensors are usually attached to the fingers. As emotional arousal increases, so does sweat gland activity, and the sweat produced increases the electrical conductivity of the child's skin. The output of the sensors provides the 'feedback' element to the child. This output can be signalled by a sound, for example a beep which decreases or increases in frequency, or by a colour display which changes across the spectrum in relation to the child's level of relaxation. The sensor output can also be used to control a computer programme. For example, a screen may display a fish that turns into scuba diver or mermaid when the child relaxes, or an egg that hatches into a bird which walks and then eventually flies and sings if the child's relaxation level increases sufficiently. There are many other options: steering a car around a course, kicking an on-screen football, or even controlling aspects of PlayStation games. However, the basic principle is that the child learns to gain control over their own physiological response. The sensitivity can be calibrated for each child as their ability to relax increases.

At a general level, these approaches can be used to teach a child how to relax, where anxiety or stress responses are an issue. There are also clinical applications related to pain management, for example migraine reduction, the improvement of concentration or the improvement of breathing or constipation. One study used biofeedback combined with relaxation training and found that the combination reduced migraine activity by 82 per cent in children between 8 and 16 years old (Hermann *et al.*, 1995).

Providing information about treatments

There are three important aspects of information supply that need to be considered with children.

1   Children are similar to adults in that they differ in the amount of information they prefer to receive about medical procedures. In addition, the amount of information preferred relates to the type of medical procedure and the timeline of treatment (Siegel and Conte, 2001). For example, children who have had a chronic illness for some time prefer more information about what is happening, or about to happen, to them.

2   The type of information and the communication medium will vary with the age of the child.

3   The information given must be related to coping in two important ways: first, the information should match the child's preferred coping style (discussed in Section 4) where an already effective coping style exists. For example, where a child prefers an avoidant style of coping information can work in two ways: it can cause greater distress by preventing the child from avoiding the issue, or it can facilitate a change in coping style, which may be adaptively functional (Christiano and Russ, 1998). Secondly, information should incorporate a consideration of coping strategies through providing ways in which the child may deal with the medical procedures to follow.

6.3 Improving children's experiences of hospitalization

Hospitalization for a child may involve removal from a safe environment, to one that is strange and frightening – an experience that the child may not associate with the illness. This potential lack of understanding and ability to communicate may produce a perception of punishment and rejection. In the 1950s, work by Bowlby (1960) and Robertson (1952, 1958) highlighted the psychological distress and disturbance caused to children by the healthcare process, particularly during hospitalization involving separation from caregivers. Robertson's (1952) now dated but impressive films of a 2 year old over a 10-day period in hospital show how an active and lively child gradually became withdrawn and clearly depressed. A variety of possible causal mechanisms for this effect have been proposed over the years including separation anxiety, painful procedures, the unfamiliarity of the environment, and fear of the unknown (Eiser, 1990).

As children get older, issues about privacy and embarrassment arise particularly related to the level of sexual awareness. Most parents will have recognized the 'closed door syndrome' as children get older and express their need for privacy (Cassidy, 1997). The age at which children begin to close doors to bathrooms and bedrooms in order to maintain privacy varies, but a great deal of distress is experienced when privacy is invaded. Invasion of privacy and personal space is often unavoidable in hospital situations but exacerbated if the patient is depersonalized (Straub, 2001).

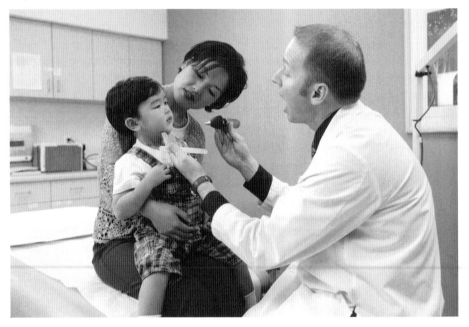

Figure 7 A visit to the doctor's surgery.

It is now common practice in hospitals to provide facilities for parents to stay with the child, or where this is not possible, to provide extended visiting periods. In some cases physical environment interventions have gone well beyond providing the space for parents to stay overnight, and have involved providing play facilities and even special children's gardens. Whitehouse *et al.* (2001) provided a post-occupancy evaluation of a children's hospital garden that had been designed for use by the sick children and their parents. It was felt to be a place of restoration and healing by those who used it.

Programmes for providing information and preparing children for hospitalization consist of five main components (Peterson and Mori, 1988). These are:

1   giving information;
2   encouraging emotional expression;
3   establishing a positive relationship between the child and staff;
4   providing the parents with information; and
5   encouraging the development of coping strategies.

(Siegel and Conte, 2001)

For infants and very young children, providing information which reduces parental anxiety can be very effective in helping the infant to cope with the stress of hospitalization and surgical procedures. Infants whose mothers had been prepared cried less and recovered more quickly following minor surgery

(Chambers *et al.*, 2002). Video material can be used to present information about treatment, coping strategies and positive models of hospitalization to children.

There is evidence that the tendency to seek information about medical procedures may reflect a stable coping style (Blount *et al.*,1999). Further, children who seek information seem to adjust better to medical procedures over time. The temperament of the child has also been linked to their adjustment to medical procedures, with adaptable children who tend to exhibit positive moods and stable behaviour and who are less reactive, coping more effectively (Blount *et al.*, 1999). The relationship between the child and parents has also been implicated in the child's experience of hospitalization (Carson *et al.*, 1991). The impact of parents on the child's adjustment to hospitalization involves an interaction between three elements: separation/non-separation from the parent; the quality of the parent–child relationship and the behaviour of the parent in the situation. Where parents can stay with the child, when the relationship is secure and positive, and where the parent is supportive and non-anxious, the child tends to respond better to the experience of hospitalization. Hospitalization does not always cause distress for children, and a positive outcome has been suggested in the development of psychological resilience and emotional development as a result of hospitalization (Siegel and Conte, 2001).

Summary of Section 6

- There are a number of age-related changes in children's understanding of illness and pain.
- Illness in childhood does impact on children's perceived quality of life and subsequent development.
- Children's experience of hospitalization can be positively influenced by the supply of appropriate information and by considering parental interactions.
- The family and social context can impact on children's perception of pain and their quality of life.

7 Children's adherence to treatment

In the previous section we examined the ways in which children's understanding of health-related situations, and their styles of interaction, influenced their response to illness and medical procedures. In this section we look at the factors that have an impact on how well they follow their treatment programmes.

A significant percentage of patients leave medical consultations not knowing what they have been told or what they are expected to do in terms of medication (DiMatteo, 1994). This includes information which is too technical or detailed for patients and the patient's inability to listen and digest information because of their emotional state. This may be further compounded if health professionals fail to check that the child or parent has really understood or is actually able to follow the treatment regimen recommended, as found in research regarding communication issues in childhood diabetes (DiMatteo, 2000). The quality of the interaction is also influenced by trust. Trust requires the health professional to show empathy for the patient's distress and life situation as well as the illness itself (DiMatteo, 2000). Children and parents often either fail to report information, or provide distorted information to health professionals because of a lack of trust in the relationship. Related to trust are patients' beliefs about the illness, the treatment and the healthcare process. Use of the health belief model (Rhodes *et al.*, 2004) has shown that beliefs about the severity of the illness and the efficacy of the treatment will influence adherence. It is here that social cognition models such as the TPB can be useful in identifying the factors that will turn beliefs into behavioural intentions. The communication process must consider whether the patient has committed to the regimen. Engagement in the healthcare delivery process and ultimately adherence will be influenced by socio-cultural norms (Rand, 2002) as there are important differences in attitudes to illness and treatment across religions and cultures (Dein, 2004).

As well as the differential attitudes that may influence adherence to medication, there is also a range of barriers faced by children and their families in coping with treatment regimens. The socio-economic status of the family, the presence of sufficient caregivers, parental alcohol or drug misuse, the health culture of the family, and many other factors will make it more difficult for a child to adhere to medical treatments. There are at least two important ways in which the problem of childhood adherence provides health professionals with challenges that are not present in adult adherence. First, there is the developmental process. The attitudes, beliefs, understanding and communication of a child undergoing medication may change over relatively short periods of time. For both parents and practitioners this may lead to under- or overestimations of how much responsibility the child can take for their own medication at particular stages. Secondly, the communication process must incorporate the health professional, the child and at least one caregiver. The propensity for misunderstanding is increased by the addition of a third person in the communication network.

For children with chronic illness, adherence to medical regimens is paramount. The problem is confounded by the fact that the child may not recognize the seriousness of over- or undermedicating and responsibility generally reverts to a parent or carer. The extent of non-adherence varies by type of illness and also across different studies, but is somewhere in the range of 25–50 per cent, with around 60 per cent overusing and about 10 per cent underusing their medication (Riekert and Drotar, 2000). As a result of non-adherence to medication treatment, significant numbers of children with chronic illness are referred to health psychologists working in paediatric hospitals, but the referrals at this point may arise when the problem has become serious and potentially irreversible (Riekert and Drotar, 2000). This indicates a need to prioritize preventive strategies.

Research on adherence to medication in the adult literature is generally rooted in the work of Ley (1981) on the cognitive hypothesis of compliance.

> Compliance implies an involuntary act of submission to authority, whereas *adherence* refers to a voluntary act of subscribing to a point of view. The difference is not just semantic; it goes right to the heart of our relationship with our patients. We need to influence our patients to become – or remain – adherents of good self-care. To do this, we need to establish three key conditions in our communication with patients: shared values, shared language, and mutual respect

(Stone *et al.*, 1998)

According to Ley (1989), compliance can be predicted by an interaction between understanding and memory mediated by satisfaction (see Figure 8). If a patient understands the information, is able to recall it, and is generally satisfied with the healthcare process, she or he will be more likely to comply with the treatment.

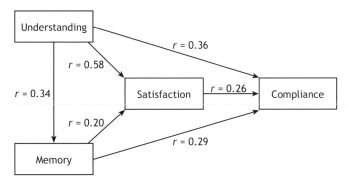

Figure 8   Ley's model of compliance.

Ley's model identifies three 'components' that influence compliance. The values shown are measures of correlation between pairs of components. The higher the value, the greater the association between these two components. Ley's model provides a broad framework for understanding the compliance process, and suggests that it is worthwhile to research the specific factors that enable individuals to understand and remember the information about medication provided and how the mode of delivery of the healthcare can increase satisfaction.

Social cognition models, such as the TPB, have been applied quite successfully to adult adherence (Riekert and Drotar, 2000). In essence, the sorts of constructs considered include the severity of the risk, perceived susceptibility (the likelihood that it could actually happen to the person), expectations about outcomes (i.e. the perceived costs and benefits of adhering), and perceived control or self-efficacy (the perception of whether the person can actually successfully adhere). Children are more likely to adhere to treatment when (a) they perceive the risk to their health as significant (b) they judge the benefits of adherence to be greater than the costs of their adherence and (c) their self-efficacy is high. In terms of perceived susceptibility, there is some conflicting evidence suggesting that for adolescents with cancer and diabetes, higher perceived susceptibility actually predicts lower levels of adherence (Bond *et al.*, 1992). When parents have a greater perception of risk, hold a more positive expectancy and have greater perceived control, the child is more likely to adhere to treatment.

DiMatteo (2000) suggests three basic recommendations for increasing adherence in childhood illness. First, the health professional should ensure that the child and caregiver fully understand what they are being asked to do. For example, in a study by Ievers *et al.* (1999) children with cystic fibrosis and their parents' level of adherence were directly related to their knowledge of the specific details associated with medically prescribed treatments. Their knowledge of the functions of what had been prescribed was a significant variable in explaining non-adherence. Secondly, the health professional needs to determine that the child and caregiver are committed to, and intend to follow the treatment programme as recommended. Estimates of non-adherence across many chronic childhood illnesses (e.g. diabetes, asthma and rheumatoid arthritis) are commonly at or below 50 per cent of prescribed dosage (Rapoff *et al.*, 2002; Rand, 2002). Thirdly, there is a need to enable the child and the carer to adhere to the regimen by fully understanding any barriers that exist and by providing the resources to overcome the barriers. This may involve practical help in developing a treatment routine, or in developing psychological resources in terms of coping strategies. In order to achieve this there needs to be effective involvement of household members and supportive links between the family, school and healthcare settings (Rand, 2002). For young children, adherence requires developmentally appropriate parent–child partnerships; for example regarding issues of self-administration of medicine.

Summary of Section 7

- Adherence to treatment is a major issue for children's health services.
- Attempts to understand and improve adherence have used different psychological models of behaviour.
- Methods that help children and their families to understand health-related information improve subsequent adherence.

8   Conclusion

Of all the models discussed in this chapter, the biopsychosocial model, by indicating the links between psychological and social and biological processes, has a major impact on how psychologists research and support the health of children. Health psychology is a growing discipline that challenges models of health, and indeed professions, grounded in a single paradigm. Although still young, health psychology offers the potential for a multilevel analysis of childhood health and illness, based on a conceptualization of child development that encompasses cultural, social and biological aspects. In doing so, it promises a uniquely holistic approach to child health. The extent to which this promise is fulfilled will require collaboration between health professionals, family, school and community (Goreczny and Gage, 1999) and transdisciplinary research (Suls and Rothman, 2004).

References

Abraham, C., Wight, D. and Scott, S. (2002) 'Encouraging safer-sex behaviours: development of the SHARE sex education programme', in Rutter, D. and Quine, L. (eds) *Changing Health Behaviour*, Buckingham, Open University Press.

Adams, R. J., Smith, B. J. and Ruffin, R. E. (2000) 'Factors associated with hospital admissions and repeat emergency department visits for adults with asthma', *Thorax*, vol. 55, pp. 566–73.

Ajzen, I. (1985) 'From intentions to actions: a Theory of Planned Behaviour', in Kuhl, J. and Beckmann, J. (eds) *Action-Control: from cognition to behaviour*, Heidelberg, Springer.

Albano, A. M., Causey, D. and Carter, B. D. (2001, 3rd edn) 'Fear and anxiety in children', in Walker, C. E. and Roberts, M. C. (eds) *Handbook of Clinical Child Psychology,* New York, Wiley.

Anand, K. J. S. and Carr, D. B. (1989) 'The neuroanatomy, neurophysiology and neurochemistry of pain, stress and analgesia in newborns, infants, and children', *Paediatric Clinics of North America,* vol. 36, pp. 795–822.

Asher, S. R. and Coie, J. D. (1990) *Peer Rejection in Childhood*, New York, Cambridge University Press.

Bandura, A. (1977) *Social Learning Theory*, New York, General Learning Press.

Bearison, D. J., Sadow, A. J., Granowetter, L. and Winckel, G. (1993) 'Patients' and parents' causal attributions for childhood cancer', *Journal of Psychosocial Oncology*, vol. 11, pp. 47–61.

Bibace, R. and Walsh, M. E. (1980) 'Development of children's conceptions of illness', *Paediatrics*, vol. 8, pp. 533–43.

Biology Dictionary: Hyperdictionary. Available from: http://www.hyperdictionary.com/dictionary/asthma [last accessed 22 August 2005].

Bird, J. E. and Podmore, V. N. (1990) 'Children's understanding of health and illness', *Psychology and Health*, vol. 4, pp. 175–85.

Blount, R. L., Smith, A. J. and Frank, N. C. (1999) 'Preparation to undergo medical procedures', in Goreczny, A. J. and Hersen, M. (eds) *Handbook of Pediatric and Adolescent Health Psychology*, London, Allyn and Bacon.

Bond G. G., Aiken L. S. and Somerville S. C. (1992), 'The health belief model and adolescents with insulin-dependent diabetes mellitus', *Health Psycholology*, vol. 11, pp. 190–8.

Bowlby, J. (1960) 'Separation anxiety', *International Journal of Psychoanalysis*, vol. 41, pp. 89–113.

Bradley, R. H. and Corwyn, R. F. (2002) 'Socioeconomic status and child development', *Annual Review of Psychology*, vol. 53, pp. 371–99.

British Psychological Society Division of Health Psychology (BPS BHP) (2005) Available from: http://www.health-psychology.org.uk/menuItems/abouttheDHP.php [accessed 22 August 2005].

Bruvold, W. H. and Rundall, T. G. (1988) 'A meta-analysis and theoretical review of school-based tobacco and alcohol intervention programs', *Psychology and Health*, vol. 2, pp. 53–78.

Buchanan-Barrow, E. A. and Barrett, M. D. (2005) 'The development of children's conceptions of mental illness' ESRC report [RES-000–22–0073]. Available from www.esrc.ac.uk [last accessed 22 August 2005].

Caplan, G. (1964) *Principles of Preventive Psychiatry*, New York, Basic Books.

Carson, D. K., Council, J. R. and Gravley, J. E. (1991) 'Temperament and family characteristics as predictors of children's reactions to hospitalisation', *Developmental and Behavioural Pediatrics*, vol.12, pp. 141–47.

Cassidy, T. (1997) *Environmental Psychology: behaviour and experience in context*, Hove, Psychology Press.

Cassidy, T. (1999) *Stress, Cognition and Health*, London, Routledge.

Cates, W. and Berman, S. M. (1999) 'Prevention of sexually transmitted diseases other than Human Immunodeficiency Syndrome', in Goreczny, A. J. and Hersen, M. (eds) *Handbook of Pediatric and Adolescent Health Psychology*, London, Allyn and Bacon.

Chambers, C. T., Craig, K. D. and Bennett, S. M. (2002) 'The impact of maternal behaviour on children's pain experiences: an experimental analysis', *Journal of Paediatric Psychology*, vol. 27, pp. 293–301.

Chen, E., Bloomberg G. R., Fisher Jr, E. and Strunk, R. C. (2003) 'Predictors of repeat hospitalizations in children with asthma: the role of psychosocial and socioenvironmental factors', *Health Psychology*, vol. 22, pp. 12–18.

Christiano, B. and Russ, S. W. (1998) 'Matching preparatory interventions to coping style: the effects on children's distress in the dental setting', *Journal of Pediatric Psychology*, vol. 23, pp. 17–27.

Cohen, L. L. (2002) 'Reducing infant immunization distress through distraction', *Health Psychology*, vol. 21, pp. 207–11.

Cohen, S. and Herbert, T. B. (1996) 'Health Psychology: psychological factors and physical disease from the perspective of human psychoneuroimmunology', *Annual Review of Psychology*, vol. 47, pp. 113–42.

Connor, M. T. and Armitage, C. J. (1998) 'Extending the theory of planned behaviour: a review and avenues for further research', *Journal of Applied Social Psychology*, vol. 28, pp. 1429–64.

Coscia, J. M., Christensen, B. K., Henry, R. R., Wallston, K., Radcliffe, J. and Rutstein, R. (2001) 'Effects of home environment, socioeconomic status, and health status on cognitive functioning in children with HIV-1 infection', *Journal of Pediatric Psychology*, vol. 26, pp. 321–29.

Cummings, E. (1987) 'Coping with background anger in early childhood', *Child Development*, vol. 58, pp. 976–84.

Dein S. (2004) 'Explanatory models of and attitudes towards cancer in different cultures', *The Lancet Oncology,* vol. 5, pp. 119–24.

Diepgen T. L and Mahler V. (2002) 'The epidemiology of skin cancer', *British Journal of Dermatology*, vol. 146, pp. 1–6.

DiMatteo, M. R. (1994) 'Enhancing patient adherence to medical recommendations', *The Journal of the American Medical Association*, vol. 5, pp. 79–83.

DiMatteo, M. R. (2000) 'Practitioner-Family-Patient communication in pediatric adherence: implications for research and clinical practice', in Drotar, D. (ed.) *Promoting Adherence to Medical Treatment in Chronic Childhood Illness*, London, Lawrence Erlbaum.

Ditto, P. H., Druley, J. A., Moore, K. A., Danks, J. H. and Smucker, W. D. (1996) 'Fates worse than death: the role of valued life activities in health-state evaluations', *Health Psychology*, vol. 15, pp. 332–43.

Ebbeling, C. B., Pawlak, D. B. and Ludwig, D. S. (2002) 'Childhood obesity: public-health crisis, common sense cure', *The Lancet*, vol. 360, pp. 473–82.

Eiser, C. (1990) *Chronic Childhood Disease: an introduction to psychological theory and research*, Cambridge, Cambridge University Press.

Eiser, C. (1997) 'Children's perceptions of illness and death', in Baum, A., Newman, S., Weinman, J., West, R. and McManus, C. (eds) *Cambridge Handbook of Psychology, Health and Medicine*, Cambridge, Cambridge University Press.

Engel, G. L. (1977) 'The need for a new medical model: a challenge for biomedicine', *Science*, vol. 196, pp. 129–36.

Evans, R. I. (2001) 'Social influences in the etiology and prevention of smoking and other health-threatening behaviours in children and adolescents', in Baum, A., Newman, S., Weinman, J., West, R. and McManus, C. (eds) *Cambridge Handbook of Psychology, Health and Medicine*, Cambridge, Cambridge University Press.

Eveleth, P. B. and Tanner, J. M. (1991, 2nd edn) *Worldwide Variation in Human Growth*, Cambridge, Cambridge University Press.

Felce, D (1997) 'Defining and applying the quality of life', *The Journal of Intellectual Disability Research*, vol. 41, pp. 126–35.

Fishbein, M. and Ajzen, I. (1975) *Belief, Attitude, Intention and Behaviour: an introduction to theory and research*, Reading, MA, Addison-Wesley.

Fitzgerald, M. (1995) 'Pain in infancy: some unanswered questions', *Pain Reviews*, vol. 2, pp. 77–91.

Fitzgerald, M. and Anand, K. J. S. (1993) 'Developmental neuroanatomy and neurophysiology of pain', in Schechter, N. L., Berde, C. B. and Yaster, M. (eds) *Pain in Infants, Children and Adolescents*, Baltimore, Williams and Wilkins.

Fonagy, P., Steele, M., Steele, H., Higgit, A. and Target, M. (1994) 'The theory and practice of resilience', *Journal of Child Psychology, Psychiatry and Allied Disciplines*, vol. 35, pp. 231–57.

Frable, D. E. S. (1997) 'Gender, racial, ethnic, sexual, and class identities', *Annual Review of Psychology*, vol. 48, pp. 139–62.

Gafney, A. and Dunne, E. A. (1986) 'Developmental aspects of children's definitions of pain', *Pain*, vol. 26, pp. 105–17.

Garmezy, N. (1991) 'Resilience in children's adaptation to negative life events and stressed environments', *Pediatric Annals*, vol. 20, pp. 459–66.

Glanz, K., Geller, A. C., Shigaki, D., Maddock, J. E. and Isnec, M. R. (2002) 'A randomized trial of skin cancer prevention in aquatics settings: the Pool Cool program', *Health Psychology*, vol. 21, pp. 579–87.

Gollwitzer, P. M. (1999) 'Implementation intentions: strong effects of simple plans', *American Psychologist* vol. 54, pp. 493–503.

Goreczny, A. J. and Gage, M. (1999) 'Pediatric and adolescent health psychology during the healthcare revolution: challenges and opportunities', in Goreczny, A. J. and Hersen, M. (eds) *Handbook of Pediatric and Adolescent Health Psychology*, London, Allyn and Bacon.

Grych, J. H. and Fincham, F. D. (1993) 'Children's appraisals of marital conflict: initial investigations of the cognitive-contextual framework', *Child Development*, vol. 64, pp. 215–30.

Hagger, M. S., Chatzisarantis, N., Biddle, S. J. H. and Orbell, S. (2001) 'Antecedents of children's physical activity intentions and behaviour: predictive validity and longitudinal effects', *Psychology and Health*, vol. 16, pp. 391–407.

Hamnett, F. S. (1921) 'Studies in the thyroid apparatus', *American Journal of Physiology*, vol. 56, pp. 196–204.

Hanley, M. (2002) 'Stress', in Brace, N. and Westcott, H. (eds) *Applying Psychology*, Milton Keynes, The Open University,

Harbeck, C. and Peterson, L. (1992) 'Elephants dancing on my head: a developmental approach to children's concepts of specific pains', *Child Development*, vol. 63, pp. 138–49.

Health Select Committee Report on Obesity (2004) May. Available from: http://www.publications.parliament.uk/pa/cm200304/cmselect/cmhealth/23/2302.htm [accessed 1 March 2005].

Hergenrather, J. R. and Rabinowitz, M. (1991) 'Age-related differences in the organization of children's knowledge of illness', *Developmental Psychology*, vol. 27, pp. 952–59.

Hermann, C., Kim, M. and Blanchard, E. B. (1995) 'Behavioural and pharmacological intervention studies of pediatric migraine: an exploratory meta-analysis', *Pain*, vol. 60, pp. 239–56.

Hofferth, S. (1987) 'Implications of family trends for children: a research perspective', *Educational Leadership*, vol. 44, pp. 78–84.

Ievers, C. E., Brown, R. T., Drotar, D., Caplan, D., Pishevar, B. S. and Lambert, R. G. (1999) 'Knowledge of physician prescriptions and adherence to treatment among children with cystic fibrosis and their mothers', *Journal of Development and Behavioral Problems*, vol. 20, pp. 335–43.

Janz, N. K. and Becker, M. H. (1984) 'The health belief model: a decade later', *Health Education Quarterly*, vol. 11, pp. 1–47.

Jenney, M. E. M. and Campbell, S. (1997) 'Measuring quality of life', *Archives of Disease in Childhood*, vol. 77, pp. 347–50.

Kibby, M. Y., Tyc, V. L. and Mulhern, R. K. (1998) 'Effectiveness of psychological intervention for children and adolescents with chronic medical illness: a meta-analysis', *Clinical Psychology Review*, vol. 18, pp. 103–17.

Kim-Cohen, J., Moffitt, T. E., Caspi, A. and Taylor, A. (2004) 'Genetic and environmental processes in young children's resilience and vulnerability to socioeconomic deprivation', *Child Development*, vol. 75, pp. 651–88.

Klonoff, E. A. and Landrine, H. (2004) 'Predicting youth access to tobacco: the role of youth versus store-clerk behavior and issues of ecological validity', *Health Psychology*, vol. 23, pp. 517–24.

Kobasa, S. C. (1979) 'Stressful life events, personality and health: an inquiry into hardiness', *Journal of Personality and Social Psychology*, vol. 42, pp. 168–77.

Kost, K. and Forrest, J. D. (1992) 'American women's sexual behaviour and exposure to risk of sexually transmitted diseases', *Family Planning Perspectives*, vol. 24, pp. 244–54.

Lazarus, R. S. and Folkman, S. (1984) *Stress, Appraisal and Coping*, New York, Springer.

Ley, P. (1981) 'Professional non-compliance: a neglected problem', *British Journal of Clinical Psychology*, vol. 20, pp. 151–4.

Ley, P. (1989) 'Improving patients' understanding, recall, satisfaction and compliance', in Broome, A. K. (ed.) *Health Psychology: process and application*, London, Chapman and Hall.

Lowrey, G. H. (1986, 8th edn) *Growth and Development of Children*, Chicago, Year Book Medical Publishers Inc.

Mannino, D. M., Homa, D. M., Pertowski, C. A. *et al.* (1998) 'Surveillance for asthma: United States, 1960–1995', *Morbidity and Mortality Weekly Reports: CDC Surveillance Summaries*, vol. 47, pp. 1–27.

Margolin, G. and Gordis, E. B. (2000) 'The effects of family and community violence on children', *Annual Review of Psychology*, vol. 51, pp. 445–79.

McCabe, M. P. and Ricciardelli, L. A. (2003) 'Body image and strategies to lose weight and increase muscle among boys and girls', *Health Psychology*, vol. 22, pp. 39–46.

McGrath, P. J., McAlpine, L. (1993) 'Psychologic perspectives on pediatric pain', *Journal of Pediatrics*, vol. 122, pp. S2–8.

McGuire, W. J. (1964) 'Inducing resistance to persuasion', in Berkowitz. L. (ed.) *Advances in Experimental Social Psychology, Vol. 1*, New York, Academic Press.

McMurran, M. (1994) *The Psychology of Addiction*, London, Taylor & Francis.

Mullins, R., Borland, R. and Hill, D. (1992) 'Smoking in Victoria: a profile from 1988–1991' in *Quit evaluation Studies, Vol. 6, 1990–1991*, Melbourne, Victorian Smoking and Health Program 1992, pp. 85–104.

Nicklas, T. A., Baranowski, T., Cullen, K. W. and Berenson, G. (2001) 'Eating patterns, dieting quality and obesity', *Journal of the American College of Nutrition*, vol. 20, pp. 599–608.

Olsson, C. A., Bond, L., Burns, J. M., Vella-Brodrick, D. A. and Sawyer, S. M. (2003) 'Adolescent resilience: a concept analysis', *Journal of Adolescence*, vol. 26, pp. 1–11.

Orford, J. (1992) *Community Psychology: theory and practice*, Chichester, Wiley.

Peterson, L. and Mori, L (1988) 'Preparation for hospitalisation', in Routh, D. K. (ed.) *Handbook of Pediatric Psychology*, New York, Guilford Press.

Peterson, L., Crowson, J., Saldana, L. and Holdridge, S. (1999) 'Of needles and skinned knees: children's coping with medical procedures and minor injuries for self and others', *Health Psychology*, vol. 18, pp. 197–200.

Phipps, S., Fairclough, D. and Mulhern, R. K. (1995) 'Avoidant coping in children with cancer', *Journal of Pediatric Psychology*, vol. 20, pp. 217–32.

Picard, E. M., Del Dotto, J. E. and Breslau, N. (2000) 'Prematurity and low birth weight', in Yeates, K. O., Ris, M. D. and Taylor, H. G. (eds) *Pediatric Neuropsychology: research, theory and practice*, London, The Guilford Press.

Rand C. S. (2002) 'Adherence to asthma therapy in the preschool child', *Allergy*, vol. 57, p. 48.

Rapoff, M. A., Belmont, J., Lindsley, C., Olson, N., Morris, J., Padur, J. (2002) 'Prevention of nonadherence to nonsteroidal anti-inflammatory medications for newly diagnosed patients with juvenile rheumatoid arthritis', *Health Psychology*, vol. 21, pp. 620–34.

Rhodes, R. E., Plotnikoff, R. C. and Spence, J. C. (2004) 'Creating parsimony at the expense of precision? Conceptual and applied issues of aggregating belief-based constructs in physical activity research', *Health Education Research*, vol. 19, pp. 392–405.

Ricciardelli, L. A. and McCabe, M. P. (2001) 'Self-esteem and negative affect as moderators of sociocultural influences on body dissatisfaction, strategies to decrease weight, and strategies to increase muscles among adolescent boys and girls', *Sex Roles*, vol. 44, pp. 189–207.

Ricciardelli, L. A. and McCabe, M. P. (2003) 'Sociocultural and individual influences on muscle gain and weight loss strategies among adolescent boys and girls', *Psychology in the Schools*, vol. 40, pp. 209–24.

Riekert, K. A. and Drotar, D. (2000) 'Adherence to medical treatment in pediatric chronic illness: critical issues and answered questions', in Drotar, D. (ed.) *Promoting Adherence to Medical Treatment in Chronic Childhood Illness*, London, Lawrence Earlbaum.

Robertson, J. (1952) *A Two-year old goes to Hospital (Film)*, New York, NYU Film Library.

Robertson, J. (1958) *Young Children in Hospitals*, New York, Basic Books.

Robinson, M. E. and Riley, J. L. (1999) 'The role of emotion in pain', in Gatchel, R. J. and Turk, D. C. (eds) *Psychosocial Factors in Pain*, New York, The Guilford Press.

Ross, M. W., Rigby, K., Rosser, B. R., Anagnostou, P. and Brown, M. (1990) 'The effect of a national campaign on attitudes towards AIDS', *AIDS Care*, vol. 2, pp. 239–46.

Ross, D. M. and Ross, S. H. (1984) 'Childhood pain: the school-aged child', *Pain*, vol. 20, pp. 207–9.

Rutter, M. (1999) 'Resilience concepts and findings: implications for family therapy', *Journal of Family Therapy*, vol. 21, pp. 119–44.

Sahinler, B. E. (2002) 'A review of pediatric pain management in acute and chronic setting', *Pain Practice*, vol. 2, pp. 137–50.

Schwimmer, J. B., Burwinkle, T. M. and Varni, J. W. (2003) 'Health-related quality of life of severely obese children and adolescents', *Journal of the American Medical Association*, vol. 289, pp. 1813–19.

Siegel, L. J. and Conte, P. (2001, 3rd edn) 'Hospitalisation and medical care of children', in Walker, C. E. and Roberts, M. C. (eds) *Handbook of Clinical Child Psychology*, New York, Wiley.

Stokols, D. (1992) 'Establishing and maintaining healthy environments: towards a social ecology of health promotion', *American Psychologist*, vol. 37, pp. 6–22.

Stone, M. A., Sheryl, J., Bronkesh, M. B. A., Zachary, B., Gerbarg, M. D. and Wood, S. D. (1998) 'Improving patient compliance', *Strategic Medicine*. Available from: http://www.hsmgroup.com/info/compli/compli.html [accessed 13 May 2005].

Straub, R. O. (2001) *Health Psychology*, New York, Worth.

Striegell-Moore, R. H., Silberstein, L. R. and Rodin, J. (1986) 'Toward an understanding of risk factors in bulimia', *American Psychologist*, vol. 41, pp. 246–63.

Suls, J. and Fletcher, B. (1985) 'The relative efficiency of avoidant and non-avoidant coping strategies: a meta-analysis', *Health Psychology*, vol. 4, pp. 248–49.

Suls, J. and Rothman, A. (2004) 'Evolution of the biopsychosocial model: prospects and challenges for health psychology', *Health Psychology*, vol. 23, pp. 119–25.

Taddio, A., Katz, J., Ilersich, A. L. and Koren, G. (1997) 'Effect of neonatal circumcision on pain response during subsequent routine vaccination', *The Lancet*, vol. 349, pp. 599–603.

Tapert, S. F., Stewart, D. G. and Brown, S. A. (1999) 'Drug abuse in adolescence', in Goreczny, A. J. and Hersen, M. (eds) *Handbook of Pediatric and Adolescent Health Psychology*, London, Allyn and Bacon.

Tapper, K., Horne, P. J. and Lowe, C. F. (2003) 'The Food Dudes to the rescue!', *The Psychologist*, vol. 16, pp. 18–21.

Tucker, C. M. (2002) 'Expanding pediatric psychology beyond hospital walls to meet the health needs of ethnic minority children', *Journal of Pediatric Psychology*, vol. 27, pp. 315–23.

Varni, J. W. and Katz, E. R. (1997) 'Stress, social support and negative affectivity in children with newly diagnosed cancer: a prospective transactional analysis', *Psycho-Oncology*, vol. 6, pp. 267–78.

Varni, J. W., Seid, M., Rode, C. A. (1999) 'The PedQL: measurement model for the pediatric quality of life inventory', *Medical Care*, vol. 37, pp. 126–39.

Varni, J. W., Katz, E. R., Colegrove, R. and Dolgin, M. (1994) 'Perceived social support and adjustment of children with newly diagnosed cancer', *Journal of Developmental and Behavioural Pediatrics*, vol. 15, pp. 20–26.

Varni, J. W., Katz, E. R., Seid, M., Quiggins, D. J. L., Friedman-Bender, A. and Castro, C. M. (1998) 'The Pediatric Cancer Quality of Life Inventory (PCQL). 1. Instrument development, descriptive statistics, and cross-informant variance', *Journal of Behavioural Medicine*, vol. 21, pp. 179–204.

Vogt, C. J. (1999) 'A model of risk factors involved in childhood and adolescent obesity', in Goreczny, A. J. and Hersen, M. (eds) *Handbook of Pediatric and Adolescent Health Psychology*, London, Allyn and Bacon.

Wallander, J. L. and Varni, J. W. (1998) 'Effects of pediatric chronic physical disorders on child and family adjustment', *Journal of Child Psychology and Psychiatry and Allied Disciplines*, vol. 39, pp. 267–78.

Wang, Y., Monteiro, C., and Popkin, B. M. (2002) 'Trends of obesity and underweight in older children and adolescents in the United States, Brazil, China, and Russia' *American Journal of Clinical Nutrition*, vol. 75, pp. 971–77.

Whitaker, R. C., Wright, J. A., Pepe, M. S., Seidel, K. D. and Dietz, W. H. (1997) 'Predicting obesity in young adulthood from childhood and parental obesity', *New England Journal of Medicine*, vol. 337, pp. 869–73.

Whitehouse, S., Varni, J. W., Seid, M., Cooper-Marcus, C., Ensberg, M. J., Jacobs, J. R. and Mehlenbeck, R. S. (2001) 'Evaluating a children's hospital garden environment: utilisation of consumer satisfaction', *Journal of Environmental Psychology*, vol. 21, pp. 301–14.

Wight, D., Raab, G. M., Henderson, M., Abraham, C., Buston, K., Hart, G. and Scott, S. (2002) 'Limits of teacher delivered sex education: interim behavioural outcomes from randomised trial', *British Medical Journal*, vol. 324, pp. 1430. Available from http://bmj.bmjjournals.com/cgi/content/full/324/7351/1430 [Last accessed 3 January 2005].

Woolston, J. L. (1987) 'Obesity in infancy and early childhood', *Journal of the American Academy of Child and Adolescent Psychiatry*, vol. 26, pp. 123–26.

Chapter 4
Autism and developmental psychology

Andrew Grayson

Contents

	Learning outcomes	145
1	Introduction	145
2	Understanding autism from the inside out	146
	2.1 First-hand accounts	146
	2.2 First-hand accounts and science	153
	2.3 The incorrigibility of first-hand accounts?	153
3	Understanding autism from the outside in	154
	3.1 Diagnosis	154
	3.2 Prevalence	156
	3.3 Causes	156
	3.4 Brain mechanisms	158
	3.5 Sensation and movement	159
	3.6 Reflecting on the different perspectives	160
4	Psychological theories	161
	4.1 Theory of mind	161
	4.2 Executive dysfunction	165
	4.3 Central coherence	168
	4.4 Early transactions	170
5	Psychological theories: a critique	171
	5.1 Evaluating psychological approaches	172
	5.2 What is said and what is heard	173
	5.3 Psychological research on autism: who is it for?	173
6	Integrating insider and outsider accounts	175
	6.1 Pretend play	175
7	Conclusions	177
	References	178
	Reading	
	Reading A: The history of ideas on autism: legends, myths and reality	183

Learning outcomes

After you have studied this chapter you should be able to:

1 describe key characteristics of autism;
2 discuss critically the characteristics of first-hand and third-party accounts of autism;
3 compare and contrast different psychological approaches to understanding autism;
4 evaluate the role that psychological research has played in relation to understanding and representing autism.

1 Introduction

So far in this book 'developmental psychology in action' has been presented in a very practical sense – in terms of applying psychological research to areas of child development to improve the way children are understood and supported in a variety of contexts. This chapter represents an additional way of interpreting the theme of this book – it looks at how developmental psychology itself is 'in action'. That is, this discussion of autism will show how psychological research itself is dynamic, with approaches to a particular topic being examined, re-evaluated and developed in the light of new knowledge and changing attitudes in society.

The chapter looks at autism from two different perspectives. First, from 'within', examining what can be learned from the observations of those who live with autism, either as people with autism, or as parents, siblings, carers or friends. The proliferation of 'insider' (or 'first-hand') accounts has been an important step in the development of scientific understandings of autism.

Second, the chapter will review 'outsider' accounts of autism that have been offered by clinical, educational, and research psychologists. The conventional literature on autism can be thought of as a source of outsider (or 'third-party') accounts of autism, because it looks at autism from the perspective of the non-autistic psychologist, looking 'in'.

The chapter offers an overview of a rapidly changing area and shows how the theories and discourses developed by psychologists create particular views of autism. These views influence how research into autism is pursued, and the image of autism that is projected in society as a whole.

2 Understanding autism from the inside out

Until relatively recently the voices of people with autism have been absent from accounts of autism, and these voices are still relatively rare in much psychological research. This has also been the case for other groups within society, such as disabled adults and children and adults with learning difficulties. However, this has begun to change. For example, people with learning difficulties are moving beyond passive involvement and it is increasingly common to find projects where they are directing the research that affects their lives (Walmsley and Johnson, 2003). The phrase 'nothing about us, without us' encapsulates this movement. Similarly, self-help and advocacy organizations for people with autism are being developed, particularly on the internet. Underpinning this development is the belief that 'Autistic people have characteristically autistic styles of relating to others, which should be respected and appreciated rather than modified to make them "fit in"' (Autistic Network International, 2005).

Therefore in seeking to consider the nature of autism this chapter begins by foregrounding the voices of people with autism. One reason for doing this is to make it clear that understanding autism is not about solving an abstract clinical or theoretical riddle. It is first and foremost about understanding people, and their lived experiences.

Activity 1

Allow about 5 minutes

Your perception of autism

This activity will help you bring together the ideas you already have about autism.

Before you read the written accounts that follow from people with autism, take a few minutes to make a note of the things you already know about autism, from whatever source.

Comment

As you read Section 2.1, you will be able to compare your ideas about autism with ideas that have been expressed by people with autism. Make further notes about key features from their descriptions.

2.1 First-hand accounts

The following accounts are excerpts of writings from a variety of people with autism or from close family members. The accounts are lengthy and are deliberately presented in full prior to the commentary to enable the voices of people with autism to emerge. All contributors are adults, reflecting on their past, apart from the first contributor, a boy from India known as Tito, who writes insightful prose and poetry.

Tito, age 8

Men and women are puzzled by everything I do. My parents and those who love me, are embarrassed and worried. Doctors use different terminologies to describe me. I just wonder. ...

That is not just wonder alone but also a reason for my worry. I think about the little boy who had a way of expressing himself, not through speech but through a frustrated temper tantrum. The language was known but it did not relate to anything.

(Mukhopadhyay, 2000, p. 5)

It pains when people avoid us and the schools refuse to take us. I faced it and felt that every day there may be others like me who are facing the social rejection like me. I must make the point clear that it is not lack of social understanding which causes the weird behaviour, but it is a lack of getting to use oneself in the socially acceptable way, which causes the weird or the undesirable behaviour.

(Mukhopadhyay, 2000, p. 57)

Tito, age 11

Sometimes I had to knock my head or slap it to feel it. Of course from my knowledge of biology I knew that I had voluntary muscles and involuntary muscles. ... I experimented with myself that when I ordered my hand to pick up a pencil I could not do it. I remember long back when I had ordered my lips to move I could not do it.

(Mukhopadhyay, 2000, p. 73)

I had a definite problem. When I concentrated on the sound, I felt my eyes and nose shutting off. I could never do everything together at the same time. That is, I could not see you and at the same time hear you. My sense of hearing was always sharper than my sight. This is the reason, I never used my eyes to interact with anybody. Psychologists call it 'lack of eye contact'.

(Mukhopadhyay, 2000, p. 74)

Donna Williams

Words were no problem, but other people's expectations for me to respond to them were. This required my understanding what was said, but I was too happy losing myself to want to be dragged back by something as two-dimensional as understanding.

'What do you think you're doing?' came the voice.

Knowing I must respond in order to get rid of this annoyance, I would compromise, repeating 'What do you think you're doing?' addressed to no-one in particular.

'Don't repeat everything I say,' scolded the voice.

Sensing a need to respond, I'd reply: 'Don't repeat everything I say.'

Slap. I had no idea what was expected of me. ...

Around this time I was again tested for partial deafness, for although I could speak I often didn't use language in the same way as others and often got no meaning out of what was said to me. Although words are symbols, it would be misleading to say that I did not understand symbols. I had a whole system of relating which I considered 'my language'. It was other people who did not understand the symbolism I used, and there was no way I could or was going to tell them what I meant. I developed a language of my own. Everything I did, from holding two fingers together to scrunching up my toes, had a meaning, usually to do with reassuring myself that I was in control and that no-one could reach me, wherever the hell I was. Sometimes it had to do with telling people how I felt, but it was so subtle it was often unnoticed or simply taken to be some new quirk that mad Donna had thought up.

(Williams, 1999, pp. 9–10, pp. 30–31)

Contributor to A is for Autism

This autobiography consists of information about my hearing and eyesight playing tricks on me. ... Let's start with what happened in pre-school times. At that time I used to hate small shops because my eyesight used to make them look as if they are even smaller than they actually were – and they looked only a metre in area. ...

I did not get on very well at nursery school. On bright days my sight blurred. Sometimes when other kids spoke to me I could scarcely hear them, and sometimes they sounded like bullets. I thought I was going to go deaf. ...

I was often lazy at school because sometimes my ears distorted the teacher's instructions, or my eyes blurred to stop me seeing the blackboard properly. I was sometimes able to hear a word or two at the start and understand it, and then the next lot of words sort of merged into one another, and I could not make head or tail of it. I can now recall that one could sometimes refer to my vision and hearing as being like an untuned television.

(*A is for Autism*, 1992)

Wendy Lawson

I always had rituals and obsessions!!! ... they changed over time. However, they were always based around my interests: animals, insects, medicine ... I like to wear clothes that are familiar ... eat foods that are the same ... . I hated it when routines changed and would become quite miserable, almost lose motivation for anything. I needed to be sure of what would happen ... I am still like this today; however, I am more adaptable now than when I was as a child. ...

My ears are very sensitive to particular sounds and certain noises really hurt me ... even today. I wear tinted glasses to help me cope with the light that hurts my eyes, and I only wear cotton next to my skin because of discomfort with how other materials feel. ...

I'm not good at 'reading' another's body language ... I often 'feel' that if someone is unhappy then it must be my fault. ... I don't 'feel' the emotions of others, unless it impacts upon myself. However, I have learnt to 'listen' to others and how to ask them how they are feeling and what this might mean for them. I am naturally inquisitive about human behaviour and driven to understand both myself and others. This means asking lots and lots of questions all of the time which can be very demanding on people and is not always appreciated!

(Lawson, 2001, pp. 180–2)

Ros Blackburn

To me, the outside world is a confusing mass of sights and sounds. It is totally baffling and incomprehensible. Try watching a soap opera on television with no volume. The characters' actions immediately become sudden and unpredictable since the meaning behind them is no longer clear. ... This is how the world appears to me most of the time. I am unable to 'read into' people's behaviour or read the intentions behind it and am therefore not able to predict their actions. It comes across as very threatening and frightening most of the time.

I have therefore developed various coping strategies.

In order to create a distraction or cut off between me and 'out there', I will flick my fingers in front of my face. My attention is drawn to my fingers rather than what is going on beyond. I can focus on what is near and close to me and what is predictable and 'me controlled' rather than what is further afield, unpredictable and therefore threatening. Sometimes 'beyond' is so penetrating, that simply flicking my fingers is not a powerful enough distraction in itself, so I may use objects as well such as a piece of paper to flick or a liquid-filled sensory toy, for example. This obviously increases the distraction level and therefore the cut off level is increased too.

(Blackburn, 2000, p. 4)

Jim

Stereotyped movements aren't things I decide to do for a reason; they're things that happen by themselves when I'm not paying attention to my body. ...

If I'm not monitoring them because I'm worn out, distracted, overwhelmed, intensely focused on something else, or just relaxed and off-guard, then stereotyped movements will occur. ...

People who are close enough for me to be relaxed and off-guard can expect to see me acting 'weird', while people who only see me in my 'public display' mode don't see such behavior.

(Cesaroni and Garber, 1991, p. 309)

Temple Grandin

This withdrawal from touch, so typical of autistic children, was followed in the next few years by standard autistic behaviours: my fixation on spinning objects, my preference to be alone, destructive behaviour, temper tantrums, inability to speak, sensitivity to sudden noises, appearance of deafness, and my intense interest in odors. ...

Up to this time, communication had been a one-way street for me. I could understand what was being said, but I was unable to respond. Screaming and flapping my hands was my only way to communicate.

(Grandin and Scariano, 1986, pp. 16–17)

Clara Claiborne Park (mother of Jessy)

We start with an image – a tiny, golden child on hands and knees, circling round and round a spot on the floor in mysterious self-absorbed delight. She does not look up, though she is smiling and laughing; she does not call our attention to the mysterious object of her pleasure. She does not see us at all. She and the spot are all there is, and though she is eighteen months old, an age for touching, tasting, pointing, exploring, she is doing none of these. She does not walk, or crawl up stairs, or pull herself to her feet to reach for objects. She doesn't *want* any objects. Instead, she circles her spot. Or she sits, a long chain in her hand, snaking it up and down, up and down, watching it coil and uncoil, for twenty minutes, half and hour, longer.

(Park, 2001, p. 6)

Activity 2   *Learning about autism from the inside out*

Allow about 15 minutes

This activity will help you to identify important features of autism based on insider (first-hand) accounts.

Review the written accounts that you have just read from people with autism. What do you learn from these accounts? Compile a list, with notes, about the key features of autism as presented to you 'from within'. From these accounts what do you consider to be the three or four most significant features of autism? In addition what do you think might be missing from these accounts, given that they are provided by people with autism who write and/or speak, while many people with autism do neither?

Looking back to the notes you made in Activity 1, consider whether these first-hand accounts have confirmed, contradicted, or complemented your prior knowledge.

Comment

There are indications in these accounts of a complex set of interrelationships between people with autism and non-autistic people. Perhaps the most apparent features of this complexity are the difficulties of communication that exist between people with autism and the non-autistic social world: hearing the words of others as jumbled up and indistinct; not being able to respond in ways that others could understand; presenting as being uninterested when interacting with others. All these aspects of behaviour and experience relate directly to the issue of communication and to the experience of living with a communication disability.

All these excerpts originate from children and adults with autism, or from their families. Words such as these give glimpses into the worlds of people with autism that are very difficult to achieve in other ways. Non-autistic people can observe the behaviour of a person with autism, and make inferences about the experiences that accompany that behaviour. But experience is only really accessible 'from within', so without first-hand accounts non-autistic people are likely to gain only a partially filled-out picture, and one that may be wrong in certain important respects. What can be picked out of these brief accounts to begin this chapter's journey of exploration into autism, and into psychologists' understandings of autism?

Experiencing others

One notable feature of the accounts that you have just read is a set of observations about interacting with others. Reference is made to the difficulties of making eye contact; there is an account of the social exclusion that often accompanies being disabled; and there are hints of the 'extreme aloneness' identified by Kanner (1943, p. 248) in his pioneering description of children with 'autistic disturbances of affective contact'. There is also mention of the notion of not being able to 'read into' the behaviour of others – an observation that links with a major area of psychological research into 'theory of mind', which is considered in Section 4.1 of this chapter.

BOX 1

Kanner and autism

Leo Kanner (1943) observed particular behaviours in eleven young children and coined the label 'early infantile autism'. Kanner chose the term 'autos' (self) to describe the children's apparent 'inward-looking' behaviour. A little later, Asperger (1944) wrote a separate account of some older children and also used the term 'autistic' as a description.

Kanner (1943) developed a list of five characteristics to define the group of children he observed:

- the inability to relate to and interact with people from the beginning of life;
- the inability to communicate with others through language;
- an obsession with maintaining sameness and resisting change;
- a preoccupation with objects rather than people;
- the occasional evidence of good potential for intelligence.

Source: Waterhouse, 2000, p. 15.

A restricted range of interests: inflexibility in thought and behaviour

There are several references in this section to some level of inflexibility in thought and behaviour, which may express itself in terms of a set of narrow, specialized interests and an apparent desire for sameness: needing to wear the same clothes, to eat the same foods, and to repeat the same movements. And there is an indication of the anxiety and unhappiness that can happen when an important routine is infringed.

Stereotypies
Repeated movements, such as hand flapping, or finger flicking.

Distal world
The world at a distance, away from the body.

Proximal world
The world in proximity to the body.

There is also mention of a 'stereotypy' – in this case hand-flapping. Stereotyped and repetitive movements are a very visible aspect of the behaviour of some people with autism. But one thing to be gained from first-hand accounts is some insight into the possible reasons for stereotyped movements. For Ros Blackburn, these movements help to shut out the confusing distal world, and to bring the more predictable proximal world to the fore. Note, however, that Jim's account of the reasons for his stereotypies is quite different from that of Ros.

Sensation and movement

A striking feature of first-hand accounts is the consistent reference to the unusual sensory world that people with autism appear to experience. Researchers and clinicians had noticed this feature of autism (for example de Meyer, 1976), but until the voices of people with autism began to be heard the significance of this aspect of autism was not fully appreciated. In the excerpts there are a number of references to sensory experiences, but later in this chapter you will see that the sensory world of the person with autism does not appear in the main diagnostic picture of autism. It also does not occupy many pages in the psychological literature.

Of particular note is the effect of these sensory experiences on the person with autism. Many of the descriptions that are given are of specific sights and sounds being intrusive, almost painful. These 'hypersensitivities' to aspects of the environment can have significant consequences for the person with autism. If the sound of another person talking is experienced as confusing and indistinct, or loud and painful, this is likely to have an effect on motivation to communicate and to interact with others. It is difficult for typically developing adults to understand the experience of a world in which certain everyday sensations cannot be modulated, and become oppressive. One way to imagine this is to think of the tangible physical response in many people to the sound of fingernails scraping on a chalk-board and to consider what it might feel like if that were the effect that human voices or a whirring fan or busy shopping centres had on you.

There are also references to difficulties in organizing physical responses. Tito (Mukhopadhyay, 2000) recalls not being able to make his body move or respond in a way that was within his control. And Jim (Cesaroni and Garber, 1991) talks about the way in which his body seems to produce movements if he is 'off guard' and not monitoring himself sufficiently closely.

Change and growth

Autism is classified as a pervasive developmental disorder (a PDD). Among other things, this means that it stays with a person for life. People with autism do not 'grow out of it'; neither are they 'cured' of it; neither is there a 'normal' child waiting to emerge from their 'shell' (Sinclair, 1993). However, this does not mean that people with autism stay the same throughout their life, nor indeed does it mean that their autism stays the same throughout their life. Many of the observations made in the first part of this section by people with autism are expressed in the past tense – describing how things were for them when they were younger, with subsequent change and growth implied.

Growth and development are just as much a feature of a life with autism as they are of a typically developing life. Indeed it may be helpful to think about autism as a *trajectory* though life (Roth, 2002). There are undoubtedly extra challenges for a person with autism in terms of growth and development, particularly with regard to their transactions with their environment and with the world of non-autistic people. There are also extra challenges for families that include one or more children with autism. But the lifelong nature of autism should not be misinterpreted as a barrier to development and growth.

2.2 First-hand accounts and science

There are many reasons for listening carefully to first-hand accounts – there are moral and political reasons for engaging with all members of society. However, the argument that is pursued in this chapter is that first-hand accounts of people with autism are a prerequisite for a *scientific* understanding of autism. How can such accounts be regarded as a legitimate component of a scientific approach? Surely they are merely 'anecdotes' – illustrative, human interest stories – not a basis for science?

There are a number of ways of answering this question depending on one's chosen definition of science. But one thing on which every definition would agree is that in order to achieve a scientific understanding of something, a clear description of the phenomenon that is being studied is required.

An argument within this chapter is that until researchers started listening, seriously, to the accounts of people with autism about their experience, they were in danger of mis-describing some fundamental elements of autism. Take the unusual sensory world that many people with autism appear to experience. How could psychologists know, for example, that the ticking of a clock can sound like a gunshot, or that the voice of a person can sound like a train rushing at them, until those experiences are described to them? All that psychologists would be able to see would be the *behaviour* of the person with autism – covering their ears, or shying away from people. And they might misinterpret that behaviour as meaningless stereotypy, or as a desire to be alone in the world.

2.3 The incorrigibility of first-hand accounts?

Incorrigible
An incorrigible account is one that is deemed to be beyond question and not subject to correction.

Saying that it is important to listen to first-hand accounts of experiences, and to afford these the significance and respect they deserve, is not the same as saying that such accounts must be taken at face value, nor that they offer some kind of direct access to the 'truth'. No single perspective can give the whole picture of something as complex as autism. A scientific approach to understanding something requires that all accounts be subject to critical scrutiny, and that none is privileged on the basis of presumed status. In psychology, the objective, outsider accounts of researchers and clinicians have historically been privileged over first-hand accounts. But the intention of this chapter is not to reverse the problem by idealizing first-hand accounts. Rather it is to balance the status of the two perspectives, and to further an understanding of autism by reference to both.

So what is the basis for subjecting first-hand accounts to critical scrutiny? Why should first-hand accounts of people with autism not be treated as incorrigible?

- If one person with autism says something about their experience, this does not mean that another person with autism will necessarily have the same experience (see Ros Blackburn's and Jim's accounts of their stereotypies).

After all, when a non-autistic person says something about the quality of their experience, people do not automatically assume that the same must be true for all non-autistic people. If enough people say the same thing about their experiences, then people start to take note.

- There are good reasons to suppose that people with autism who publish engaging books about their experiences are in many important respects not typical of 'people with autism' in general, in the same way that published non-autistic authors are not typical of non-autistic people in general (see the sophistication of Tito Mukhopadhyay's prose at age 8 and 11!). There is a great deal of diversity among those diagnosed as having an autism spectrum disorder. For example, many people with autism do not themselves speak or write, and the extent to which they can be 'spoken for' by others with (or without) autism is unclear.

The challenge of integrating insider preferences with the traditional outsider perspective of clinical and research psychology is further examined in Section 6.

Summary of Section 2

- People with autism write and talk about a variety of ways in which their experiences differ from those of typically developing people.
- A key feature of these insider accounts is the distinctiveness of the sensory world that people with autism can experience.
- First-hand accounts of a condition such as autism should be regarded as an important component of a scientific understanding of that condition.
- From a scientific perspective, first-hand accounts should not be idealized nor treated as incorrigible.

3 Understanding autism from the outside in

Section 2 provided a view of autism constructed out of the first-hand accounts of people with autism (an account of autism 'from the inside out'). This section seeks to provide a description of autism from the point of view of non-autistic researchers and clinicians – a third-party perspective which has been constructed by 'looking in' on autism, from the outside.

3.1 Diagnosis

According to psychologists, autism is seen as one of the set of pervasive developmental disorders. It is classified as such because it is characterized by pervasive impairments in several areas of development, notably in terms of social interaction and communication skills. A variety of systems are used for diagnosing

Autism spectrum disorders (ASD) A group of identified disorders of development with lifelong effects, which have in common the 'triad of impairments' (Wing, 1998). ASD includes children and adults with autism and those with Asperger Syndrome.

autism, but the most widely cited is the *Diagnostic and Statistical Manual of Mental Disorders* prepared by the American Psychiatric Association (2000) and known as DSM-IV-TR. According to DSM-IV criteria, for a child to be diagnosed as having 'autistic disorder', there must be evidence of the following, normally by the time the child reaches 3 years of age:

> a qualitative impairment in social interaction;
> qualitative impairments in communication;
> restricted repetitive and stereotyped patterns of behavior, interests and activities.
>
> (American Psychiatric Association, 2000, p. 75)

Diagnoses are made on the basis of behaviour, by noting the things the children do and do not do as they develop, and comparing this with a list of diagnostic criteria. There is no 'test' that can identify autism.

Activity 3   *Learning about autism from the outside in*

Allow about 20 minutes

This activity will help you to broaden your understanding of autism.

Turn to the end of this chapter and read the Reading, 'The history of ideas on autism: legends, myths and reality', by Lorna Wing (1997). This reading provides an overview of ideas about autism by a highly respected researcher–practitioner who is also the parent of a child with autism.

Review the Reading and write a list, with notes, of features of autism as described 'from the outside'.

Comment

Wing's personal and professional involvement with autism highlights the fact that although this chapter sets up a distinction between 'insider' and 'outsider' accounts, the two perspectives should not be seen as 'in opposition' to each other. The distinction between them is emphasized in this chapter for the sake of clarity of exposition. In reality things are not so clear cut.

Note Wing's use of the phrase 'triad of impairments' to describe three key features of autism (impairments in social interaction, communication, and imagination). Note also the way in which she talks of the 'spectrum of disorders' associated with autism.

Phenotype The set of observable characteristics associated with a particular 'genotype'.

Since the 1990s it has become usual to speak of 'autism spectrum disorders' (ASD) rather than 'autistic disorder' (AD). This reflects the fact that there is a broader phenotype of autism than is defined by the strict diagnostic criteria for AD in instruments such as the DSM-IV – one that includes people with Asperger Syndrome. The diagnosis of Asperger Syndrome is made where children possess many of the developmental patterns of children with autism, but where there is no clinically significant delay in cognitive or language development (American Psychiatric Association, 2000).

One important thing to note in relation to this is that the voices heard in Section 2 are those of people who may only represent one section of the wider population of people with ASD. For example, it has been estimated that approximately 80 per cent of children with autism have severe or profound learning difficulties, scoring below 70 on psychometric tests of intelligence (Jordan, 1999; Peeters and Gillberg, 1999). Although some researchers contest the strength of the association between ASD and profound learning difficulties (Biklen and Cardinal, 1997; Grayson *et al.*, 2004), the apparent range of abilities and disabilities within the spectrum means that caution is needed when making general statements about 'people with autism'.

3.2 Prevalence

A most striking thing about the prevalence of autism is the increase that started towards the end of the twentieth century. For the 25 years to 1991, rates of 4.4 cases per 10,000 people were recorded by large population surveys. In the 10 years to 2001 the rate was 12.7. Volkmar *et al.* (2004) suggest that a prevalence rate of 10 cases per 10,000 people is a realistic estimate for autistic disorder (autism spectrum disorders would therefore have a somewhat higher prevalence because of the broader definition). Accounting for this increase is difficult. It may be that the actual incidence of autism is increasing. Or it may be that diagnostic practices (for example, the broadening of the label into a 'spectrum') have had the effect of pulling more people under the umbrella of autism. Alternatively, perhaps greater public awareness of the condition has led to more cases of autism (that would previously have been hidden) being discovered.

Organic disorder
A disorder that has a biological (not necessarily genetic) cause.

Perinatal
During childbirth.

Triangulation
A metaphor from navigation which refers to the notion of using more than one source of data to support an assertion.

3.3 Causes

There is a large body of evidence to show that autism is an organic disorder. That is, autism is caused by some type of prenatal, perinatal, postnatal or early childhood damage or disruption to the developing central nervous system. The likelihood is that autism results from a variety of different causal pathways (Baird *et al.*, 2003). Furthermore, twin and family studies (triangulated against other sources of evidence) support the view that there is probably a genetic susceptibility which increases the likelihood of some children developing autism (Szatmari, *et al.*, 2003). For example, in one study a concordance rate of 36 per cent was found for identical twins, and 0 per cent for fraternal twins (see Box 2). When taken in the context of the pattern of findings from several studies this is 'strong evidence of genetic causes' (Frith, 1989, p.77).

BOX 2

Twin studies

Identical (monozygotic) twins share an identical genetic make-up. Fraternal (non-identical or dizygotic) twins are no more genetically similar than ordinary siblings. A concordance rate of 36 per cent in Frith's study (1989) means that of eleven children with autism who had an identical twin, four had an identical twin who also had autism. Not one of the children with autism who had a fraternal twin had a twin with autism (a 0 per cent concordance rate). The fact that genetically identical individuals were more likely to 'share' autism than genetically non-identical individuals is suggestive of a genetic susceptibility.

Psychogenic disorder
A psychological disorder that is not principally to do with physical damage to the body.

It is not the role of this chapter to debate the details of the causes of autism. But it is important to distinguish between organic and psychogenic causes. Accounts based on the latter hold that autism is caused by psychological factors. For example, it has been argued that autism results from certain types of parent–infant relationships. 'The precipitating factor in infantile autism is the parent's wish that his [sic] child should not exist' (Bettelheim, 1967). It is hard to imagine the effect that such accounts had on parents of children with autism, who were being told that their children's autism was caused by the way in which they related to them as parents.

BOX 3

The 'take-home message' of psychogenic explanations

However much psychogenic theorists tried to reassure parents (particularly mothers) that their theories were not meant to imply that it was the fault of the parents that a child had autism, the message heard by the parents was quite different. In the words of Clara Claiborne Park, whose daughter, Jessy, has autism:

> It is painful to return to the book Bettelheim, with his gift for metaphor, called *The Empty Fortress* – and thank God and the rules of evidence, it has become unnecessary. Autism is now almost universally recognized as a developmental disorder, multiply caused: genetic predisposition, pre- or postnatal viral infection, chromosomal damage, biological agents still unknown. ...

> Kanner ... had thought that such a profound inability to relate to others was probably 'innate'. But he had also speculated in a different direction; the phrase 'refrigerator parents' was also his. Twenty-five years later, before the newly formed National Society for Autistic Children ... he would repudiate this explanation in words none of us who heard him would ever forget: 'Herewith I especially acquit you people as parents.' But ... the ghost of parental responsibility was not so easily laid to rest.

Source: Park, 2001, pp. 7, 10–11.

Although the overwhelming weight of evidence points to organic causes, this does not rule out the influence of early social and environmental factors. For example, there is an unexpectedly high percentage of blind children who have autism. This has led Hobson and Bishop (2003) to examine the role that early social and environmental factors might play in the development of autism:

> ... one might consider that there are several sources of social impairment in blind children, including both physical and environmental factors, and that when potentiated by the children's lack of vision, these result in specific forms of impoverishment in interpersonal experiences that have developmental consequences which include several autistic-like features.
> (Hobson and Bishop, 2003, p. 342)

However, they acknowledge (p. 342) how such factors might interact with organic explanations. Perhaps there exists 'some form of minimal brain damage associated with the conditions that led to blindness (Cass *et al.*, 1994) that predisposes both to the social impairments of these children and to their "autistic-like" clinical features'.

3.4 Brain mechanisms

SG

Since 1990 there have been significant developments in the technology of neuroimaging, which have made it possible to map brain structures and functions with increasing accuracy and sophistication. Neuroimaging allows for comparisons to be made between the brains of typically developing children and children with autism, though the interpretation of data from these rapidly developing technologies is a complex process.

There is evidence that the brains of very young children with autism are larger than the brains of typically developing children of the same age, but that this size difference decreases with age. Courchesne *et al.* (2001) found that 90 per cent of the 30 boys with autism (aged between 2 and 4 years) whom they studied using magnetic resonance imaging (MRI) had a larger brain volume than normal. There had been no neonatal evidence in these children of larger-than-average brains. It seems that there may be early overgrowth in the brain of the child with autism, together with disruption of the typical course of programmed cell death and synaptic pruning. One brain structure that has attracted interest is the cerebellum. For a long time this area of the brain has been linked with the control of movement, though more recently it has also been found to be associated with attention (Allen *et al.*, 1997). When adolescents and adults with autism were compared with matched control participants using fMRI, the former showed evidence of less activation in the cerebellum relating to attention and more activation relating to motor activity (Allen and Courchesne, 2003). This suggests that there may be differences in the way that the cerebellum works in people with autism compared with typically developing people. Abnormalities in the cerebellum are of particular interest to those interested in motor dysfunction in autism (Bauman, 1992).

Other brain structures that have received attention are areas of the prefrontal cortex that are considered to be associated with aspects of social cognition and with executive functions, and the amygdala and hippocampus, which are

Magnetic resonance imaging (MRI)
A non-invasive method of creating a 'map' of the brain or other part of the body by measuring blood flow.

Synaptic pruning
The process by which the total number of connections between brain cells ('synapses') decreases during early childhood (after rapid prenatal and postnatal increases).

implicated in emotional arousal. Caution is needed in assigning clear roles to these complex brain structures, especially when thinking about autism. One reason for this is the sheer complexity and interconnectedness of the human brain. Another reason is that a number of studies have shown that localization of brain function is less consistent in people with autism (Pierce *et al.*, 2001), who show more 'individually variable and scattered functional brain organization' (Müller *et al.*, 2003, p. 1847).

Although the precise brain mechanisms associated with autism have not been definitively established, the overwhelming message of neuro-psychology is that there are structural and functional differences between the brains of people with and without autism. This does not in itself mean that autism is caused by such brain differences (brain differences can *result* from a condition, as well as being the *cause* of a condition). However, when viewed together with other bodies of research, it adds considerable weight to the argument that autism is, essentially, an organic disorder.

3.5 Sensation and movement

Although most of the information about the sensory worlds of people with autism comes from first-hand accounts, there is a small but growing 'conventional' literature on this topic. This 'outsider' perspective is important because, as you have seen, the autism spectrum is very broad, and it should not be assumed that the experiences of a small number of people with autism who write about this topic necessarily hold for all people with autism.

In one study, 26 children with autism (average age 31 months) were reported by parents to respond differently to taste and smell, and to show different levels of tactile sensitivity and auditory filtering, when compared to matched control children (Rogers *et al.*, 2003). From her study based on a retrospective video analysis of home videos of eleven children with autism, Baranek (1999) concluded that early assessment procedures for children aged between 9 and 12 months should take into account sensory processing and sensory motor functions, as well as social responses.

Magneto-encephalo-graphic measurements (MEG)
A technique that detects changes in the magnetic field corresponding to the brain's electrical activity.

In another study Tecchio *et al.* (2003) used magneto-encephalographic measurements (MEG) to record aspects of cortical processing of auditory stimuli in fourteen children and adults who met the diagnostic criteria for autistic disorder. A dysfunction of auditory discrimination was found, suggesting that it may not just be intellectually able people with autism who experience distinctive sensory worlds. In short, there is a body of evidence, from a variety of sources, to show that any account of autism must include reference to sensory processing, as well as to the triad of impairments.

When Asperger first described his group of four children he noted clumsiness. For many years it was accepted that some level of motor impairment was evident in children and adults with Asperger Syndrome. Furthermore, it has become increasingly clear that there is a motor impairment in the majority of people with autism, across the whole spectrum (Manjiviona and Prior, 1995; Bauman, 1992). For example, Goin and Myers (2004) used a multi-method approach in a study of early detection of autism. They concluded (p. 5, emphasis added) that infants and toddlers who went on to become diagnosed with autism showed marked differences 'in their social, affective, *motor,* play, and communication skills' in comparison with those children who were not subsequently diagnosed with autism.

Some researchers see the motor impairments associated with autism as a core feature of the condition, which may underlie other disabilities (Donnellan and Leary, 1995). For example, Page and Boucher (1998) call for more research to investigate whether oral and manual dyspraxia underlies the impairments in speech and signing among children with autism. Jones and Prior (1985) also question whether relatively poor performance in motor imitation underlies some of the difficulties that are observed in children with autism in terms of learning to use gesture.

Dyspraxia
An impairment in the ability to plan and carry out sequences of co-ordinated movements to achieve an objective.

3.6 Reflecting on the different perspectives

One aim of this chapter is to highlight that both insider and outsider perspectives are necessary if a grounded account of autism is to be achieved. There are many points of strong agreement between the two sets of perspectives, with respect to the identification of characteristic features of autism. Conversely there are some areas in which the two sets of perspectives diverge, particularly with respect to emphasis (in terms of which features are viewed as the most significant) and also with respect to the meanings that are ascribed to observable behaviours.

Activity 4   *Integrating insider and outsider accounts*

Allow about 15 minutes

This activity will help you to reflect on different perspectives on autism.

Compare and contrast the lists and notes that you drew up in Activities 1, 2 and 3. Identify points of convergence. What do insiders and outsiders agree on? What are the most significant points of divergence across the different perspectives? What does one set of perspectives add that the other one does not or cannot?

Summary of Section 3

- Autism has traditionally been regarded as a condition characterized by a 'triad of impairments'.
- Autism is a predominantly organic disorder.
- The number of people diagnosed with autism and autism spectrum disorders rose dramatically in the final years of the twentieth century.
- Advances in neuroimaging technology may lead to better insights into the organic basis of autism.
- There is a small but increasingly important literature on sensory and motor aspects of autism.

4   Psychological theories

This section examines three major theoretical approaches to understanding autism that have emerged from the work of developmental psychologists. These three approaches propose that autism is characterized by:

1   a theory of mind deficit;
2   executive dysfunction;
3   a weak drive for central coherence.

The section concludes with a brief examination of some aspects of early social transactions in infancy that might shed further light on autism.

4.1 Theory of mind

In 1985, Baron-Cohen *et al.* published an influential paper which suggested that a core, distinctive feature of autism may be a difficulty in understanding the thoughts and feelings of other people. They found that 80 per cent of participants with autism (aged between 6 and 16 years) failed a false belief task known as the 'Sally/Anne Task' (or the 'unexpected transfer task' see Box 4). This finding was interpreted as an indication that children with autism have difficulty in understanding other minds – a theory of mind deficit (Baron-Cohen *et al.*, 1985).

BOX 4

The unexpected transfer task

In this task a child is presented with the story as shown in Figure 1 (overleaf). It is usually acted out using dolls or puppets. The story concerns two characters, Sally and Anne (Figure 1, Frame 1). Sally puts a marble in the basket (Frame 2) and then leaves the room (Frame 3). While Sally is out of the room, Anne removes the marble from the basket and puts it in a box (Frame 4). The child is then told that Sally has returned and wants to find her marble (Frame 5).

Sally, of course, does not know that the marble has been moved; she still thinks that it is in the basket. Therefore she holds a false belief, i.e. a belief about the world that is incorrect. The child is then asked 'Where will Sally look for her marble?' To answer this successfully children need to understand that Sally did not see the marble being moved and therefore will hold a false belief about its location. Typically developing children of 4–5 years who have been following the story will be able to answer this question correctly, saying that Sally will look for her marble in the basket.

Figure 1   The unexpected transfer task (adapted from Frith, 1989, p. 160).

In the wake of the study by Baron-Cohen and colleagues came a proliferation of research studies into autism and theory of mind, which saw the findings replicated and triangulated. The extensive series of replications that have been undertaken mean that the experimental procedures can be regarded as reliable. The efforts to triangulate the findings, by using different methods to tackle the same question, address the more complex question of their validity – the extent to which the findings mean what they appear to mean. Do children with autism tend to do poorly on false belief tasks because they have a theory of mind deficit? Or are there other reasons for their relatively poor performance? For example, in the 'Sally/Anne' version of the unexpected transfer task dolls are used, and participants have to make judgements on the basis of what the dolls 'believe' to be true about the location of a marble. Perhaps the participants with autism found it difficult to attribute any kind of belief to a doll. Failure for this reason might be more to do with having difficulties imagining dolls as social actors, rather than having anything to do with a theory of mind deficit. However, this particular interpretation was ruled out by using real people in place of the dolls in a later study (Leslie and Frith, 1988).

There is certainly a lot of evidence from a variety of different types of studies that supports the idea that people with autism typically have some difficulty with reading the thoughts and feelings of others (so-called 'mind-reading'). For example Perner *et al.* (1989) found that children with autism did not perform as well as matched children with a specific language impairment on the deceptive box task. This task aims to create the experience of a false belief within the child who is being tested. Failure on the task may suggest that the child has difficulty in understanding the status of their own beliefs.

In the deceptive box task children are asked to guess what is inside a tube of Smarties (see Figure 2, Frame 1). Most children answer 'Smarties'. They are then shown that the tube actually contains pencils (Frame 2). The child is shown the closed tube and asked, once again, what is inside, even though they cannot see the pencils (Frame 3). The child is then introduced to a Sooty puppet who has been asleep in the toy box (Frame 4). The child is asked what Sooty will say is in the tube. They are also asked what they thought was in the tube before they looked inside it. For a child to pass this task they must say that Sooty will believe there to be Smarties inside the tube, even though the child now knows that this is not the case.

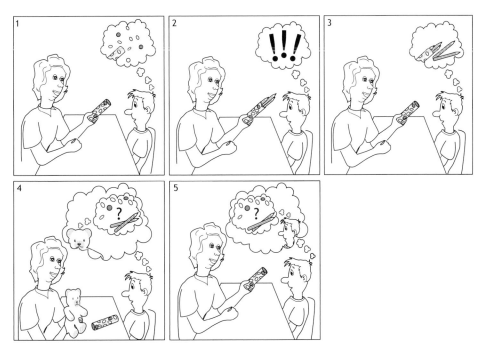

Figure 2   The deceptive box task.

Children with autism also tend to perform less well than children with learning difficulties on the 'seeing-leads-to-knowing' task (Baron-Cohen and Goodhart, 1994). In this task children are shown a doll that touches a box, and one that looks inside the box. The children are then asked 'Which one *knows* what's inside the box?' The children with autism seemed to have greater difficulty than the children with learning difficulties in saying what kind of knowledge would be in the mind of each of the dolls, one having looked in the box, and the other having only touched it.

Other evidence that supports a theory of mind deficit in autism comes from studies by Baron-Cohen and Cross (1992), and Tager-Flusberg (1992) (see Research summary 1). Baron-Cohen and Cross showed that children with autism did not correctly identify which of two pictures showed a person who was thinking (Figure 3). Typically developing children of 4 years of age were better able in this test to make inferences about the *mental state* of the boy in the picture from looking at his direction of gaze, showing that they recognized that the eye-region of the face gives clues about what is going on in another person's mind.

Figure 3   The 'which one is thinking?' test.

RESEARCH SUMMARY 1

Mean length of utterance

Six children with autism (aged between 3 and 7 years) were matched with six children with Down Syndrome, on the basis of a measure of language development, mean length of utterance (MLU).

Records of spontaneous speech were collected from each participant every 2 months. The researchers noted terms that the children used that related to psychological states (desire, perception, emotion and cognition).

There were no differences between the two groups of children in the frequency with which desire or emotion terms were used. However, there were differences for certain types of perception and cognition terms. As shown in Table 1 (in the scores for 'Attention' and 'Mental'), children with autism used significantly fewer terms that had the function of calling for another person's attention, and also fewer terms referring to mental states. These differences may be taken as one indication that calling for attention from another person, and thinking about the mental state of another person, are two areas of impairment in early childhood autism.

Table I   Mean frequency of functional uses of psychological state terms

	Children with autism		Children with Down Syndrome	
	M	(SD)	M	(SD)
Perception terms				
Vision	10.95	(9.91)	4.19	(2.59)
Hearing	.59	(.52)	.44	(.42)
Touch	5.01	(3.04)	2.62	(1.73)
Smell	.46	(.83)	.05	(.12)
Taste	.27	(.58)	.00	(.00)
Attention	1.10	(1.02)	**10.40	(5.02)
Cognition terms				
Idiom	2.58	(3.35)	4.27	(3.76)
Conversational	.40	(.56)	2.28	(2.66)
Mental	.17	(.20)	*1.66	(2.46)

*$p < 0.05$; ** $p < 0.01$

Source: adapted from Tager-Flusberg, 1992 (table from p. 167).

Furthermore, the notion of finding it difficult to 'read into' the minds of others is a feature of many first-hand accounts of autism (Blackburn, 2000; Lawson, 2001). So there is little doubt that psychological research has identified an important feature of autism – the notion that autism is associated with some difficulties in tuning into the minds of others – a feature that may indeed help non-autistic people to understand more clearly the experience of a person with autism.

4.2   Executive dysfunction

SG

Theory of mind research has tackled autism at a socio-cognitive level. Other psychological perspectives have focused on more general learning and information-processing mechanisms – working from the assumption that the social challenges faced by people with autism are consequences of difficulties with various aspects of cognitive function. One such perspective sees autism as associated with underdeveloped or disrupted executive functions.

Given that executive function has to do with (among other things) flexibility of thought, then it is not a surprise that psychologists began to relate executive *dys*function to autism. A difficulty with disengagement from a strand of thought or behaviour (perseveration), an apparent mental rigidity, problems with switching attention flexibly from one thing to another, problems with planning and delivering intended actions – all of these are signs of executive dysfunction, and all of these can be features of the cognitive style of a person with autism.

Perseveration
The continuous, insistent performance (repetition) of a behaviour.

Prepotent stimulus
A stimulus that draws a person's attention towards it, and which seems to cause the person to behave in a particular way (the prepotent response).

Furthermore it appears that people with autism can experience difficulties with inhibiting responses to prepotent stimuli (see Research summary 2). Note that inhibitory control is a central feature of executive function (Hughes *et al.*, 2004).

RESEARCH SUMMARY 2

The strategic deception task: theory of mind versus executive function

Strategic deception – planting a false belief in the mind of another – requires a theory of mind. Typically developing children above the age of 4 years can succeed on strategic deception tasks. Typically developing children of 3 years of age, and children with autism, tend not to succeed on these tasks. The question that Hughes and Russell set out to investigate was whether failure on a strategic deception task really was due to a theory of mind deficit, or whether it was better understood in terms of executive dysfunction.

The 'windows task' is a task where the participant plays against an experimenter. Both 'players' close their eyes while one of two boxes is 'baited' with a chocolate. The participant opens their eyes and has to point at one of the two boxes. Whichever box the participant points to, the opponent looks in. If the chocolate is in that box, the opponent keeps it. If it is in the other box, the participant keeps it. The participant cannot see which box the chocolate is in. This guessing game goes on for 15 trials. For the 16th trial (the first experimental trial) the boxes are replaced by ones with a window that faces the participant. Now, when they come to point, they can see which box contains the chocolate. Four year olds who understand deception will point to the box that does *not* contain it, thus tricking the opponent, and keeping it for themselves. Three-year-old children and children with autism tend to point to the box with the chocolate. This might be interpreted as indicating that children with autism find deception difficult because of theory of mind difficulties.

However, Hughes and Russell noticed that children with autism tended to continue to point to the box *with* the chocolate for the next 20 trials. This led them to ask whether it might be some other factor that was causing the children not to learn an apparently simple rule: 'point to the box without the chocolate and I get the chocolate'. They wondered whether the chocolate was acting as a prepotent stimulus, and whether the children with autism found it difficult to inhibit a response to it (by pointing *away* from it). This alternative theory could also explain the children's failure on the task, in a way that has nothing to do with theory of mind. In effect this left two theories competing to explain the data from the windows task: the theory of mind theory, which explained failure on the task as a socio-cognitive failure to deceive another person, and the executive dysfunction theory, that focused on the problems of disengagement from a prepotent stimulus.

An experiment was set up to test these two competing theories. If the theory of mind theory offered the better explanation, then children with autism ought to do better on a similar task, if the requirement to deceive another person was removed. So they simply compared performance for 60 children with autism (and for 60 control children) with and without an opponent. When there was no opponent the participant just had to learn that to get the chocolate they had to point to the box where it was *not*. Table 2 shows a summary of the results. The no-opponent condition did not make the task easier for participants with autism. Approximately one-third of participants with autism failed on the sixteenth trial whether or not an opponent was present. Note also that not one of the non-autistic control participants continued to give the incorrect response on all subsequent trials. This suggests that failure on the windows task has more to do with a failure to disengage from an object, than it has to do with a restricted theory of mind.

Table 2   **Number of participants who indicated the incorrect ('baited') box on the first experimental trial**

	Participants with autism		Control participants	
	N	Perseverating participants*	N	Perseverating participants*
No opponent	23	14	14	0
Opponent	19	7	8	0

* number of participants who perseverated on the incorrect response on all trials

Source: Hughes and Russell, 1993.

The kinds of difficulties that are now referred to as executive dysfunctions have long been associated with autism. For example, Hermelin and O'Connor (1970) noted a tendency to stick with one response during a task (perseveration), rather than to shift to another. More recently, many studies have shown consistent patterns of relatively poor performance among people with autism on tasks that purport to measure executive functions (Pennington and Ozonoff, 1996); for example, on the Wisconsin Card Sort Test and the Tower of Hanoi task. Ruble and Scott (2002) studied the behaviour of children with autism in naturalistic settings and found that, relative to control children, they showed less persistence in goal-directed behaviours, and were less able to engage with more than one activity at a time (suggesting a difficulty with the flexible switching of behaviour and attention).

On the basis of a relatively large body of available evidence Hughes (2001) has argued that executive dysfunction could be the cause of many everyday problems experienced by people with autism and observed in young children with autism, such as difficulties with pretend play and joint attention. For example, a typically developing 1-year-old child may draw their parent's attention to a toy with which they are playing. The parent and child then share an interaction that focuses on the toy (joint attention), pointing to it, and 'discussing' it. In order to do this the child must, among other things, switch attention flexibly between the parent and the object. If the child does not 'disengage' from the object, as might happen for a child with autism, the quality of the interaction will be affected.

As noted with regard to theory of mind, there are plenty of examples of first-hand accounts of people with autism that 'fit' with the notion of executive dysfunction. In Section 2 of this chapter you read Tito's description of the difficulties he experiences in switching between hearing and seeing 'at the same time'. Note also the description of Jessy at the age of 18 months provided by her mother, Clara.

4.3 Central coherence

Another psychological theory of autism that comes from an information processing perspective has been labelled the hypothesis of weak central coherence or a weak drive for central coherence. Happé (1994) has argued that any useful psychological theory relating to autism must be capable of explaining not only deficits, but also areas of strength. It has long been observed that people with autism tend to show particular strengths at picking apart the details of things, such as visual arrays. For example, on the block design test of the Wechsler Intelligence Scale for Children (WISC; Wechsler, 1974), children with autism consistently show better performance than on other sub-tests of the WISC, and often better performance relative to matched control children (see Figure 4). Similarly, Shah and Frith (1983) found that their participants with autism outperformed matched control children on an embedded figures task (see Figure 5).

Figure 4   Block design test from the WISC.

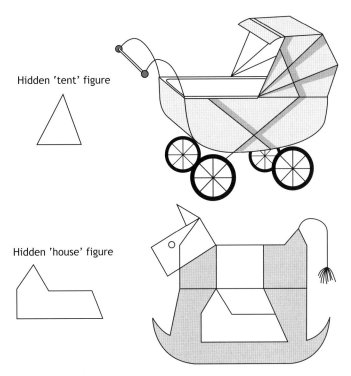

Hidden 'tent' figure

Hidden 'house' figure

Figure 5   The embedded figures test (from Frith, 1989, p. 96, by special permission from Consulting Psychologists Press, Inc, Palo Alto CA, USA).

Both of these tasks are done best when the overall meaning of each stimulus figure is ignored, and when the objects are seen as a collection of discrete parts – in other words, when the global *context* for each individual part of the figure is ignored. Typically developing children and adults tend to find this difficult to do. The triangle in Figure 5 is 'overwhelmed' by the whole image of the pram, such that it is difficult to locate it. But there is a tendency for children with autism to 'see' the triangle more quickly than their typically developing counterparts. This may be because they are seeing the figure not so much as a pram, but as a collection of individual shapes.

So weak central coherence refers to the idea that people with autism may be better able than non-autistic people at seeing the component parts of things. To frame this in a more negative way, people with autism may not be so good at 'seeing the bigger picture'. They may have difficulties in putting things together to make up a meaningful, coherent whole (see for example Tito's comments about his own body, in Section 2). It might be more accurate to refer to this as a distinct cognitive style rather than as a deficit. Indeed, there are arenas of human activity (areas of engineering and scientific research, for example) in which an ability to focus on one thing for a long time, or to decompose complex arrays into their constituent parts, is a distinct advantage.

On the other hand, there are disadvantages to a cognitive style that does not enable the effective use of context as a route to meaning. For example, understanding language – that is, understanding what people *mean* by the words that they use – involves more than just attending to the meaning of each individual word. Words have to be understood in the context of phrases, which have to be understood in the context of whole utterances, which in turn have to be understood in terms of the intentions of the speaker and in terms of local social, and wider cultural contexts.

An indication that weak central coherence may be one cause of difficulties for people with autism in terms of understanding language is provided by Frith and Snowling (1983) who used a 'disambiguation of homographs' procedure. Homographs are words that are pronounced differently according to the different meanings that they can have. One example is 'lead' – something to put around a dog's neck – and 'lead', a metal. In order to find the correct pronunciation, the word has to be interpreted in context. Happé (1994, p. 122) gives an example item from such a task as: 'Mary took the dog for a walk. She went to fetch the lead.' Pronunciation of the final word (it can either be made to rhyme with 'feed' or with 'red') depends on a person's ability to interpret the meaning of the previous sentence, and to hold that interpretation in mind when the target word is reached. Children with autism who were tested on this task supplied fewer correct pronunciations than matched typically developing children, and children with dyslexia. They tended to give the more common of the two possible pronunciations, irrespective of the sentence context. It appears that they were more inclined to read the words one by one, without putting them together into a meaningful whole – without finding coherence in the stimulus materials as a whole.

4.4 Early transactions

One of the ways in which research in developmental psychology is driven forward is by the search for 'precursors'. For example, if there really is a theory of mind deficit in people with autism, where does it come from? Is it a case of a theory of mind 'module' simply not switching on in the brain at a pre-determined developmental stage? Or are there features of the child's early development that relate to later theory of mind deficits? Furthermore, there is a clear need in the field of autism to develop methods for the earlier diagnosis of autism – earlier diagnosis means earlier intervention and there is general agreement that the earlier an intervention can start, the more effective it is likely to be. Additionally, there has been a growing realization that a single core deficit is unlikely to be able to account for neuroimaging findings that implicate 'broader and developmentally interrelated neural systems' (Volkmar *et al.*, 2004, p. 142). These three factors have led to a renewed interest in very early aspects of social development. One focus for this work has been joint attention, particularly triadic joint attention (Flynn, 2004) or secondary intersubjectivity (Trevarthen, 1979).

 Joint attention behaviours, such as pointing, showing gestures and gaze monitoring are seen to develop between the ages of 9 and 14 months in typically developing children. It is argued that this capacity to engage with another person about something – to experience shared attention with that person – plays an important role in the development of thought, language and social behaviour. Furthermore, joint attention is argued to be a precursor to theory of mind development (Charman *et al.*, 2000) and may be related in typical development (as noted earlier) to the executive function of attentional flexibility – also known as 'set-shifting' (Stahl and Pry, 2002).

Sigman *et al.* (1986) noted significantly fewer 'attention-sharing behaviours' in a group of children with autism (aged between 3 and 6 years), than in matched typically developing children, and in matched children with learning difficulties. The observation of fewer behaviours signifying joint attention in children with autism has been replicated a number of times (Barrett *et al.*, 2004; Dawson *et al.*, 2004). This apparent deficit is regarded by researchers and practitioners as a key feature in the developmental story of autism: 'From early in life, children with autism have failed to connect with people mentally' (Hobson, 2002, p. 189).

Summary of Section 4

- Psychological approaches to understanding autism have focused on theory of mind deficits, executive dysfunction, a weak drive for central coherence, and early social transactions.
- The theory of mind approach holds that children with autism find it hard to 'read into' the mental life of another person.
- The executive dysfunction approach highlights difficulties with regard to the flexibility of thought and behaviour.
- The central coherence approach suggests that people with autism may be particularly good at working in fine detail, and perceiving component parts of things.
- Research into social behaviour in infancy may lead to earlier diagnosis as well as an enhanced understanding of the developmental course of autism.

5   Psychological theories: a critique

Section 4 explored three major psychological perspectives on autism. This section builds on that material, by taking a critically evaluative stance towards psychological research into autism. Historically, the fields of autism and psychology have had a complex 'relationship' – and this complexity remains. However, it is a relationship that has on balance been mutually beneficial. Understanding of the nature and causes of autism has been enhanced. With the current valuing of first-hand accounts, and with new technologies (such as neuroimaging), psychology promises to offer much to autism in the future. Equally, autism has contributed to the stock of knowledge within developmental psychology. Much theoretical work, into issues such as theory of mind, modularity, and brain structure and function, has been undertaken with people with autism – a fact that is given some detailed consideration in this section.

5.1 Evaluating psychological approaches

As this chapter has shown, there is a considerable amount of evidence in support of the notion that children with autism have difficulty with 'mind-reading', with some aspects of executive function, and with the social interaction aspects of early development (such as joint attention). There is rather less evidence relating to the hypothesis of a weak drive for central coherence.

Critics of research in these areas point to a number of problems with each of the accounts. Neither theory of mind deficit, nor executive dysfunction is specific to autism, so neither is capable of distinguishing it from other developmental disorders. Furthermore, executive function is a very general term that incorporates several different cognitive phenomena ('fractionated' is the positive way of framing this; 'poorly-defined' is a rather more negative way), and reliable measurement of dysfunction, especially among children, is problematic. The central coherence approach has a high level of 'clinical face validity' (Volkmar *et al.*, 2004, p. 142), but its empirical basis requires further development, and there are conflicting empirical findings with which it has to deal. For example, Mottron *et al.* (2003) present findings that are 'inconsistent with the common assumption that persons with autism display a tendency to focus on minute details rather than on a more general picture' (p. 910). Perhaps the approach that promises most in terms of enhancing understanding of autism, and for facilitating effective early intervention methods, is the one that focuses on social transactions in infancy and early childhood. This approach is already intimately linked with theory of mind and executive function approaches.

Psychology tends to be somewhat atomistic in its treatment of topics. Its preferred methods of experimentation and systematic observation encourage the asking of highly specific and narrowly focused questions. It may be that findings about theory of mind, executive function and central coherence are all in their own way valid, but that they miss out on a bigger picture of autism. Perhaps findings related to theory of mind and executive dysfunction are really just re-descriptions of detailed aspects of autism – re-characterizations of symptoms that can sit comfortably alongside each other – rather than explanatory tools that are capable of explaining autism at a psychological level. Is it in fact *psychology* that has a tendency to be drawn into a perseverative response to the 'prepotent' stimulus of an elegant experimental paradigm (such as the 'false belief task')?

The explication and investigation of detailed aspects of autism are in themselves potentially useful things to do. The fact that theory of mind deficits and executive dysfunction are not specific to autism only matters when trying to use these features to discriminate among different conditions. If the intention is simply to describe the difficulties and challenges that people with autism face, then the fact that people with other conditions face the same sorts of problems is neither here nor there. Where things do become problematic is when the significance of detailed aspects of symptoms are over-played – when the weight of *empirical* evidence behind a set of findings becomes confused with the *conceptual* weight of those findings – and a 'core' status is misattributed to them. It can be argued that this has happened in the psychology of autism, particularly in relation to theory of mind approaches.

5.2 What is said and what is heard

Whatever the intentions of researchers in this field, a 'fact' that tends to be expressed about children with autism is that they lack a theory of mind (for example, Kanazawa, 2004) as if this has been shown to be true in the same way that the chromosomal abnormality underlying Down Syndrome has been demonstrated. It is true to say that psychological research supports the notion that children with autism tend to have difficulty 'reading into' the thoughts and behaviour of others, but this is not the same as *lacking* a theory of mind. Furthermore, this 'fact' is sometimes expressed rather as if it is something that can define children with autism. Disabled activists and organizations run by people with learning difficulties (such as People First) have reacted strongly against the characterization of a group principally in terms of a medical or psychological deficit.

The messages that are *heard* from a discipline are just as important as the messages that are *intended*. Proponents of early psychogenic explanations of autism, based on family systems theories, argued that their assertion that autism emerged out of a family system was not in any way intended to blame the family. But the message that was heard was that autism *was* the fault of the family, and at heart, the fault of the mother (see Box 3). There may also be issues with the 'take-home message' of theory of mind research.

What are the unintended sub-texts of the theory of mind account of autism? There is only room to mention one of these here. An important precursor to theory of mind research, as applied to autism, is the work of Premack and Woodruff (1978). They published a paper entitled 'Does the chimpanzee have a theory of mind?' It makes for uncomfortable reading to see here, in the same paragraph, the title of the paper by Baron-Cohen *et al.* (1985), 'Does the autistic child have a "theory of mind"?' There is something in this line of research that implies that a theory of mind is a distinctively human-like characteristic. So when research findings are strongly interpreted in the wider psychological literature as showing that children with autism lack a theory of mind, this has consequences for society's attitudes to, and understanding of, people with autism.

Quasi-experiment
Participants in a quasi-experiment 'allocate themselves' to the experimental conditions by having some kind of inherent characteristic (e.g. autism). In an experiment proper, researchers can allocate participants to any condition.

5.3 Psychological research on autism: who is it for?

There is an impression in some areas of the autism literature that the studies that have been undertaken have not always sought to further understanding of autism per se, and have not been directed towards goals identified as important by people with autism. Some studies of autism appear to be more to do with testing hypotheses about human behaviour and communication (in general) by recruiting people with autism (particularly 'high-functioning' people) as a naturally occurring comparison group in the design of quasi-experiments. The phrase 'high-functioning' is commonplace in the psychological literature on autism. It is often used to refer to people with Asperger Syndrome, or to those with a diagnosis of ASD who are evidently intellectually able. The implicit (and sometimes explicit) contrast that the phrase sets up is clearly 'low-functioning'. It is worth considering how it would feel to be described as 'low-functioning'.

The theory of mind literature is one area in which research *on* people with autism has not always been *about* people with autism. People with autism were discovered to have difficulties performing on theory of mind tasks. Researchers then set out not only to try to understand autism better, but also to test theories about brain and cognitive development (particularly with regard to the issue of modularity and domain specificity) by comparing people with typical theory of mind task performance and people with atypical theory of mind task performance.

In other words, there is an extent to which people with autism have been recruited to studies that may in truth have been more to do with testing general theories of human development, rather than testing specific questions about autism. If this point is only partly true of people with autism (by and large psychological research into autism *does* try to advance understandings of autism), it is more true of children with Down Syndrome, and especially true of children with Williams Syndrome and of those with general learning disabilities, who are often recruited to studies as 'non-autistic controls' – that is, the studies in which they participate in the literature on autism are not concerned to develop an enhanced understanding of Down Syndrome, or Williams Syndrome, or learning disability, but to enhance understanding of autism, or of some general theory of human development.

General theoretical work of this type is important, and this critique does not intend to argue otherwise. The aim of the critique is simply to pose the question, 'For whose benefit is psychological research undertaken?' The fact that a research study includes a sample of a specific group of people does not necessarily mean that the study is *for* that group.

One particularly important aspect of this is the gaining of genuinely informed consent from participants – consent that is sought and given in relation to the aims of a particular research study or programme. Indeed, much recent autism research, including psychological research, has been funded by advocacy groups and ethical guidelines for approaches that are autism-focused have been developed (Chen *et al.*, 2003). Where research is related to the lives of people with learning difficulties, including autism, psychologists are increasingly employing co-operative and consultative ways of working (Goodley, 2004).

Summary of Section 5

- The fields of autism and psychology have been intertwined since the work of Kanner (1943).
- All the psychological approaches examined in Section 4 say something valid about autism, but none is capable of explaining autism on its own.
- The 'take-home message' of research, whether intended or unintended, reflects and influences how people with autism are seen in society.
- Psychological research on autism has not always been for people with autism. The recent influence of advocacy groups is beginning to shape more inclusive research methods.

6 Integrating insider and outsider accounts

This section aims to illustrate how an interpretation of insider and outsider perspectives is required in order to move an understanding of autism forward. It takes as its focus the issue of pretend play, an issue that has received considerable attention from psychologists.

6.1 Pretend play

One of the 'triad of impairments' identified by Wing and Gould (1979) is an apparent difficulty with imagination. Difficulties with imagination are thought to relate to stereotyped and repetitive behaviours, and to a preference for 'sameness' – key diagnostic features of autism. But they also relate to aspects of play, particularly pretend play. It has been observed that children with autism do not engage in as much pretend play as do typically developing children.

Pretend play in typical development appears to relate to receptive language development (Lewis *et al.*, 2000) so, when making experimental comparisons between children with and without autism, it is important to ensure that they are matched on their level of receptive language ability. Studies that have controlled for receptive language development have shown that children with autism show less spontaneous pretend play than matched typically developing children (Jarrold *et al.*, 1996).

However, this does not necessarily mean that children with autism are less *able* to engage in pretend play than typically developing children. Lower levels of spontaneous pretend play can be explained in a number of ways. One of the operational definitions that is employed in research studies on this topic is the child's use of one object to stand for another object (for example, using an upturned stool as a boat, or a cardboard box as a car). However, it appears to be the case that many people with autism interpret the world around them in a concrete, relatively literal sense and prefer not to entertain alternative understandings of situations that may have multiple possible meanings (or they may not be very good at entertaining them). Perhaps it is this that makes them less willing or able to engage in spontaneous pretend play, rather than having a 'deficiency' in pretend play, per se. Or maybe children with autism just enjoy pretend play less, and therefore do it less.

Another explanation of the observation of lower levels of pretend play in children with autism is that these children might have difficulties in initiating and executing the behaviours that researchers take as evidence of pretend play. Certainly some type of executive dysfunction (difficulties in initiating planned actions, for example) might account for this kind of difficulty. Furthermore, Jarrold *et al.* (1994) were able to show that children with autism were just as good as typically developing children at *understanding* pretend play when exposed to it. This suggests that it might be something to do with *doing* pretend play (such as motivation, or planning and initiating actions) that accounts for the observation that children with autism engage in it less frequently than typically developing children.

One reason for the uncertain interpretations of observational and experimental data is that it is not possible directly to observe someone 'pretending'. This is a familiar issue in psychology and has to do with operational definitions. Operational definitions are the ways in which researchers take a behaviour (or a set of behaviours) to represent a hidden, psychological process. So researchers of pretend play might define 'pretence' as using one object in place of another (a banana being used as a telephone), or as invoking the presence of an absent object or power ('I'm superman so I can fly ...'). But how would they know that using a banana as a telephone is really 'pretending'? Could it simply be 'imitating', or the performance of an action that has been taught? Furthermore, as Jarrold points out, pretence might be happening internally, with or without accompanying behaviour. 'If I stare intently at an empty cup on my desk I might be pretending that it contains tea, or I might simply be lost in thought' (Jarrold, 2003, p. 385).

It may be, then, that pretence is one of those things that really needs to be studied from both outsider and insider perspectives. The observation (from an outside perspective) that children with autism exhibit fewer behaviours that are indicative of spontaneous pretend play is an important one. It can be useful in diagnostic terms and it accurately reflects the lived experience of families with autism. It may be highly reassuring and helpful for a parent of a child newly diagnosed with autism to know that their child's behaviour is, in fact, typical of children with autism. However, it is very difficult to know what this observation really means at both theoretical and experiential levels. Does it, for example, give evidence at a theoretical level for a deficit of imagination, as specified in Wing's triad of impairments? At an experiential level, it could be that the lack of behaviour misrepresents highly active – but private – imaginary worlds in children with autism:

> I understand why there is a need to develop typical play skills, but I was developing my skills at my rate for being the person on the autism spectrum that I am.

> Imagination is something that is different in each person. For me, it was making my lists, creating fictional genealogies of characters, planning imaginary ball games with players on baseball cards, creating different languages, and the list goes on. Each person is different and imagination is different for each person.

> (Jean-Paul Bovee, in Donnelly and Bovee, 2003, p. 476)

Summary of Section 6

- Children with autism have been observed to engage in less spontaneous pretend play than typically developing children.
- From an 'outsider' perspective cognitive and emotional states can only be inferred on the basis of behaviour – which can be misleading.
- It is necessary to integrate insider and outsider accounts of key features of autism in order to advance scientific understanding.

7   Conclusions

This chapter has been about how developmental psychologists can come to a better understanding of autism. Since Kanner's account of his clinical work in 1943, an impressive amount of psychological research into autism has been undertaken. Most of that research has been conducted with the intention of achieving a better all-round understanding of the condition, in terms of causes, prevalence, core features, and clinical and educational interventions. But, like many domains in the human sciences, the research has often been conducted from an ethnocentric stance: from the position of members of the majority, typically developing, non-autistic community. A consequence of this is that assumptions are made that may not readily apply to the world of people with autism. By engaging with the voices and perspectives of children and adults with autism psychologists will strengthen our understanding of it, help to develop a critical perspective on how autism is constructed in society, and inform the development of appropriate and beneficial psychological interventions.

References

A is for Autism, video animation, directed by Tim Webb, UK, Channel 4, 1992.

Allen, G. and Courchesne, E. (2003) 'Differential effects of developmental cerebellar abnormality on cognitive and motor functions in the cerebellum: An fMRI study of autism', *American Journal of Psychiatry*, vol. 160, pp. 262–73.

Allen, G., Buxton, R. B., Wong, E. C. and Courchesne, E. (1997) 'Attentional activation of the cerebellum independent of motor involvement', *Science*, vol. 275, pp. 1940–3.

American Psychiatric Association (2000) *Diagnostic and Statistical Manual of Mental Disorders* DSM-IV-TR ⓉⓂ (4ᵗʰ edn) Washington, DC, American Psychiatric Association.

Asperger, H. (1944) in Waterhouse, S.W. (2000) *A Positive Approach to Autism*, London, Jessica Kingsley.

Autistic Network International (2005) 'Introducing ANI', [online] http://ani.autistics.org/intro.html [accessed 20 June 2005].

Baird, G., Cass, H. and Slonims, V. (2003) 'Diagnosis of autism', *British Medical Journal*, vol. 327, pp. 488–93.

Baranek, G. T. (1999) 'Autism during infancy: a retrospective video analysis of sensory–motor and social behaviors at 9–12 months of age', *Journal of Autism and Developmental Disorders*, vol. 29, pp. 213–24.

Baron-Cohen, S. and Cross, P. (1992) 'Reading the eyes: evidence for the role of perception in the development of a theory of mind', *Mind and Language*, vol. 7, pp. 172–86.

Baron-Cohen, S. and Goodhart, F. (1994) 'The "seeing-leads-to-knowing" deficit in autism: the Pratt and Bryant probe', *British Journal of Developmental Psychology*, vol. 12, pp. 397–401.

Baron-Cohen, S., Leslie, A. M. and Frith, U. (1985) 'Does the autistic child have a "theory of mind"?', *Cognition*, vol. 21, pp. 37–46.

Barrett, S., Prior, M. and Manjiviona, J. (2004) 'Children on the borderlands of autism', *Autism*, vol. 8, pp. 61–87.

Bauman, M. L. (1992) 'Motor dysfunction in autism' in Joseph, A. B. and Young, R. R. (eds) *Movement Disorders in Neurology and Neuropsychiatry*, Oxford, Blackwell Scientific Publications.

Bettelheim, B. (1967) *The Empty Fortress: infantile autism and the birth of the self*, New York, NY, The Free Press.

Biklen, D. and Cardinal, D. N. (eds) (1997) *Contested Words, Contested Science: unraveling the facilitated communication controversy.* New York, NY, Teachers College.

Blackburn, R. (2000) 'Within and without autism', *Good Autism Practice*, vol. 1, pp. 2–8.

Cass, H. D., Sonksen, P. M. and McConachie, H. R. (1994) 'Developmental setback in severe visual impairment', *Archives of Disease in Childhood*, vol. 70, pp. 192–6.

Cesaroni, L. and Garber, M. (1991) 'Exploring the experience of autism through firsthand accounts', *Journal of Autism and Developmental Disorders*, vol. 21, pp. 303–13.

Charman, T., Baron-Cohen, S., Swettenham, J. *et al.* (2000) 'Testing joint attention, imitation, and play as infancy precursors to language and theory of mind', *Cognitive Development*, vol. 15, pp. 481–98.

Chen, D. T., Miller, F. G. and Rosenstein, D. L. (2003) 'Ethical aspects of research into the etiology of autism', *Mental Retardation and Developmental Disabilities Research Reviews*, vol. 9, pp. 48–53.

Courchesne, E., Karns, C. M., Davis, H. R. *et al.* (2001) 'Unusual brain growth patterns in early life in patients with autistic disorder: An MRI study', *Neurology*, vol. 57, pp. 245–54.

Dawson, G., Toth, K., Abbott, R. *et al.* (2004) 'Early social attention impairments in autism: social orienting, joint attention, and attention to distress', *Developmental Psychology*, vol. 40, pp. 271–83.

de Meyer, M. K. (1976) 'Motor, perceptual–motor and intellectual disabilities of autistic children', in Wing, L. (ed.) *Early Childhood Autism: clinical education and social aspects*, Oxford, Pergamon Press.

Donnellan, A. M. and Leary, M. R. (1995) *Movement Differences and Diversity in Autism/mental retardation: appreciating and accommodating people with communication and behavior challenges*, Madison, WI, DRI Press.

Donnelly, J. and Bovee, J. P. (2003) 'Reflections on play: recollections from a mother and her son with Asperger Syndrome', *Autism*, vol. 7, pp. 471–6.

Flynn, E. (2004) 'Understanding minds' in Oates, J. M. and Grayson, A. (eds) *Cognitive and Language Development in Children*, Oxford, Blackwell.

Frith, U. (1989) *Autism: explaining the enigma*, Cambridge, MA, Blackwell.

Frith, U. and Snowling, M. (1983) 'Reading for meaning and reading for sound in autistic and dyslexic children', *British Journal of Developmental Psychology*, vol. 1, pp. 329–42.

Goin, R. P. and Myers, B. J. (2004) 'Characteristics of infantile autism: moving toward earlier detection', *Focus on Autism and Other Developmental Disabilities*, vol. 19, pp. 5–12.

Goodley, D. (2004) 'Disability studies and research: introduction to this special issue', *British Journal of Learning Disabilities*, vol. 33, p. 49.

Grandin, T. and Scariano, M. M. (1986) *Emergence Labelled Autistic*, New York, NY, Warner Books.

Grayson, A., Barton, L. and Howard-Jones, P. (2004) 'Can I see where I look because I am interested?: eye-tracking research and communication, evidence from an inclusive project', paper presented at the Common Solutions: Inclusion and Diversity at the Center Conference, Syracuse University, 2004.

Happé, F. G. E. (1994) *Autism: an introduction to psychological theory*, London, UCL Press.

Hermelin, B. and O'Connor, N. (1970) *Psychological Experiments with Autistic Children*, New York, NY, Pergamon.

Hobson, P. (2002) *The Cradle of Thought: exploring the origins of thinking*, London, Macmillan.

Hobson, R. P. and Bishop, M. (2003) 'The pathogenesis of autism: insights from congenital blindness,' *Philosophical Transactions of the Royal Society B*, vol. 358, pp. 335–44.

Hughes, C. (2001) 'Executive dysfunction in autism: its nature and implications for the everyday problems experienced by individuals with autism' in Burack, J. and Charman, T. (eds) *The Development of Autism: perspectives from theory and research*, pp. 255–75, New York, NY, Erlbaum.

Hughes, C. and Russell, J. (1993) 'Autistic children's difficulty with mental disengagement from an object: its implications for theories of autism', *Developmental Psychology*, vol. 29, pp. 498–510.

Hughes, C., Graham, A. and Grayson, A. (2004) 'Executive functions in childhood: development and disorder' in Oates, J. M. and Grayson, A. (eds) *Cognitive and Language Development in Children*, pp. 205–30, Oxford, Blackwell.

Jarrold, C. (2003) 'A review of research into pretend play in autism', *Autism*, vol. 7, pp. 379–90.

Jarrold, C., Boucher, J. and Smith, P. K. (1996) 'Generativity defects in pretend play in autism', *British Journal of Developmental Psychology*, vol. 14, pp. 275–300.

Jarrold, C., Smith, P., Boucher, J. and Harris, P. (1994) 'Comprehension of pretense in children with autism', *Journal of Autism and Developmental Disorders*, vol. 24, pp. 433–55.

Jones, V. and Prior, M. (1985) 'Motor imitation abilities and neurological signs in autistic children', *Journal of Autism and Developmental Disorders*, vol. 15, pp. 37–46.

Jordan, R. (1999) *Autism Spectrum Disorders: an introductory handbook for practitioners*, London, David Fulton.

Kanazawa, S. (2004) 'General intelligence as a domain-specific adaptation', *Psychological Review*, vol. 111, pp. 512–23.

Kanner, L. (1943) 'Autistic disturbances of affective contact', *Nervous Child*, vol. 2, pp. 217–50.

Lawson, W. (2001) *Understanding and Working with the Spectrum of Autism: an insider's view*, London, Jessica Kingsley.

Leslie, A. M. and Frith, U. (1988) 'Autistic children's understanding of seeing, knowing and believing', *British Journal of Developmental Psychology*, vol. 6, pp. 315–24.

Lewis, V., Boucher, J., Lupton, L. and Watson, S. (2000) 'Relationships between symbolic play, functional play, verbal and non-verbal ability in young children',

International Journal of Language and Communication Disorders, vol. 35, pp. 117–27.

Manjiviona, J. and Prior, M. (1995) 'Comparison of Asperger Syndrome and high-functioning autistic children on a test of motor impairment', *Journal of Autism and Developmental Disorders*, vol. 25, pp. 23–39.

Mottron, L., Burack, J. A., Iarocci, G. *et al.* (2003) 'Locally oriented perception with intact global processing among adolescents with high-functioning autism: evidence from multiple paradigms', *Journal of Child Psychology and Psychiatry and Allied Disciplines*, vol. 44, pp. 904–13.

Mukhopadhyay, T. R. (2000) *Beyond the Silence: my life, the world and autism*, London, National Autistic Society.

Müller, R. A., Kleinhans, N., Kemmotsu, N. *et al.* (2003) 'Abnormal variability and distribution of functional maps in autism: an fMRI study of visuomotor learning', *American Journal of Psychiatry*, vol. 160, pp. 1847–62.

Page, J. and Boucher, J. (1998) 'Motor impairments in children with autistic disorder', *Child Language Teaching and Therapy*, vol. 14, pp. 233–59.

Park, C. C. (2001) *Exiting Nirvana: a daughter's life with autism*, London, Back Bay Books.

Peeters, T. and Gillberg, C. (1999) *Austism: medical and educational aspects*, London, Whurr publishers.

Pennington, B. F. and Ozonoff, S. (1996) 'Executive functions and developmental psychopathology', *Journal of Child Psychology and Psychiatry*, vol. 37, pp. 51–87.

Perner, J., Frith, U., Leslie, A. M. and Leekam, S. R. (1989) 'Exploration of the autistic child's theory of mind: knowledge, belief, and communication', *Child Development*, vol. 60, pp. 689–700.

Pierce, K., Müller, R. A., Ambrose, J. *et al.* (2001) 'Face processing occurs outside the fusiform "face area" in autism: evidence from functional MRI', *Brain*, vol. 124, pp. 2059–73.

Premack, D. and Woodruff, G. (1978) 'Does the chimpanzee have a theory of mind?', *Behavioral and Brain Sciences*, vol. 1, pp. 515–26.

Rogers, S. J., Hepburn, S. and Wehner, E. (2003) 'Parent reports of sensory symptoms in toddlers with autism and those with other developmental disorders', *Journal of Autism and Developmental Disorders*, vol. 33, pp. 631–42.

Roth, I. (2002) 'The autistic spectrum: from theory to practice' in Brace, N. and Westcott, H. (eds) *Applying Psychology*, pp. 243–314, Milton Keynes, The Open University.

Ruble, L. A. and Scott, M. M. (2002) 'Executive functions and the natural habitat behaviors of children with autism', *Autism*, vol. 6, pp. 365–81.

Shah, A. and Frith, U. (1983) 'An islet of ability in autistic children: a research note', *Journal of Child Psychology and Psychiatry and Allied Disciplines*, vol. 24, pp. 613–20.

Sigman, M. D., Mundy, P., Sherman, T. and Ungerer, J. (1986) 'Social interactions of autistic, mentally retarded and normal children and their caregivers', *Journal of Child Psychology and Psychiatry and Allied Disciplines*, vol. 27, pp. 647–56.

Sinclair, J. (1993) 'Don't mourn for us', *Autism Network International Newsletter* vol. 1, [online], http://web.syr.edu/~jisincla/dontmourn.htm [accessed 20 June 2005].

Stahl, L. and Pry R. (2002) 'Joint attention and set-shifting in young children with autism', *Autism,* vol. 6, pp. 383–96.

Szatmari, P., Bryson, S. E., Boyle, M. H., Streiner, D. L. and Duku, E. (2003) 'Predictors of outcome among high-functioning children with autism and Asperger Syndrome', *Journal of Child Psychology and Psychiatry and Allied Disciplines*, vol. 44, pp. 520–28.

Tager-Flusberg, H. (1992) 'Autistic children's talk about psychological states: deficits in the early acquisition of a theory of mind', *Child Development*, vol. 63, pp. 161–72.

Tecchio, F., Benassi, F., Zappasodi, F. *et al.* (2003) 'Auditory sensory processing in autism: a magnetoencephalographic study', *Biological Psychiatry*, vol. 54, pp. 647–54.

Trevarthen, C. (1979) 'Communication and co-operation in early infancy: a description of primary intersubjectivity' in Bullowa, M. (ed.) *Before Speech*, Cambridge, Cambridge University Press.

Volkmar, F. R., Lord, C., Bailey, A. *et al.* (2004) 'Autism and pervasive developmental disorders', *Journal of Child Psychology and Psychiatry and Allied Disciplines*, vol. 45, pp. 135–70.

Walmsley, J. and Johnson, K. (2003) *Inclusive Research with People with Learning Difficulties: past, present and future*, London, Jessica Kingsley.

Waterhouse, S. W. (2000) *A Positive Approach to Autism*, London, Jessica Kingsley.

Wechsler, D. (1974) *Wechsler Intelligence Scale for Children – Revised*, New York, NY, The Psychological Corporation.

Williams, D. (1999) *Nobody Nowhere*, London, Jessica Kingsley.

Wing, L. (1997) 'The history of ideas on autism', *Autism*, vol. 1, pp. 13–23.

Wing, L. (1998) 'Classification and diagnosis: looking at the complexities involved', *Communication: the magazine of the National Autistic Society*, Winter, pp.15–19.

Wing, L. and Gould, J. (1979) 'Severe impairments of social interaction and associated abnormalities in children: epidemiology and classification', *Journal of Autism and Developmental Disorders*, vol. 9, pp. 11–29.

Reading

The history of ideas on autism: legends, myths and reality

Lorna Wing

Abstract

The development of ideas about the nature of autism is described, covering myths and legends, accounts of individuals in the historical literature, the search for identifiable subgroups, Kanner's and Asperger syndromes, and the current view of a wide autistic spectrum. Changes in theories of aetiology are outlined, including the early magical and mystical beliefs, the era when purely psychological and emotional causes were promulgated, and the present day research into biological mechanisms. The major advances in understanding the neurological and psychological aspects of autism, which have led to the development of special methods of education, are discussed. The rate of increase in knowledge in recent years gives hope for future progress in understanding and treatment.

Introduction

As everyone in the field knows, Leo Kanner (1943) was the first person to describe and name a pattern of behaviour he observed in a small group of young children, which he termed 'early infantile autism' (derived from the Greek word autos meaning 'self'). However, Asperger (1944), one year after Kanner's original paper, wrote about another behaviour pattern in older children and adolescents, which, though different in detail, clearly overlapped with Kanner's accounts. Asperger also used the term 'autistic' in relation to the behaviour he saw.

Legends and history

The history of autistic disorders stretches far back into the mists of time, long before Kanner's and Asperger's insights (Brauner and Brauner, 1986). Some versions of the myths of changeling children, left in place of real human babies who had been stolen by fairies, sound remarkably like children with autism. The legends concerning the followers of St Francis of Assisi include stories of one Brother Juniper, who was naively innocent and lacking in any social intuition or common sense (Frith, 1989). At the time, his oddity was considered to be due to his saintliness, even though it often exasperated the other brothers. Nowadays he may well have been diagnosed as having Asperger syndrome.

In factual history, scattered examples of individuals who seem to have had autistic disorders can be found. Kanner (1964) quotes Martin Luther's reported account of a child whose behaviour suggests that he might have been severely autistic (though Kanner did not mention this possibility). Luther recommended that the child be taken to the nearby river and drowned, because he was possessed of the Devil and had no soul. This harsh view, held by a man of the sixteenth century, is in stark contrast to the care and concern shown by J.M.G. Itard (1801/1807), the physician who devised methods of educating Victor, the boy found living wild in the woods of Aveyron in south-central France at the end of the eighteenth century. Itard described Victor's behaviour in detail (see Lane, 1977). There can be no doubt that Victor was autistic. Itard went on to work with other children who failed to develop speech. He was in the forefront in designing methods to educate those with severe hearing impairments (see Lane, 1977). He was also a pioneer in differentiating mutism due to severe generalized mental retardation from that due to more specific causes. The diagnostic categories used now were unknown in Itard's time but, among the children he described, there were some who probably had developmental dysphasia and others who would now be recognized as autistic (see Carrey, 1995).

Accounts of persons with one remarkable skill at a much higher level than their other abilities and with very strange behaviour can be found in the past and present literature. Treffert (1989) described a number of such individuals. He noted that, in 1887, Langdon Down, who is most famous for his writings on Down's syndrome, gave a lecture on individuals with isolated skills, many of whom would now be diagnosed as autistic savants.

Early psychiatric literature

Despite some very vivid descriptions by earlier writers of what we now know to be autistic behaviour (for example, Haslam, 1809), no one saw any connections among the individual cases until the last half of the nineteenth century. Then Henry Maudsley (1867), after whom the Maudsley Hospital was named, suggested that children with very strange behaviour could all be classified as suffering from childhood psychosis. This was, at first, greeted as a shocking idea because it disturbed the romantic notions about childhood current at the time (at least among the upper middle classes). However, Maudsley's idea gradually came to be accepted. Psychoses were, at that time, considered to be due to physical causes affecting the brain.

In the first half of the twentieth century, workers in the field of abnormal child development began to try to define subgroups within so-called childhood psychoses. De Sanctis (1906, 1908) and Heller (see Hulse, 1954) described children who seemed to develop normally for a time and then lost language, social and other skills. Margaret Mahler (1952) described children who insisted on clinging to their carers but without any real feeling and who had other abnormalities of behaviour. Potter (1933) wrote about children whom he said had a childhood form of schizophrenia. Earl (1934) described a group of adolescents who were mentally retarded and who developed behaviour that he called catatonic but which had major similarities to severe autistic behaviour.

Leo Kanner and Hans Asperger

Kanner (1943) was one among this group. He wrote his classic description of young children who were socially aloof and indifferent, who were mute or had echolalia and idiosyncratic speech, were intensely resistant to change in their own repetitive routines, and who had isolated skills in visuo-spatial or rote memory tasks against a background of general delay in learning. He emphasized their attractive, alert, intelligent appearance. He considered his form of autism to be unique and different from any other disorder in childhood. Asperger (1944; Frith, 1991) was another of this group of workers. He described older children and adolescents who were naive and inappropriate in social interaction, had good speech but used it for monologues on their own special interests, had poor intonation and body language, were absorbed in their circumscribed interests, and often had poor motor coordination. They were of borderline, normal or superior intelligence but often had specific learning difficulties.

James Anthony (1958a, 1958b), a child psychiatrist, discussed these attempts at defining subgroups. He pointed out that, although there were some differences, all the subgroups that were suggested overlapped with each other to a very great extent. He also noted that there were not enough symptoms to go round among all the authors who wanted to name a syndrome!

It is interesting that, out of all the workers writing in this field, Kanner and Asperger are the only ones whose names have become generally well known throughout the world. Kanner was the first to have his work widely recognized. Asperger achieved this status in the English language literature much later than Kanner, though his work was known earlier in mainland Europe. In 1962, the Dutch workers Van Krevelen and Kuipers published a paper in English on Asperger syndrome because they considered that Asperger's ideas were insufficiently known in English speaking countries. Van Krevelen wrote on the syndrome in English again in 1971, but it was not until the 1980s that interest in Asperger's work began to grow in the UK (Frith, 1991; Tantam, 1991; Wing, 1981).

The reason why Kanner's and Asperger's papers continued to capture interest, while other early workers in the field tended to fade into obscurity, is probably because both described the children they saw in such vivid detail. The children come alive from the pages of their papers. Although Kanner and Asperger each thought their syndromes were special and unique, we now know that they overlap with each other and that many children have a mixture of features of both conditions.

The influence of psychoanalysis

The twentieth century gave us the concept of autism and autistic disorders but it also gave a darker twist to the story. The theories of Freud and of other schools of psychoanalysis were developing in Europe during the early years of the century and became strongly influential in the USA during and after the Second World War.

Leo Kanner (1949) suggested that genetic factors played a part in the causation (an insightful guess in the light of recent research). However, he was also influenced by the psychoanalytic theories that had taken such a hold upon the psychiatric profession, especially in the USA. He suggested that the children's condition was also due to being reared by cold, detached, humourless, rigid parents who were perfectionists, caring for their children like attendants caring for a machine. He noted that almost all the parents he saw had academic qualifications and professional occupations. He thought that the children were potentially normal and of good intelligence but were emotionally damaged. He firmly believed that there was no physical pathology in the brain. Kanner's ideas about the parents of autistic children were accepted uncritically by many psychiatrists. Professionals in other branches of medicine, nursing and teaching, also adopted these ideas. Even parents themselves were indoctrinated by the prevailing theories.

The results were devastating. Many parents were overwhelmed with guilt and families were split by attempts to assign blame to one or other partner. Some families spent large sums of money on psychoanalytical treatment for their children. If they improved over time, the therapist took the credit. If there was no change or a deterioration the parents took the blame. The children suffered because they were not given the type of education and help they needed. I have been unable to find any single attempt at scientific evaluation of such treatment in the years when psychoanalytical theories were at their height, up to the end of the 1950s. Nor was there any study of the natural history of autism when no treatment was given, which is an essential basis for evaluation of methods of intervention.

Another thread in the story is the theory that autism is the earliest form of schizophrenia, also once thought to have emotional causes. Kanner at first wrote that autism and schizophrenia were quite separate but, later, he wavered under the influence of child psychiatrist colleagues (Kanner, 1949).

The re-emergence of theories of physical causes

Fortunately not everyone had faith in the theory of the emotional causes of autism. Some workers recognized the large overlap with mental retardation (now referred to as 'learning disability' in the UK). Some were interested in the abnormalities of language development. Others felt that the neuropathology should be explored.

The champions of the emotional theories had dismissed the possibility of any physical abnormalities in the brain because no specific lesions had then been revealed. Looking back now, it seems remarkably arrogant of anyone to assume that the techniques available in the 1940s and 1950s for examining the brain could never be improved.

It is of interest that, in 1932, Critchley and Earl had described tuberose (or tuberous) sclerosis, a condition in which recognizable brain pathology occurs. The behaviour pattern in this condition is, in a significant proportion of cases, that of typical autism (Hunt and Shepherd, 1993). In the metabolic disorder called phenylketonuria, if it is untreated by a special diet, the behaviour is also like that in autism (Jervis, 1963).

It is curious that Kanner did not mention these neurological conditions that overlap in their behaviour pattern with autism. This may have been because he was convinced of the uniqueness of his syndrome and the high intellectual potential of the children.

New influences produce new ideas

The tide began to turn in the 1960s for two main reasons. First, parents who were independently minded enough to reject the idea that they were to blame for their children's condition came together to form parents' associations. The first of these (by a small margin) was the British Society for Autistic Children, now known as

The National Autistic Society. Parents in other countries followed suit and now societies are to be found in very many countries throughout the world. Their influence has been of major importance in changing ideas on autism and the needs of the children and their families.

The second factor was the introduction of more rigorous scientific studies. Prior to the 1960s, papers on autism were either clinical case descriptions or what can only be called armchair theorizing. In 1961 , Mildred Creak, well known for her interest in autistic disorders, chaired a committee of professionals in the field who produced a set of criteria that defined what they called 'childhood schizophrenia' (Creak, 1964). Despite the terminology, it is clear that they were describing disorders we now refer to as autistic. Unfortunately the nine criteria, known as the 'Nine Points', were an unsatisfactory mixture of observation and interpretation, which proved hard to apply in practice.

Nevertheless, the work represented the first serious attempt to define a range of disorders including Kanner's autism. The confusion between autism and schizophrenia occurring in childhood continued to affect the field until, early in the 1970s, Kolvin (1971) and his colleagues carried out a study comparing the two groups of conditions and listed the many differences.

A major contribution to the scientific study of autistic disorders was made by Victor Lotter (1966). He carried out, in the former English county of Middlesex, the first ever epidemiological study of Kanner's autism. He used as the crucial defining features the two criteria selected by Kanner and Eisenberg (1956) as the most important, that is, social aloofness and indifference to others, and resistance to change in elaborate repetitive routines. He found that nearly 5 in 10,000 children had this syndrome.

Michael Rutter and his colleagues also began their series of studies in typical autism in the 1960s. They described in detail the clinical features, they investigated the children's profiles on intelligence tests and they followed them up into adolescence and adult life (Rutter, 1970).

Other workers have studied the parents and found no evidence that they caused their children to be autistic through abnormal child-rearing practices (DeMyer, 1975, 1979). Most of the studies that examined the parents' occupations found that they came from all walks of life (Wing, 1993). Kanner's theory that the parents were mostly of high social class was not upheld.

The theory of the autistic spectrum

Following Victor Lotter's work, there have been a number of other studies of the prevalence of autism defined in various ways (Wing 1993). My colleague Judith Gould and I carried out a study in one area of London of children with all kinds of disabilities (Wing and Gould, 1979). We looked for children who had any feature of autistic behaviour, not just those who had typical Kanner's autism. As a result of this, we developed the hypothesis of a wide spectrum of autistic conditions of which Kanner's autism was only one small part. We found a total of 20 per 10,000 children with autistic spectrum disorders combined with mental retardation (IQ below 70). It was during the course of this study that we first saw a few children with the pattern of behaviour described by Hans Asperger. It was a great pleasure to me that I was able to meet Dr Asperger when he visited London, even though we disagreed because he thought his syndrome was separate from Kanner's autism and I thought it was part of the spectrum.

In the 1980s Christopher Gillberg and his colleagues developed and extended work on the autistic spectrum. Gillberg (1992) has hypothesized that there is a range of disorders of empathic understanding of which the autistic spectrum is a part but not the whole. Ehlers and Gillberg (1993) have also studied Asperger syndrome among children in mainstream schools and found a prevalence of at least 36 in 10,000, that is nearly 4 per 1000. They found nearly the same number (35 per 10,000) who would fit into the wider autistic spectrum, including those studied by Sula Wolff. In 1995, Wolff published a book in which she brought together the results of 30 years of research and clinical experience with a group of children and young adults, whom she originally classified as having 'schizoid personality disorder of childhood'. They were characterized by being 'loners' from birth onwards and tended to be egocentric and eccentric in their interests and activities. Most were more able than many people diagnosed as having Asperger syndrome but Sula Wolff, as she explains in her book, considers that they come within the borderlines of the wider autistic spectrum.

The present and the future

The 1990s have brought advances in understanding of the cause and underlying neuropathblogy of typical autism, although there is still a long way to go. Michael Rutter and his colleagues have shown the importance of genetic factors in autism and probably other autistic spectrum disorders as well (Bolton *et al.*, 1994). There has also been a growth of interest in the various developmental syndromes in which aspects of autistic behaviour, or even the full picture of typical autism, can occur. From the point of view of the neuropathology, there is growing evidence of possible involvement of parts of the limbic system, the cerebellum and the frontal and temporal cortex in autism. It appears likely that the abnormalities occur at the cellular level and date from very early in development (Bauman and Kemper, 1994).

Psychological aspects of autistic disorders are being examined, including abnormalities of language and communication. Uta Frith and her colleagues have shown the difficulty the children have in understanding other people's minds (Frith, 1989).

Another advance promises to aid early recognition. Simon Baron-Cohen and his colleagues (1996) have developed a brief screening instrument that appears to be able to identify children who are autistic at the age of 18 months. The basis of the examination is the ability to engage in joint referencing and pretend play.

Parallel with the increasing knowledge of the nature of autistic disorders there has been a steady development of methods of educating (Jordan and Powell, 1995) and caring for people with these conditions (Howlin, 1997a; Wing, 1996).

We have come a long way from the era of myths and legends, through the unhappy deviation into psychoanalysis, to the practical realism of the present day that is accepted by most, though sadly not all, professionals in the field. We now know that there is a wide spectrum of autistic conditions, with Kanner's and Asperger syndromes each forming only a part of these. The whole spectrum is united by the presence of underlying impairments of three aspects of psychological function, namely, social interaction, communication and imagination. When this 'triad of impairments' is present, the individual's pattern of activities is rigid, narrow and repetitive. The triad can occur alone or in association with any other physical or psychological disorder. Conditions in the spectrum can occur together with any level of ability from profound mental retardation up to superior levels of intelligence. The outcome in adult life is closely related to level of ability in childhood. Only those with average or high intelligence have any prospect of becoming independent in adult life. However, much can be done through education to improve quality of life for all those affected, regardless of ability. Autistic spectrum conditions are developmental disorders caused by physical abnormalities in parts of the brain. Complex genetic factors are important in the causation but there are other physical causes that can lead to autistic conditions. Adding together the prevalence of all autistic disorders in people of all levels of ability, the total is probably around 9 in every 1000.

Despite claims that have been made for a variety of methods, no curative treatment has yet been found that stands up to proper investigation (see Howlin, 1997b). However, we have a great deal of knowledge about methods of education and how to structure the environment and daily programme to increase skills and diminish disabilities and disturbed behaviour.

The hope for the future is that we will identify the precise causes and find effective methods of prevention and treatment of those autistic disorders that are linked with severe disabilities and distress. Where autism is linked to high ability and unusual forms of creativity, the hope is that we will develop our understanding of ways to make life happier for the individuals concerned while valuing and encouraging their special contribution to human life.

Acknowledgement

This paper was first presented at the Fifth Congress of *Autisme-Europe*, Barcelona, 1996.

References for Reading

Anthony, E. J. (1958a) 'An Etiological Approach to the Diagnosis of Psychosis in Childhood', *Revue de Psychiatrie Infantile* 25: 89–96.

Anthony, E. J. (1958b) 'An Experimental Approach to the Psychopathology of Childhood Autism', *British Journal of Medical Psychology* 21: 211–25.

Asperger, H. (1944) 'Die autistischen Psychopathen im Kindesalter', *Archiv für Psychiatrie und Nervenkrankheiten* 117: 76–136. Trans. U. Frith in U. Frith (ed.) (1991) *Autism and Asperger Syndrome*, pp. 37–92. Cambridge: Cambridge University Press.

Baron-Cohen, S., Cox, A., Baird, G., Swettenham, J., Nightingale, N., Morgan, K., Drew, A. & Charman, T. (1996) 'Psychological Markers in the Detection of Autism in Infancy in a Large Population', *British Journal of Psychiatry* 168: 158–63.

Bauman, M. & Kemper, T. (1994) 'Neuroanatomic Observations of the Brain in Autism', in M. Bauman & T. Kemper (eds) *The Neurobiology of Autism*, pp. 119–45. Baltimore, MD: Johns Hopkins.

Bolton, P., Macdonald, H., Pickles, A., Rios, P., Goode, S., Crowson, M., Bailey, A. & Rutter, M. (1994) 'A Case-Control Family History Study of Autism', *Journal of Child Psychology and Psychiatry* 35: 877–900.

Brauner, A. & Brauner, F. (1986) *L'Enfant déréél: Histoire des autismes depuis les contes de fées.* Toulouse: Privat.

Carrey, N. J. (1995) 'Itard's *Mémoire* on "Mutism Caused by a Lesion of the Intellectual Functions": A Historical Analysis', *Journal of the American Academy of Child and Adolescent Psychiatry* 34: 1655–6 1.

Creak, E. M. (1964) 'Schizophrenic Syndrome in Childhood: Further Progress Report of a Working Party (April 1961)', *Developmental Medicine and Child Neurology* 6: 530–5.

Critchley, M. & Earl, C. J. C. (1932) 'Tuberose Sclerosis and Allied Conditions', *Brain* 55: 311–46.

Demyer, M. K. (1975) 'Research in Infantile Autism: A Strategy and its Results', *Biological Psychiatry* 10: 433–52.

Demyer, M. K. (1979) *Parents and Children in Autism.* Washington, DC: Winston.

Desanctis, S. (1906) 'Sopra alcune varietà della demenza precoce', *Rivista Sperimentale di Freniatria e di Medicina Legale* 32: 141–65.

Desanctis, S. (1908) 'Dementia praecocissima catatonica oder katatonie des fruheron kindesalters?', *Folia Neurobiologica* 2: 9–12.

Earl, C. J. C. (1934) 'The Primitive Catatonic Psychosis of Idiocy', *British Journal of Medical Psychology* 14: 230–53.

Ehlers, S. & Gillberg, C. (1993) 'The Epidemiology of Asperger Syndrome: A Total Population Study', *Journal of Child Psychology and Psychiatry* 34: 1327–50.

Frith, U. (1989) *Autism: Explaining the Enigma*, pp. 42–3. Oxford: Blackwell.

Frith, U. (ed.) (1991) *Autism and Asperger Syndrome.* Cambridge: Cambridge University Press

Gillberg, C. (1992) 'The Emmanuel Miller Memorial Lecture 1991. Autism and Autistic-Like Conditions: Subclasses among Disorders of Empathy', *Journal of Child Psychology and Psychiatry* 33: 813–42.

Haslam, J. (1809) *Observations on Madness and Melancholy*, pp. 185–206. London: Haydon.

Howlin, P. (1997a) *Autism: Preparing for Adulthood.* London: Routledge.

Howlin, P. (1997b) 'Prognosis in Autism: Do Specialist Treatments Affect Outcome?', *European Child and Adolescent Psychiatry.*

Hulse, W. C. (1954) 'Dementia Infantilis', *Journal of Nervous and Mental Diseases* 119: 471–7.

Hunt, A. & Shepherd, C. (1993) 'A Prevalence Study of Autism in Tuberous Sclerosis', *Journal of Autism and Developmental Disorders* 23: 323–40.

Itard, J. M. G. (1801/1807) *The Wild Boy of Aveyron*, trans. G. & M. Humphrey (1967). New York: Appleton, Century, Crofts.

Jervis, G. A. (1963) 'The Clinical Picture', in F. L. Lyman (ed.) Phenylketonuria, pp. 52–61. Springfield, IL: Charles C. Thomas.

Jordan, R. & Powell, S. (1995) *Understanding and Teaching Children with Autism*. Chichester: Wiley.

Kanner, L. (1943) 'Autistic disturbances of Affective Contact', *Nervous Child 2*: 217–50.

Kanner, L. (1949) 'Problems of Nosology and Psychodynamics in Early Childhood Autism', *American Journal of Orthopsychiaty* 19: 416- 26.

Kanner, L. (1964) *A History of the Care and Study of the Mentally Retarded*, p. 7. Springfield, IL: Charles C. Thomas.

Kanner, L. & Eisenberg, L. (1956) 'Early Infantile Autism 1943–1955', *American Journal of Orthopsychiatry* 26: 55–65.

Kolvin, I. (1971) 'Studies in the Childhood Psychoses. I: Diagnostic Criteria and Classification', *British Journal of Psychiatry* 118: 381–4.

Lane, H. (1977) *The Wild Boy of Aveyron*. London: Allen and Unwin.

Lotter, V. (1966) 'Epidemiology of Autistic Conditions in Young Children. I: Prevalence', *Social Psychiatry* 1: 124–37.

Mahler, M. S. (1952) 'On Child Psychoses and Schizophrenia: Autistic and Symbiotic Infantile Psychoses', *Psychoanalytic Study of the Child* 7: 286–305.

Maudsley, H. (1867) 'Insanity of Early Life', in *The Physiology and Pathology of the Mind,* 1st edn, pp. 259–386. New York: Appleton.

Potter, H. W. (1933) 'Schizophrenia in Children', *American Journal of Psychiatry* 12: 1253–69.

Rutter, M. (1970) 'Autistic Children: Infancy to Adulthood', *Seminars in Psychiatry* 2: 435–50

Tantam, D. (1991) 'Asperger Syndrome in Adulthood', in U. Frith (ed.) *Autisim and Asperger Syndrome*, pp. 147–83. Cambridge: Cambridge University Press.

Treffert, D. (1989) *Extraordinary People*, pp. 3–15. New York: Bantam.

Van Krevelen, D. A. (1971) 'Early Infantile Autism and Autistic Psychopathy', *Journal of Autism and Childhood Schizophrenia* 1: 82–6.

Van Krevelen, D.A. & Kuipers, C. (1962) 'The Psychopathology of Autistic Psychopathy', *Acta Paedopsychiatrica* 29: 22–31.

Wing, L. (1981) 'Asperger Syndrome: A Clinical Account, *Psychological Medicine* 11: 115–29.

Wing, L. (1993) 'The Definition and Prevalence of Autism: A Review', *European Child and Adolescent Psychiatry* 2: 61–74.

Wing, L. (1996) *The Autistic Spectrum: A Guide for Parents and Professionals.* London: Constable.

Wing, L. & Gould, J. (1979) 'Severe Impairments of Social Interaction and Associated Abnormalities in Children: Epidemiology and Classification', *Journal of Autism and Developmental Disorders* 9: 11–29.

Wolff, S. (1995) *Loners: The Life Path of Unusual Children.* London: Routledge.

Source: Wing, L. (1997) 'The history of ideas on autism: legends, myths and reality', *Autism*, vol. 1, pp. 13–23.

Chapter 5
Psychology and education: understanding teaching and learning

Karen Littleton and Clare Wood

Contents

	Learning outcomes	195
1	What is 'education'? Notions of teaching and learning	195
2	Behaviourism and education	197
	2.1 Applying operant conditioning to the classroom	198
	2.2 Evaluating behaviourist approaches to education	199
3	Constructivism and education	201
	3.1 Applications of Piagetian ideas	202
	3.2 The significance of peer interaction	205
	3.3 Evaluating constructivism	208
4	Socio-cultural approaches	210
	4.1 Teaching as assisted performance	213
	4.2 The application of Vygotsky's ideas to classroom practice	215
	4.3 Reflections on the socio-cultural approach	219
5	Learning communities and cultures of learning	220
	5.1 Situated learning	221
	5.2 Identity and learning	222
	5.3 Reflecting on psychological accounts of learning	224
6	Conclusion	225
	References	226

Learning outcomes

After you have studied this chapter you should be able to:
1   describe and contrast different psychological accounts of teaching and learning;
2   discuss how such accounts have informed the development of initiatives designed to support children's learning.

1   What is 'education'? Notions of teaching and learning

Extract 1

Learning is to go to school and remember new things that teachers tell and drive into our heads.

Extract 2

Learning is trying to answer your own questions or acquiring a new skill. It is also investigating to increase your knowledge of a subject to gain qualifications or because it interests you.

(Berry and Sahlberg, 1996)

These extracts, from 14–15 year-old children, were taken from a study of children's ideas about learning (Berry and Sahlberg, 1996). Taken together, they illustrate that while teaching and learning can be activities that are directed by adults and focused on outcomes and meeting expectations, they can also be personally motivated processes of cognitive change. Both types of experience are commonplace in children's experiences of attending school. However, the child's description in Extract 2 implies that learning is something that is not confined to formal settings, and it is this broader conception of learning that has been explored by psychologists since the late nineteenth century.

This chapter is concerned with the contributions that psychology and psychologists have made to the field of children's education; specifically, what psychological theory and research has to say about the nature of teaching and learning. However, before we can engage in such a discussion, it is necessary to reflect on the nature of education itself.

Activity I

Allow about
10 minutes

What is 'education'?

This activity will start you thinking about the meanings attached to education.

What does the word 'education' mean to you? What images come to mind? What kinds of things do you think of when you think about your own education? What would you say are the defining features of children's educational experiences?

Comment

Perhaps one image that came to mind was that of a classroom or a teacher. When people think about education they are more likely to focus on teaching in a formal environment or some other kind of planned, adult-led activity. Another common image is of school work or taking examinations. However, this is a rather narrow conception of education. Education can also be thought of as encompassing more informal and spontaneous events and experiences, many of which may be initiated by children themselves, either during solitary activities or when accompanied by other children or adults. Such images also emphasize the importance of learning experiences, which are valued for their own sake, rather than being seen as a means to an end (i.e. acquiring knowledge).

Many ideas emerge as a result of thinking about the meanings associated with education. One useful way of organizing these is to think of them as six dimensions that constitute different aspects of educational experience (see Figure 1). Within each of these dimensions there are tensions that exist. For example, many psychologists are concerned with the 'outcomes' of education; that is, the end products of learning, such as increases in ability, or skills gained. However, as you will see, other psychologists take issue with such a narrow focus, arguing that the very processes of learning can be valued for their own sake (irrespective of the degree of gain obtained as a result). Moreover, the ability to reason or work out a solution can be viewed as an outcome of education just as test scores or qualifications are. Psychologists are therefore increasingly concerned with capturing and understanding the *processes* of teaching and learning in an attempt to resolve the perceived imbalance in the psychology of education literature.

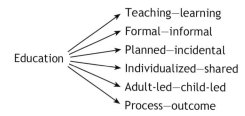

Figure 1   Dimensions of educational experience.

Research into the psychology of education has acknowledged and sought to explore these various dimensions of educational experience, although various traditions of research focus on the interplay between some elements more than others. This chapter will introduce you to three key theoretical traditions in the psychology of education that have influenced approaches to teaching and learning, both within the classroom and outside it. These are *behaviourism, constructivism* and *socio-cultural approaches*.

Summary of Section 1

- Education is a broad term that captures a variety of experiences, both formal and informal.
- Psychologists are interested in all aspects of educational experience, although theoretical perspectives differ in terms of which aspects of education they place emphasis on.
- The three main theoretical traditions considered in this chapter are behaviourism, constructivism and socio-cultural approaches.

2 Behaviourism and education

SG

Behaviourism refers to an approach to learning that emphasizes the role of external, environmental factors on an individual's behaviour. It describes how a seemingly neutral aspect of someone's environment (e.g. being in a playground) can become associated with another aspect (e.g. being bullied) that reliably produces an involuntary reaction (e.g. anxiety). The association means that, over time, the mere presence of the previously neutral stimulus is enough to trigger the involuntary behaviour (e.g. being in the playground is enough to prompt a feeling of anxiety). This involuntary reaction may even generalize to other related stimuli (e.g. going to school). This type of simple associative learning is known as classical conditioning.

Classical conditioning
The learning of an association between a reflex behaviour and a previously unrelated environmental stimulus.

However, the form of behaviourism that has been most productive with respect to classroom practice is that of operant conditioning, outlined by the influential psychologist B. F. Skinner (1905–90). Put simply, operant conditioning is concerned with:

- the various features of the environment immediately prior to a person producing a particular behaviour (so-called *antecedents*);
- the *behaviour* itself; and
- the *consequences* for the person as a result of producing that behaviour (Skinner, 1938).

So, for example, take the case of a girl working individually in a quiet room, who produces a good piece of writing and is praised by her parents as a result. In this case the antecedents would be *working on her own* and *being in a quiet place*, the behaviour is the production of *good work*, and the consequence is the *praise from her parents*.

According to this approach, both the antecedents that prompted the behaviour, and the consequences of the behaviour, determine whether the behaviour will be produced again in the future. So the girl in our example, in having received praise for her good work in the past would be motivated to try to do the same again, but would also need to have access to the same environmental conditions as before (i.e. being able to work alone somewhere quiet).

2.1 Applying operant conditioning to the classroom

The application of operant conditioning in the classroom takes two main forms. The first is concerned with managing and modifying 'problem' behaviour in the classroom, and motivating children to stay 'on task' (e.g. Wheldall *et al.*, 1986). The second centres on the potential of operant conditioning to improve academic achievement (Skinner, 1954). Skinner's approach to teaching is known as 'programmed instruction' (also referred to as 'programmed learning'). Programmed instruction follows the following sequence:

1. The child is given some information to learn.
2. The child's knowledge of that information is tested through a question.
3. If the correct answer is given, the child's behaviour is reinforced through a reward, such as praise.
4. If an incorrect answer is given, the original information is repeated, or presented in a simplified form.

Some early forms of programmed instruction were presented via 'teaching machines', which presented the teaching materials in the correct sequence. These were, in a way, precursors to some of today's educational computer software, which operate on the same behaviourist principles of reinforcement and immediate feedback. For example, behaviourist models of learning underpin the design of contemporary educational software known as integrated learning systems (ILS). These are computer systems that present students with 'individualized' teaching materials for a range of curriculum areas. The computer has a large database of tutorial activities, plus a mixture of self-assessments and formally graded assessments of the student's ability, and maintains a record of the child's progress. The system directs the student through the teaching and assessment materials depending on the student's progress and ability. Seated at computers, the students learn individually, isolated from the social context of the classroom in what the designers of the software consider to be an idealized learning environment. As Wood *et al.* (1999) note in their evaluation of such software, such an approach sees technology as:

> One means of separating the learning process from the irrationalities, vicissitudes and distractions of the social environment ... the basic conception [is] of learning as a solitary process, best supported through individualised instruction.

(Wood *et al.*, 1999, p. 95)

2.2 Evaluating behaviourist approaches to education

During the 1960s and 1970s programmed instruction was found to achieve more rapid gains in knowledge than traditional classroom teaching (Jamieson *et al.*, 1974). It was found to be the most effective technique for remediating difficulties in literacy and numeracy at that time (Kennedy, 1978). Nevertheless, it has its critics. First, the emphasis it places on individualized instruction runs counter to other approaches that value interpersonal communication as a necessary element of effective teaching and learning (see Section 4). Consistent with such criticisms, evaluations of ILS suggest that, overall, the children gain little in terms of knowledge and skills from this approach compared to that of traditional, teacher-led teaching practices (Wood *et al.*, 1999). A further criticism is that programmed instruction might position learners as 'deficient' (Littleton and Hoyles, 2002). It also has been said to inhibit the development of children's spontaneous motivation to learn, especially as the content of the sessions is determined in advance, instead of being responsive to what the children find interesting (Lepper and Greene, 1978). A further issue with this approach is the degree of careful observation that is needed to apply the principles of operant conditioning in an appropriate way. Consequently, one source of criticism has been the observation that principles of reinforcement and punishment are often applied in lax, oversimplified or inappropriate ways (Travers, 1983). While this should not be seen as a criticism of behaviourist approaches to teaching and learning per se, it does highlight a limitation of them: namely, that the degree of care and precision with which its principles need to be applied are such that it is extremely difficult to operationalize behaviourist principles appropriately outside of a controlled setting. Farnham-Diggory (1981) in particular has criticized proponents of behaviourism for supporting an over-simplified view of learning processes, saying that 'If they really want to help children learn, then why are they so quick to avoid the hard work of understanding what learning – especially their own learning – really involves?' (Farnham-Diggory, 1981, p. 60).

However, it is important to recognize, in the context of such discussions, that Skinner (1968) acknowledged that 'it is quite possible that the behavior of a man thinking is the most subtle and complex phenomenon ever submitted to scientific analysis' (Skinner, 1968, p. 140). For Skinner, thought is a behaviour, and therefore subject to the same operant principles that other behaviours are; namely, it is a response to an aspect or aspects of one's environment. Skinner's views on teaching and learning were, however, not so very out of step with the conclusions of other theorists, as you will see in the following sections. In particular, he believed that 'It is important that the student should learn without being taught, solve problems by himself, explore the unknown, make decisions, and behave in original ways, and these activities should, if possible, be taught' (Skinner, 1968, cited in Bigge and Shermis, 1999, p. 116).

Principles of teaching and learning that have their origins in programmed instruction, such as the need for immediate feedback and the need to tailor the information to be learned to the learner's current level of knowledge, are commonly reflected in other theorists' work (e.g. Kamii, 1994) and continue to be influential.

Activity 2   *Dimensions of education and behaviourism*

Allow about
10 minutes

This activity will help you consider the dimensions of education and how these relate to behaviourist theory.

Look back at the aspects of education summarized in Figure 1. Which elements are emphasized in behaviourist approaches to teaching and learning?

Comment

In terms of the aspects of education that were introduced in Figure 1, behaviourist approaches relate to both teaching and learning. However, they relate most closely to formal contexts and where there is a planned sequence of adult-led or adult-controlled activities, which children are expected engage in on an individual level. The success of such approaches is measured by their outcomes, both in terms of amount learned, and the speed of learning.

In Section 3, we consider constructivist approaches, which place less emphasis on environmental influences on learning, and see children as active in their intellectual development.

Summary of Section 2

- Behaviourism is a theoretical approach to learning that emphasizes the role of external, environmental factors on an individual's behaviour.
- The principles of operant conditioning have been used to develop an approach to teaching known as 'programmed instruction' in which information is presented, knowledge about it is tested and feedback is immediate.
- Principles of operant conditioning are also reflected in more recent computer-based instructional systems.
- Behaviourist approaches to education have been criticized for downplaying the role of interpersonal communication in effective learning, for being unresponsive to children's spontaneous interests and desire to learn, and for being difficult to operationalize effectively.

3 Constructivism and education

SG

The early 1960s saw a particular interest in approaches to learning and development that focused less on behaviour and its environmental influences and more on understanding the cognitive processes that underpin learning. The clearest example of this was the rise to prominence of the work of Jean Piaget (1896–1980). Piaget's work was concerned with the nature of children's mental representations of the world around them. According to Piaget, the fundamental issue for educationalists is to understand the nature of knowledge and intelligence. This is called genetic epistemology, and because Piaget argued that it is best approached by studying the origins, or genesis, of intelligence in childhood he is sometimes referred to as a 'genetic epistemologist' (note that genetic does not have anything to do with genes or inheritance in this context).

Genetic epistemology Piaget's term for the study of the origins and development of knowledge.

At the heart of Piaget's theory is the idea that intelligence derives from the co-ordination of *action* in the child's environment. Through such action children come to explore and build personal representations of how the world 'works'. These representations become progressively less dependent on physical experience as rules are abstracted, ultimately leading to the ability to make predictions about aspects of the environment without needing to have had direct experience of them. The development and education of the intellect are thus a matter of active discovery of reality. According to Piaget, intellectual development occurs through maturation of the nervous system but also through the 'logico-mathematical experience' which children gain by actively experimenting with their environment. Teaching may have a place, but what is learned is ultimately dependent on what children are able to assimilate into their emerging mental schemas – and 'all assimilation is a restructuration or a reinvention' (Piaget, 1969, cited in Light *et al.*, 1991, p. 14). Intellectual development is therefore a process of self-regulation and adaptation to one's environment. It is this sense of children reinventing and constructing knowledge for themselves that gives this approach the name 'constructivism'.

Piaget uses the term 'learning' rather narrowly to refer to knowledge acquired by transmission from one person to another, and contrasts this with the internal cognitive process of equilibration:

> Equilibration is a creative process of invention for Piaget, who goes farther than almost anybody in asserting the individual construction of general logical principles. In fact he argues that direct instruction will actually inhibit the child's understandings if instruction gets in the way of the child's own exploration.

(Newman *et al.*, 1989, p. 92)

Piaget's work offers what might be called a horticultural analogy, suggesting that adults should largely restrict themselves to providing a rich, stimulating and generally supportive environment for children just as a gardener provides good conditions for a plant to grow well. The health and vigour of the plant and the speed of its growth are determined from within. Indeed, just as excessive pruning, shaping or interference on the part of the gardener might well prejudice the plant's development, so direct or intrusive adult intervention could be harmful to the natural trajectory of children's intellectual development.

3.1 Applications of Piagetian ideas

During the 1960s Piaget's views on child development were used to support educational ideas of 'progressive' education in the UK and also influenced the development of the curriculum. For example, the following quotation is from a popular mathematics scheme of the day:

> The stress is on *how* to learn, not what to teach. Running through all the work is the central notion that the children must be set free to make their own discoveries and think for themselves, and so achieve understanding, instead of learning off mysterious drills.

> (Nuffield Mathematics Project, 1967, cited in Davis, 1991, p. 21)

Piaget's ideas also gave rise to notions of 'readiness' where it was suggested that to learn effectively, educational experiences need to be matched to a child's current level of understanding and acknowledge that children's interests and ways of learning are diverse and subject to change. This view may now seem to be rather obvious, however it was not a common view at the time when Piaget was proposing it. Indeed, some education systems, most notably in the USA, were implementing curricular reforms in which abstract mathematical reasoning was taught to children very early in their academic careers, at a point when most would be at Piaget's concrete operational stage.

Piaget believed that the ability to reason in an abstract way did not emerge until around the age of 11 years. As a result, proponents of Piaget's ideas were, and continue to be, highly critical of attempts to 'hothouse' children into ways of thinking that are set as targets by adults (e.g. Kohlberg and Gilligan, 1971). This argument views 'formal' methods of instruction, such as worksheets and reference textbooks, as unsuitable for young children's ways of learning, and only teaches them that learning is a stressful experience (Elkind, 1981). As Ginsberg and Opper comment, 'What is needed is sensitivity and flexibility on the teacher's part – a willingness to look closely at the child's actions, to learn from the child, and to be guided by the child's spontaneous interests' (Ginsberg and Opper, cited in Crain, 2005, p. 139). In fact, the American 'new maths' curriculum of the 1950s and 1960s was judged to be largely unsuccessful, and this was attributed to the fact that it ignored the developmental level of the children being taught (Ginsberg and Opper, cited in Crain, 2005).

Many attempts have been made to develop educational approaches that apply Piaget's ideas to classroom activity. An excellent example of such an application is the work of Constance Kamii (1985, 1994, 2004) who has applied Piagetian ideas to the teaching of mathematics. She argues that children need to rediscover and reinvent mathematical principles for themselves, but that the ways in which numbers are represented (by digits) and the mathematical procedures that are taught inhibit children's ability to do so.

The result is that children learn mathematical procedures in the absence of genuine conceptual understanding of why the answer they have produced is 'correct'. By teaching children 'adult' procedures for representing numbers and making calculations, children are forced to reject their own ways of reasoning about numbers, and become dependent on tools and methods that can be counterproductive, such as the spatial arrangement of digits, the use of pen and paper to solve problems, or the presence of adults. For example, Kamii notes that when children, aged around 9 years, begin to add or subtract numbers such as:

18 +

<u>17</u>

the children's preference is to add the columns working from left to right, whereas the adult procedure is opposite.

> Children's first methods are admittedly inefficient. However, if they are free to do their own thinking, they invent increasingly efficient procedures ... by trying to bypass the constructive process, we prevent them from making sense of arithmetic.

(Kamii, 1994, p. 32)

Her position is supported by evidence from US classrooms where 8-year-old children were either taught standard adult procedures for solving addition problems, or were encouraged to develop their own approaches to mathematical reasoning. They were later given some written addition problems to solve verbally and overall there was little difference between the groups in terms of the number of problems solved correctly. However, one of the problems:

7 + 52 + 186

was presented twice, once in a 'vertical' format (as shown earlier) and once in the 'horizontal' format (shown in this paragraph). Again, there were no differences in the children's ability to solve the problem when it was presented in the vertical format, but when it was presented in the more unfamiliar horizontal format some striking differences emerged. Forty-five per cent of the children who had not been taught adult procedures for solving addition problems (and who were not coached at home in them, as the teacher was in contact with the parents and actively prohibiting this) solved the problem correctly. These children typically began their solution along the lines of '180 and 50 is 230 ...'. Their incorrect answers were more often than not in an appropriate number range (between 255 and 235).

In the class where the children had been taught formal procedures, the children typically got around 12 per cent of the answers right, with some children protesting that they needed a pencil, or 'We haven't had this kind in class' or 'I forgot what the teacher said'. Their incorrect solutions were either very high (between 9308 and 295) or very low (200 to 29), with none in the mid-range. Their difficulties appeared to be the result of adding numbers in the wrong way (e.g. adding the '7' to the '1' in '186'), or adding them as if they were single digits (i.e. 7 + 5 + 2 + 1 + 8 + 6 = 29) and not realizing that this cannot be possible because the answer they arrived at was lower than two of the numbers they had started with!

Kamii argues that instead of teaching children 'accepted' adult procedures for solving mathematical problems, children should be allowed to devise their own procedures. Teachers are encouraged to provide the children with activities that they enjoy and are motivated to complete for their own sake. The role of the teacher during these activities is to prompt the children to reflect on their own thinking, rather than correct errors or provide answers. Kamii (1994) notes that children particularly like spontaneously occurring 'problems' in which the teacher prompts the children to answer a question that is part of the classroom activity they are currently engaged in, such as calculating how many things are needed for a particular type of activity, or working out how many people will be going on the class trip from the amount of money that has been paid in.

Kamii (1994) also uses commercially available number orientated games (e.g. Yahtzee, Rummikub) and has devised some of her own (see Box 1) that are intended to stimulate children into spontaneously thinking about and reflecting on number and calculations.

BOX 1

Leapfrog

Materials: Any commercially made or home-made board; one or more markers for each player; two 10- or 12-sided dice.

Play: The players take turns rolling the dice. If the total is an even number, the player advances by half of this total. (For example, if a 6 and an 8 are rolled, the player advanced 7 spaces). If the total rolled is an odd number, the player does not move at all. The first person to reach the goal is the winner. The total of 13 is lucky, and the player can advance 13 spaces.

Source: Kamii, 1994, p.107.

Kamii describes the advantages of activities like those in Box 1 as follows:

> Few children ever ask for worksheets, but they often beg to play math games and protest when the teacher's response is 'no'. For children's development of autonomy, it is important that they work and learn for their own satisfaction, without being manipulated with extrinsic motivators.
>
> Games are better than worksheets also because feedback is immediate and from peers. Immediate feedback is obviously more effective than a reaction that comes the next day, when children do not care what happened any more. Moreover, with games, unlike with worksheets, each child has the possibility of supervising everyone else's work and learns to be critical and self-reliant. Furthermore, games provide opportunities for creating strategies.

(Kamii, 1994, p. 99)

Kamii's (1994, 2004) evaluations of her approach show that there is little difference in the levels of attainment achieved by the children who experienced her methods of teaching compared to those who experienced traditional teaching approaches. However, as the children's performance during the verbal problem solving assessments described earlier demonstrated, the children taught by her methods showed greater levels of understanding, and demonstrated a more autonomous approach to their learning.

3.2 The significance of peer interaction

Piaget's account of the development of human reasoning paid little attention to the question of what particular types of experience were necessary to facilitate progress. Where particular experiences were referred to these tended to be encounters between the child and the physical world. Piaget and his co-workers paid limited attention to the *social* dimensions of experience, such that the Piagetian child could be regarded almost as a child-scientist, single-handedly (re)discovering physics and mathematics by grappling with the puzzles and paradoxes of the natural world.

Although this is something of a simplification of Piaget's position, it serves to contrast this later Piagetian work with his earliest research conducted in the 1920s and 1930s. In these early studies, based for the most part on observations of his own children, Piaget developed the key concept of egocentrism. Both in his work on *The Language and Thought of the Child* (1926) and on *The Moral Judgement of the Child* (1932), he saw the principal barrier to the pre-school child's progress as being an inability to 'decentre'; to take account of other people's points of view. The egocentric child, he suggested, does not understand other points of view, and takes his or her own view for reality. This egocentrism limits moral thinking and communication in fairly obvious ways, but it also limits cognitive development in other more subtle ways. Since children cannot appreciate that the first thing that strikes them about a problem might not be the *only* way the problem can be thought about, they cannot reflect on alternatives or understand how different factors might interact with one another. Importantly, Piaget saw this egocentrism of children's thinking as being overcome through social experience of a particular kind.

Egocentrism
The inability to understand the existence and/or nature of points of view other than one's own.

Piaget regarded children's relations with adults (whether parents or others) as inherently asymmetrical, and the difference in power and status was such that children could not balance their own views against those of adults. However, in more symmetrical relationships between the child and his or her peers, differences of viewpoint could provide the foundations for intellectual progress. When children interact with one another on more or less equal terms there are opportunities for a divergence of views and also a social need to reach a resolution of this difference of view. Thus, peer interaction was seen to hold a very special potential for helping egocentric ('pre-operational') children to overcome their egocentrism and make progress towards higher level ('operational') thinking.

This idea lay dormant for many years, little explored in subsequent work either by Piaget or by his co-workers. However, in the 1970s, at a time when social psychology was establishing itself in Geneva, these social dimensions of Piaget's theory began to be researched more systematically. In these explorations some of the 'classic' tests of operational thinking devised by Piaget were used to explore the argument that he had himself advanced many years earlier regarding the facilitatory role of peer interaction. The principal architect of these experiments was Willem Doise, together with Gabriel Mugny and Anne-Nelly Perret-Clermont. These researchers used the three mountains task, in which the children were required to indicate what could be seen from the viewpoint of another person, and adapted the procedure so that the effects of peer interaction on children's developing cognition could be directly assessed (see Research summary 1).

RESEARCH SUMMARY 1

Egocentrism and socio-cognitive conflict

As a pre-test, 100 children, aged between 5 and 7 years, were shown, on their own, a model village with buildings arranged around a pond. On another table next to the child was a base, with the pond marked on it, but no buildings. The orientation of the pond might be the same as the original, or rotated by 180 degrees (see Figure 2). The child was then asked to reconstruct the village on the second board so that the two were identical. Generally, the children found it difficult to reconstruct the village accurately when the board was rotated. Such difficulties indicate a degree of egocentrism, as the correct arrangement required the children to decentre from their own viewpoint.

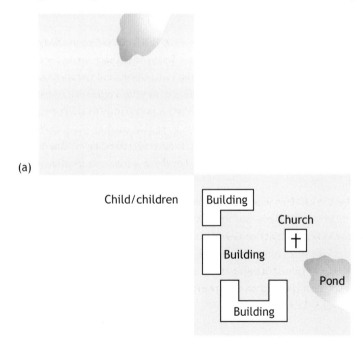

(a)

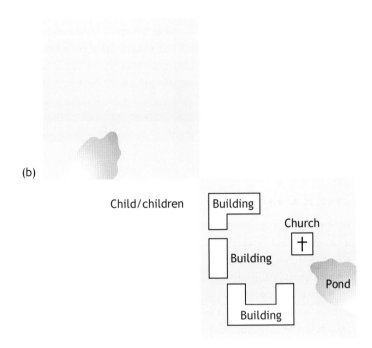

(b)

Child/children

Building

Church

Building

Pond

Building

Figure 2 Village representations. (a) The pond in the same position for viewing two tables. (b) The pond has been rotated 180 degrees.

The next phase of their study involved the children either working alone on the task (the control group) or working in pairs. Some of the pairs were constructed so that the children working together were of the same ability and some of the pairs were based on a mismatch of ability on the task. There were two types of mismatched pairs – in one case the least able children (Level 1) were matched with children at the next level of ability (Level 2), in the other case the least able children were matched with children who were even more advanced in their understanding of the task (Level 3). The mismatched pairs would expose the Level 1 children to a different viewpoint, thereby inducing a degree of socio-cognitive conflict.

Socio-cognitive conflict
Exposure to conflicting ideas presented by a peer that force a child to reconsider their own understanding.

Finally, the children were all re-assessed on the task individually as they had been in the pre-test to see if there was any change in their individual ability to solve the task. The results indicated that the Level 1 children who gained the most from pre to post test were those who were paired with a Level 2 partner. Those children working with a Level 3 child gained little from this exposure, as the Level 3 children tended to impose their solution rather than engage in the discussion and disagreement that characterized the Level 1–Level 2 pairs.

Source: adapted from Doise and Mugny, 1984.

Doise and colleagues interpreted their findings in terms of socio-cognitive conflict. A Level 1 child paired with a Level 2 child finds themselves confronted with a solution which conflicts with their own. This conflict, and the socially engendered need to resolve it, prompts the child to re-examine his or her own initial response, and may lead the child to recognize a higher order solution to the problem which resolves the apparent conflict (Mugny *et al.*, 1981). Note that for this to occur, it is necessary that the children's initial solutions differ, but it is not necessary for any one solution to be more advanced than another, or for any of them to be correct. What drives the process is that resolution of children's partial or centred solutions can in the end only be found by adopting a higher level, more decentred solution, thus ensuring cognitive progress.

Figure 3   Peer interaction offers children the opportunity to experience a variety of different viewpoints.

This work and other related studies lent weight to the idea that peer facilitation could have effects on children's cognitive development. More generally, it also helped to stimulate a much wider interest in research into the ways that peer interaction can facilitate individual cognitive development, some of which will be considered in Section 4.

3.3   Evaluating constructivism

Piaget's theories are not without their critics. Some have highlighted an over-emphasis on the cognitive and individualized nature of development and learning, indicating that it is also possible, as we shall see in the next section, to conceive of these as primarily social activities taking place between individuals situated in specific cultural contexts.

Cultural transmission becomes identified with a coercive social process of direct instruction. The possibility that there are cultural transmission processes that are (in part) not experienced coercively and that these processes require the child's active participation are not considered.

(Newman *et al.*, 1989, p. 92)

Another criticism of Piaget's view of development and learning is that it offers a very limited view of the intellectual 'product'. Piaget's theory was rooted in his interest in how intelligence is a form of 'adaptation' to the environment. His theory implies that by the time we reach physical maturity we also reach intellectual maturity, and that this is characterized by the use of reasoned logic and 'scientific' thought. However, it has been suggested that this is a highly ethnocentric view as other types of intelligence and thought, such as the ability to reflect on one's own thought processes, are valuable but not acknowledged in Piaget's conception of intellectual development (Kincheloe and Steinberg, 1993).

If you reconsider the various dimensions of education outlined in Figure 1 at the beginning of the chapter, you can see that Piaget's discussion of children's intellectual development centres on a very different set of concerns compared to those of Skinner. In Piaget's account the emphasis is very much on learning to the exclusion of teaching, which he considered to be potentially detrimental. This learning was primarily conceived of as informal and incidental, with the focus on the individual child leading their own learning experiences, which are sometimes influenced by contact with peers, although the resolution of cognitive conflict is always a personal process. However, there appears to be an equal emphasis on processes of learning and the outcomes of those processes.

Summary of Section 3

- Piaget's approach to child development, referred to as constructivism, emphasizes the cognitive processes that underpin learning and sees the child as actively constructing their own learning, independently of adults.
- Constructivism leads to an emphasis on learning rather than teaching in classrooms. Activities from which children are able to develop their own strategies and ideas are valued.
- Peer interaction is seen as important in leading children to overcome egocentric ways of reasoning.
- Kamii has demonstrated that a constructivist approach to teaching mathematics promotes greater understanding of mathematical concepts than traditional approaches.
- Constructivist approaches have been criticized for emphasizing learning as an individualized process, thereby downplaying the social and cultural context it occurs within.

4   Socio-cultural approaches

'Socio-cultural' approaches have their origins in the work of the Russian developmental psychologist Lev Vygotsky (1896–1934). Like Piaget, Vygotsky was interested in the development of cognitive processes (which he termed the 'higher mental functions'– thinking, reasoning and understanding) and adopted a constructivist approach. However, there are some important differences between the two theorists. Piaget viewed development as a process which starts from an infant who is 'autistic' (not in the clinical sense we tend to use today but in the sense of being inwardly focused), 'wrapped up in him/herself' and in this sense profoundly separate from others. Development is seen as progressing through a long period in which the child remains relatively egocentric, to an eventual condition in which the child's thinking and behaviour effectively becomes socialized. Development thus proceeds from the individual to the social. Vygotsky, however, turns this process on its head, seeing even the youngest infant as a comprehensively social organism. From this perspective it is through interaction with others that the child comes to have a growing awareness of self and a capacity for reflection. For Vygotsky, development proceeds from the social to the individual.

Furthermore, the achievement of individuality and mental maturity depends not only on interaction with others (as in the peer interactions we described in the previous section), but on interaction with others who are more advanced and capable members of the society in which the child is growing up. Any society contains a wealth of 'tools for thought', the most obvious example being its language. The developmental task is conceived as a kind of apprenticeship, served by the child under the tutelage of adults, whereby these 'cultural tools' become part and parcel of the child's own mental resources. Consider, for example, the interaction reproduced in Box 2 where a 4-year-old child is learning how to trace the shape of letters with his finger.

Tracing letters made from sandpaper

Teacher: Do it one more time Matty because you did it so nicely (pause) always start at the top (pause) that's it

Matty: [While tracing the letter 'p' with his index finger] /p/ /p/ /p/

[NB. '/ /' denotes that the child is making the sound associated with the letter]

Teacher: Beautiful so we've got /p/ (pause) and

Matty: /e/

Teacher: /e/ and (pause)?

Matty: /s/

Teacher: /g/ I'm going to move them right in front of you Matty okay so you can see them more easily sit back a little bit [moves letters in front of Matty] okay /p/ /e/ and /g/

Matty: /p/ /e/ /g/

Teacher: Yes

Matty: Do you know what?

Teacher: What Matty?

Matty: Does that spell 'trace'? /p/ /e/ /g/

Teacher: /p/ /e/ /g/

Matty: /p/ /e/ /g/ does does that spell 'trace'?

Teacher: It doesn't spell 'trace'. It does spell a word though funnily enough.

Matty: Erm what does it spell?

Teacher: Let's see /p/ /e/ /g/ (pause) /p/ /e/ /g/

Matty: Mud!

Teacher: [Laughs] Good try!

Matty: Er 'mud' has M in it

Teacher: It does doesn't it. Does this one have M in it?

Matty: No

Teacher: No it does /p/ /e/ /g/ (pause) /p/ /eg/ /p/ /eg/

Matty: Egg (pause) peg!

Teacher: Yes you've actually got 'peg' there.

In this example, the adult is teaching the child how to form letters as an introduction to writing, as well as teaching him about letter sounds in readiness for learning to read. Although she is not attempting to teach him to read, the context of the activity prompts the child to guess at the meaning of the shapes he is forming. Although his initial guess is wrong, with help from the adult he arrives at the correct answer without being told it first. The child is clearly 'apprenticed' to the adult and the various forms of learning going on in this extract (learning how to write, the sounds made by letters, how to 'decode' words from letters) all are literacy skills learned in a specific cultural and interpersonal context, rather than an individual one.

Source: The Open University, 2002.

Vygotsky proposed that the processes which go on *between* the child and others become the basis for processes which subsequently go on *within* the child. Discussion, interaction and argument become internalized as the basis for reflection and logical reasoning. Language is seen to hold the key to the processes of internalization. Language originally is a social means of communication, but it becomes the chief means by which individuals become able to reason and regulate their own behaviour. Language is thus significant because it mediates much of our experience of the world and how we come to understand it. Consequently, meanings constructed through social interaction become embedded in individual thought processes.

Vygotsky's approach proposes a more central and positive role for adults in fostering children's learning. The learning process is, as in Piaget's theory, seen as a constructive one, but it is not the child alone who is doing the constructing. Instead, the construction of knowledge and understanding is seen as a fundamentally *social* activity, through which the cognitive resources of society are gradually made available to the child. In this way Vygotsky offers the possibility of keeping Piaget's emphasis on the constructive and creative aspects of mental development without relegating 'social transmission' and 'instruction' to the status of irrelevant and interfering factors.

As noted above, Vygotsky clearly saw interaction with adults as a key element of successful mental development. In relation to this he talked about children's zone of proximal development (ZPD), which refers to the difference between what a child can do unaided, and what they can achieve with the support of a more knowledgeable other. While 'ability' is typically measured by what children can achieve by their own efforts, Vygotsky argued that what they could achieve with support was a more sensitive measure of children's intellectual potential. The ZPD is well illustrated by Matty and his teacher in Box 2, where the adult guides Matty to answer his own question through careful use of repetition and verbal prompts, but without actually telling him the answer.

The metaphor that has been most widely used to capture the sort of guidance that supports learners in their progress through the ZPD is that of 'scaffolding'. Introduced by Wood *et al.* (1976), it captures the sense in which, through encouragement, focusing, demonstration, reminders and suggestions, a learner can be supported in mastering a task or achieving understanding. As the name suggests, scaffolding is strictly temporary, although without it the child's learning would have been impossible to construct. The role of the adult in scaffolding the child's learning is to lend support to the child's own constructive activity.

Psychologists have attempted to study scaffolding in order to define what constitutes 'effective tuition'. Related to this is the notion of *contingency*, which refers to the way that the degree of help offered by the adult is adjusted in response to the progress of the child. For example, Wood and Middleton (1975) carried out an experimental study designed to capture how adults give over more of a task to a child as they becomes more competent (see Research summary 2).

Zone of proximal development (ZPD)
The difference between what a child can do unaided, and what the same child can do with the help of more able others.

RESEARCH SUMMARY 2

Studying contingent instruction

In a classic study, Wood and Middleton (1975) looked at the different ways in which an adult can help a child to complete a task. They asked the mothers of 4-year-olds to teach their child to complete a three dimensional jigsaw puzzle in the shape of a stepped pyramid. The task is a complex one for a child of this age, and those who attempt it alone are not usually successful until the age of 7–8 years. However, when asked to complete the puzzle alone just after having been taught how to do it, those 4 year olds who were taught well by their mothers were able to complete most or all of the puzzle.

In order to decide what being taught 'well' entailed, Wood and Middleton classified the different types of tuition into five levels as follows:

Level 1   General verbal encouragement.

Level 2   Specific verbal instruction.

Level 3   Assists in choice of material.

Level 4   Prepares material for assembly.

Level 5   Demonstrates an operation.

Note that as the level increases, the specificity of the help given to the child also increases, whilst the amount of responsibility taken by the child lessens.

The children who were most successful had mothers who used a variety of these levels of instruction. However, what was important was that the type of instruction used by the adult was dependent on the preceding success of the child. If the child could not understand the last instruction, his mother would immediately offer a higher level of help. For example, a child who could not correctly put together the pieces of the puzzle his mother had pointed out for him (Level 3) would get more help. His mother might put the correct pieces next to each other in the correct orientation (Level 4). On the other hand, if the child was successful with the 'Level 3 ' instruction, she might tell him what type of pieces he needed to put together next, but would leave him to select them (Level 2). In this way, the mother ensured that her response was contingent on the child's previous action. A failure by the child resulted in an instruction from the mother that increased the level of control, whereas a success resulted in a decrease in control: this is what Wood and Middleton refer to as *contingent instruction*.

Source: Wood and Middleton, 1975.

Although contingent instruction sounds easy, in practice it is quite hard to achieve. In a later study Wood and his colleagues (1978) found that an experimenter who had been trained to teach contingently did so only 85 per cent of the time.

> Monitoring children's activity, remembering what one had said or done to prompt that activity, and responding quickly to their efforts at an appropriate level is a demanding intellectual feat. Effective teaching is as difficult as the learning it seeks to promote.

(Wood, 1998, p. 164)

4.1 Teaching as assisted performance

Two researchers, Tharp and Gallimore (1998), have extended Vygotsky's notion of the ZPD and have drawn upon Wood *et al.*'s (1976) conception of 'scaffolding' to present what they call a theory of *teaching as assisted performance*. Tharp and Gallimore characterize the ZPD not as a single growing point for an individual, but as a multitude of 'growing edges' which relate to all areas of developing competence:

There is no single zone for each individual. For any domain of skill, a ZPD can be created. There are cultural zones as well as individual zones, because there are cultural variations in the competencies that a child must acquire through interaction in a particular society ... Boys in Micronesia, where sailing a canoe is a fundamental skill, will have a ZPD for the skills of navigation, created in interaction with the sailing masters. A girl in the Navajo weaving community will have experiences in a zone not quite like any encountered by the daughters of Philadelphia. Whatever the activity, in the ZPD we find that assistance is provided by the teacher, the adult, the expert, the more capable peer.

(Tharp and Gallimore, 1998, p. 96)

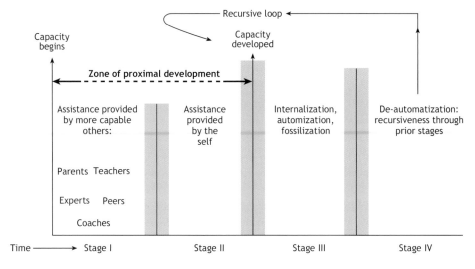

Figure 4   Progression through the ZPD and beyond.

Tharp and Gallimore also see progression through the ZPD in terms of four stages (see Figure 4). In Stage 1 performance is directly assisted by more capable others through scaffolding of one kind or another. In Stage 2 the learner effectively takes over the role of the scaffolder in relation to his or her own learning. This often means 'talking oneself through' a task, remembering requests, reminders and injunctions previously given, and so on. Stage 3 is marked by the falling away of such self-guidance, as performance becomes automatic. The fourth stage recognizes the fact that individuals can be thrown back to earlier stages of the acquisition process by such stressors as tiredness, or by changes in the precise conditions of the task.

Activity 3   *Learning a skill*

Allow about   *This activity will help you to consider how well Tharp and Gallimore's account relates to your own*
10 minutes   *experiences of learning.*

Go through some of your more recent learning experiences, particularly any which involved new skills such as learning to drive a car, or use a new piece of equipment or other technology. How well does an account in terms of a ZPD, or more specifically in terms of Tharp and Gallimore's stages, fit with your recollection of your learning experience?

Comment

Ontogenetic
Relating to the
developmental
history of an
individual.

Microgenetic
Relating to the
developmental
history of a
particular
psychological
process, at a
particular point in
time and in a
particular context.

The fact that we can see some of these processes at work in our own experiences as adults raises an important issue. The whole history of development in the child could be viewed as a single, age-related process, going from Tharp and Gallimore's Stage 1 (where assistance is provided by more capable others) through Stage 2 (where assistance is provided by the self) to eventual internalization in Stage 3. In some ways this seems to fit facts: infants and younger children are obviously heavily dependent on others for help; around 4 to 6 years of age they engage in a great deal of 'talking to themselves' out loud, which diminishes as they become more self-sufficient learners during the school years. Equally, however, we could take the view that these stages apply to learning at whatever age it occurs. Even as adults when we encounter a new learning situation our learning experience can be described in the same terms. Looked at from this point of view, age may in fact make rather little difference and what is at issue is the level of one's expertise in relation to a particular problem. Tharp and Gallimore suggest that while there is an overall *ontogenetic* development which follows the course that they outline, this outline will also apply equally well to the *microgenetic* processes in learning at any point in the lifespan.

4.2 The application of Vygotsky's ideas to classroom practice

Much of the research conducted from a Vygotskian standpoint has tended to see effective teaching and learning exchanges as essentially incidental to ongoing joint engagement in activities. These exchanges can be between mothers and children in the home (e.g. Rogoff and Gardner, 1984, Rogoff, 1990) or between experts and novices in traditional craft practices such as tailoring or weaving (Greenfield and Lave, 1982; Lave and Wenger, 1991). Such work has typically emphasized the interpersonal, informal and incidental nature of teaching and learning. It has also stimulated a strong tradition of research that seeks to understand teaching and learning as both cultural activity, and one that is necessarily 'embedded' in an immediate social context which enables children to make sense of their new experiences. Efforts have been made to use a Vygotskian approach to illuminate what goes on in the classroom and this line of work has reported mixed success. For example, attempts to apply the concept of 'scaffolding' more directly in relation to classroom practice have, in at least some cases (e.g. Bliss *et al.*, 1996), been unable to find any evidence of scaffolding by teachers.

One of the most successful applications of Vygotskian theory to classroom practice has involved researchers exploring how, by skilfully guiding classroom discussion, the class teacher can establish and maintain a focus of shared attention, provide children with a language in which to describe their own experiences and, using that language, build up a body of 'common knowledge' about the topic in hand (Edwards and Mercer, 1987; Mercer, 1995, 2000). Mercer's work (1995, 2000) places particular emphasis on the communication process he calls the *guided construction of knowledge* – a process encompassing both teaching and learning (which he suggests are often talked about as though they are two separate processes) and which sits at the heart of 'education'. He has drawn on detailed observations of teaching–learning interactions made in classroom contexts to highlight a number of key strategies used by teachers to guide the construction of knowledge (see Box 3).

BOX 3

Guiding the construction of knowledge

Teachers in schools and other educational institutions use language to pursue their professional aims and goals. One of their aims is to guide the learning activity of their students along directions required by a curriculum, and to try to construct a joint, shared version of educational knowledge with their students. There are certain common techniques that teachers use to try to achieve this. Teachers may not necessarily be self-consciously aware of the techniques they use; and teachers will vary as to how much and how well they use any of them. But these techniques are intentional, goal-directed ways of talking nevertheless, which reflect the constraints of the institutional setting in which schoolteachers work. In attempting to guide learning, they use talk to do three things:

elicit knowledge from students, so that they can see what students already know and understand and so that the knowledge is seen to be 'owned' by the students as well as teachers;

respond to things that students say, not only so that students get feedback on their attempts but also so that the teacher can incorporate what students say into the flow of the discourse and gather students' contributions together to construct more generalized meanings;

describe the classroom experiences that they share with students in such a way that the educational significance of those joint experiences is revealed and emphasised.

Source: Mercer, 1995, pp. 25–6.

While the emphasis in guiding the construction of knowledge is on the teachers' contribution, Mercer's ongoing programme of work, inspired by Vygotskian theory, also considers the learners' contribution and the educational significance of the collaborative talk between learners. As has been seen, Vygotsky's work directs attention to asymmetrical interactions; that is, those that occur between individuals who differ in knowledge or ability. His theory offers an account of tutoring, and draws attention to the fact that most of what children have to learn, the adults around them already know. But the concepts of negotiation of meaning and co-construction of shared understanding can be applied to peer interaction as well as to adult–child interaction. This leads us to consider the significance of collaborative processes and in particular to focus on the constructive role of discussion.

Since the early 1990s, Mercer and his colleagues have analysed the talk of children working together in classroom settings (see Mercer, 1995, 2000) and he has suggested that 'while encouraging talk between learners may help the development of understanding, not all kinds of talk and collaboration are of equal educational value.' (Mercer, 1995, p. 98). Mercer's (1995) analyses reveal that three types of talk can be identified in children's joint discourse, namely, *disputational, cumulative* and *exploratory* talk. Disputational talk is characterized by disagreement and individualized decision-making. Cumulative talk is positive but uncritical comment, usually indicated by repetition, agreement and elaboration of what has already been said. Exploratory talk is where there is constructive criticism of other people's ideas; any challenges are justified, explained and solutions or fresh ideas are offered. Progress thus emerges from the joint construction of solutions and acceptance of suggestions. Mercer argues that exploratory talk, although infrequent, is an ideal form of educational discourse as it makes thought processes explicit for all children participating in the group such that reasoning is visible in talk.

Activity 4   *Classifying classroom talk*

Allow about
10 minutes

This activity will help you consider the use of different types of talk identified by Mercer.

Read the extract below of four children classifying animals into 'herbivores' or 'carnivores'. Which of Mercer's different types of talk can you see evidenced in this exchange of ideas?

Emmeline:	Now we've got a fish – uh – the ...
Oliver:	What sort, the piranha?
Emmeline:	No, the little, not the scaly one.
Maddy:	Lun, lungf ... (*hesitating*)
Oliver:	Lungfish.
Maddy:	It probably feeds on things in the river, because it's not going to go out and catch a monkey or something, is it? (*all laugh*)
Emmeline:	Yeah. Could bri ...
Oliver:	(*interrupting*) There is of course river plants, some of them do feed on river plants, and leaves that fall in the river.
Maddy:	Yeah, it's probably a herbivore.
Ben:	We haven't got anything to tell.
Emmeline:	What do you think it should be?
Oliver:	No, actually I think we should put it in 'carnivore', most fish are.
Emmeline:	No, because, ma ...
Oliver:	(*interrupting*) It's our best, and most fish are, isn't it?
Emmeline:	(*interrupting*) Yeah, but we've got this one here, and this one here (*she indicates some fish cards in both 'carnivore' and 'herbivore' piles on the table*).

(Mercer, 1995, p. 111)

Comment

This extract reveals some cumulative talk (e.g. 'Yeah, its probably a herbivore') and also some evidence of exploratory talk. For example, in the second half of the extract Emmeline and Oliver disagree with each other and even interrupt each other, but provide reasons for their counter positions.

▲

While Mercer and colleagues acknowledge that all three types of talk are appropriate in certain circumstances, their work has demonstrated that exploratory talk offers a potential for learning over and above that offered by the other types. This is because exploratory talk involves partners explicitly presenting ideas and reasoning together. According to this analysis, children should be inducted into educationally effective ways of talking and working together and collaborative activities should be designed to foster children's use of exploratory talk. As Jackson (1987) stresses, until 'children are able to use language as a resource for negotiation with others and as a means for establishing collaborative learning, the pattern of learning in the (primary) classroom remains inaccessible' (Jackson, 1987, p. 85).

Mindful of this, Mercer and colleagues have been involved in a sustained programme of classroom intervention work, called the *Thinking Together* approach, in which children are explicitly inducted into the use of exploratory talk. The approach (see Dawes *et al.*, 2000; Littleton *et al.*, 2005) provides a framework for the direct teaching of the speaking and listening skills children and young people need in order to learn from and with each other. In this way, learners can add educationally effective ways of talking and thinking together to their talk repertoire. Key features of the approach are:

1   Children follow a series of *Thinking Together* lessons. Aims for group talk are made explicit in the whole class introduction. During plenary sessions, groups reflect on the quality of their talk.

2   In these lessons, the class are directly taught speaking and listening skills (such as challenging with respect, reasoning, negotiating ideas) and are provided with contexts for collaboration in which they can apply such skills.

3   Classes create and agree on a shared set of ground rules for exploratory talk to use when working with one another in groups.

Children form specific expectations and beliefs about teaching and learning relationships and 'are motivated to understand the social rules and relationships of their cultural world' because they 'need to get things done' in classroom contexts (Dunn, 1988, p. 189). Teachers make a powerful contribution to the creation of contexts for learning in their classrooms and the ways in which they talk, act and structure classroom activities convey powerful messages regarding how learning and talking are to be done in such contexts. The pedagogy inherent in the *Thinking Together* approach is thus designed to enable children's participation in ongoing learning conversations where opportunities for structured dialogue with peers are frequent and where ground rules for exploratory talk are modelled in the talk of the teacher. This is because, as Gee notes, 'Any efficacious pedagogy must be a judicious mix of immersion in a community of practice and overt focusing and scaffolding from "masters" or "more advanced peers" who focus learners on the most fruitful sorts of patterns in their experience' (Gee, 2000, pp. 201–2).

4.3 Reflections on the socio-cultural approach

The emphasis on instruction that characterizes much research undertaken within the post-Vygotskian tradition and the associated interest in the concept of 'scaffolding' has attracted some critical comment from researchers. For example Mariette Hoogsteder and colleagues (Hoogsteder *et al.*, 1998) argue that research in the post-Vygotskian tradition has emphasized the uni-directional transmission of skills and knowledge from adult to child. They suggest that the metaphor of scaffolding conveys an image of the child's learning being 'propped up' by an omniscient adult who invariably directs and controls the interaction with the result that the contributions of the child have been ignored. The allocation of a passive role to the child, these researchers argue, oversimplifies the nature of teaching and learning interactions. Their own work suggests that teaching and learning interactions are 'exercises in collectivity' which involve both child and adult in processes of negotiation, disagreement, the exchange and sharing of information, judgement and decision making and evaluation of one another's contributions.

Socio-cultural research focuses on different dimensions of educational experience relative to both behaviourism and constructivism. It offers an account of both teaching and learning processes, with the emphasis firmly on understanding these as processes without undue emphasis on the products of those experiences. It values experiences that are either planned or incidental, although the emphasis is always on shared activity that is adult-led.

We will now extend our discussion of teaching and learning to consider a way of viewing educational contexts that have become increasingly influential. Rooted in socio-cultural ideas, it emphasizes the need to see learning as situated in particular contexts and communities that have the potential to impact on what is learned, how it is learned and the identity of the learner.

Summary of Section 4

- Socio-cultural approaches have their origins in the work of Vygotsky, who, like Piaget, was interested in cognitive development. However, according to this view development is seen as inherently social – it is through interaction with more able others that children acquire reasoning skills, which eventually become internalized.
- The zone of proximal development (ZPD) refers to the difference between what children can do unaided and what they can achieve with the support of a more knowledgeable other.

- The term 'scaffolding' is used to refer to the support given to a child by a more able person.
- It is argued that for teaching to be effective it should be contigent on a child's actions, supporting more if the child struggles with a task, and controlling less if the child is succeeding.
- A socio-cultural analysis of classroom talk has identified different kinds of peer dialogue, some of which are more desirable than others in an educational context.
- Aspects of the socio-cultural approach have been criticized for emphasizing the idea of a uni-directional transfer of knowledge and skills from adult to child.

5 Learning communities and cultures of learning

While a concern with promoting effective reasoning in talk sits at the heart of the *Thinking Together* approach, the programme is based on more than just cognitive accounts of how group-work works. The processes of knowledge construction that Mercer and his colleagues aim to foster are inextricably interwoven with the construction of social understanding and the experience of being a pupil participating in the ongoing life of the classroom. Thus, while the *Thinking Together* approach is concerned with promoting the guided construction of knowledge, it aims to do so in part through the creation of a positive culture of collaboration and community of enquiry in the classroom. Such a culture of collaboration is founded on mutual respect and trust among teachers and learners – such that learners feel able to take the risks inherent in opening up their thinking to their peer group (Underwood and Underwood, 1999). This approach therefore highlights a view that education is not about the transmission of specific bodies of knowledge and skills. Rather, as Wells and Claxton (2002) comment: 'it is about the development of understanding and the formation of minds and identities' (Wells and Claxton, 2002, p. 2).

The notion of 'community' touched on briefly in the account of the *Thinking Together* approach is an important one for researchers interested in understanding education. This is because 'communities' (which are defined as groups of people who share experiences and interests and communicate among themselves to pursue those interests) offer members distinctive resources for knowledge construction. Presented in Box 4 is a synopsis developed by Mercer (2000) which summarizes how he believes communities can enable collective thinking.

Many of these ideas concerning the potential value of communities for learning are reflected in one contemporary and influential extension of Vygotsky's theory, namely the idea of situated learning (Lave and Wenger, 1991).

BOX 4

How communities resource collective thinking

The kind of groups I call 'communities' offer their members the following resources for joint intellectual activity:

A history. Groups which persist over time accumulate a body of shared experience. Members will be likely to recall that experience together and reflect on it, and so gain a history. Shared experience will generate information and expertise, on which members can draw and which can be passed to new members.

A collective identity. By sharing a history, knowledge, aims and the experience of doing things together, members can find meaning, purpose and direction for their own endeavours and relate these to the special contributions that others in the community make. Joining the community may involve some initiation or admission process.

Reciprocal obligations. Members will have responsibilities towards each other, and so can expect to have access to each other's intellectual resources. There will be roles and ground rules for specifying appropriate behaviour.

A discourse. Communities use language to operate, but they do not simply take language 'off the peg' and use it as given. One of the marvellous and distinctive design features of language is what is usually called its 'openness'. That is, language can be reshaped to suit new communicative demands as they emerge. New words and new ways of putting words together can be generated if people consider it necessary. If a group of people are striving to communicate about their special interests, they can adapt and extend language as a tool for doing so. The specialized language of a community can be called its *discourse*. Fluency in the discourse is likely to be one of the obvious signs of membership.

Source: Mercer, 2000, pp. 106–7.

5.1 Situated learning

Lave and Wenger argue that learning is an inherently social activity. According to their account, learning occurs all the time, is an aspect of all activity and is usually unintentional. Learning occurs as a result of participating in what they call 'communities of practice', in which novices are inducted into ways of thinking and doing things by more experienced members of the group. Participation leads to the transition from being a novice member to being able to participate fully in the community in question. So, for example, a family unit may be considered a community of practice in which children learn about various aspects of daily activity through interaction with their parents and siblings, and consequently come to participate fully in the various aspects of family life having acquired the skills and knowledge needed to do so. In this way, learning is seen as 'situated' in the social context and social practices of the group.

Schools too may be regarded as communities of practice. In this instance, both teachers and older pupils can be seen to induct children into full participation in school activities. Teachers are often seen to limit access to resources and structure this access as part of the process of formal tuition, and this has led Lave and Wenger (1991) to note the element of power that is held by the experienced members of the community. Moreover, Lemke (1997) has attempted to broaden the idea of situated learning by noting that it is not just situated in its immediate social context, but in a cultural and historical one too. That is, Lemke argues that cultures and history attach certain meanings to objects, words and actions.

Wenger has advanced what is described as a 'social theory of learning', which sees learning as a 'process of being active participants in the *practices* of social communities and constructing *identities* in relation to these communities' (Wenger, 1998, p. 4). The characterization of learning offered here moves beyond the emphasis on learning as a process of knowledge building. It recognizes, for example, that part of being seen as 'knowledgeable' is being competent in activities that are culturally valued. An example of this in British school culture might be the way that academic ability is often valued more highly than physical skills such as manual trades or sporting ability.

5.2 Identity and learning

Wenger's account of learning (1998) also emphasizes how it is a process of 'becoming' – it changes who we are. The significance of identity in accounts of learning is illustrated by recent work by Wirtanen and Littleton (2004), who interviewed adult students at the Sibelius Academy in Finland about their experiences in relation to their piano studies.

In Box 5, one of the students, Tuomas, talks about the dilemmas and delicate processes involved in negotiating a position between the teacher's suggested interpretation of a musical piece and his own creative ideas. His comments are made in the context of a discussion relating to learning together, with the teacher (see Box 5).

BOX 5

Learning and identity

And in reality, if telling it straight now, so, I have very often had a kind of period of what to do when you don't appreciate fully what the teacher says? It is quite dangerous. And even if you have a different opinion of things and you would like to do it another way ... so you know that when you go to the next lesson, so, you play according to your own ideas but that is not, like, right either. However, it is quite an uncomfortable situation when it doesn't ... like, how do you make sense of it that you play how another person

wishes? It is the biggest possible deception that can exist. Let them play then like that ... but of course you have to consider that there surely is a good idea behind it, but digging it out then.

(Tuomas)

In 'telling it straight' Tuomas discloses his dilemma about what to do when he does not fully embrace the perspective on interpretation the teacher is advocating. He characterizes this as a dangerous situation, although he does not expand on the potential losses or risks inherent in it. If he plays according to his own interpretation, it is deemed 'not right'. It is an uncomfortable situation. Tuomas suggests that to play how another person wishes involves deception and perhaps a betrayal of one's own self – it is the biggest possible deception that can exist. He struggles towards understanding the rationale for the teacher's advocacy of his particular stance and uses the archaeological metaphor of having to uncover, through 'digging out', the reasons underpinning the interpretation that his teacher is advocating. [...] Tuomas struggles to give voice to his own interpretations. However, his own creative interpretations are in direct conflict with the guidance being given by the teacher who is working with the student within the framework afforded by a particular system of assessment carrying the weight of historical tradition, oriented to the forms of expression valued by an established classical music community. To adhere unquestioningly to these valued forms of expression is somehow considered by Tuomas to be dishonest – and creates a situation in which inherent in the simple, unquestioning adoption of an interpretation, is the risk of taking on a troubled identity.

Source: Wirtanen and Littleton, 2004, pp. 33–4.

Work such as this demonstrates how approaching the study of learning in social and cultural contexts involves abandoning 'the conventional demarcation between cognitive, social and emotional development' (Woodhead *et al.*, 1999, p. 1). It would also suggest that it is perhaps inappropriate to talk about the social and emotional *dimensions* of learning as if such dimensions were analytically separate and distinct from the activity of learning itself. One of the key features of a situated approach to cognition is the recognition that the processes of thinking and identity construction go hand in hand:

> To think or to reason well in a situation is, by definition, to take on the forms as well as the substance of a community of reasoners and, thus, to join that community. Much of discourse, and thus [much] of cognition, serves to situate an individual with respect to others, to establish a social role or identity.

(Resnick *et al.*, 1997, p. 9)

The importance of identity, and the way in which a learner positions him- or herself with respect to a task or their peers, is crucial. For example, from a very early age children are engaged in the construction of their identities as pupils. They construct and participate in discourses about ability and effort (Bird, 1994) and are motivated to understand what it means to be a learner and what it means to succeed at educational tasks. The social climate of comparison, competition, success, failure and issues of relative status in the classroom rapidly becomes established within the early years of schooling (Crocker and Cheesman, 1988) and remains a powerful interpersonal dynamic throughout learners' educational careers.

5.3 Reflecting on psychological accounts of learning

The view of development and learning being described here has far reaching implications for the way developmental psychologists 'do' their science. What moves to the fore is a detailed understanding of issues of subjectivity, intersubjectivity and social construction. Seen from this perspective, educational and developmental psychologists are not engaged in the activity of discovering the 'real' capabilities of the child. Rather they are involved in the business of constructing particular accounts and representations of the child and notions of competence (Woodhead *et al.*, 1999). The representations they create are historically located, culturally determined and value laden, as are the very issues they choose to investigate. As Burman comments, 'the developmental psychology we know is tied to the culture which produced it' (Burman, 1999, p. 177). Much of the work reported in this chapter has clearly been shaped by unarticulated cultural preconceptions about the contexts, goals and processes of learning and development in Western society at this time (see also Woodhead *et al.*, 1999).

Seen from this perspective, psychologists do not exist in isolation from the social contexts they study. They too are 'situated' in particular institutional, cultural and historical contexts and it is in such contexts that they actively create their subject. Educational theories and research shape the environments in which children develop and learn, and to this extent psychologists participate in the construction of contemporary reality (Rose, 1990; Woodhead *et al.*, 1999). Thus, learning, is a process of engagement with culturally elaborated and socially mediated reality. The social processes which shape and constitute learning can be powerful in their effects. The harnessing of these processes to support children's learning holds the key to enhancing the effectiveness of their education, in the widest sense.

Summary of Section 5

- Some socio-cultural researchers see communities as offering their members important resources for joint intellectual activity. The potential value of communities for learning is explored in one contemporary extension of Vygotskian theory known as situated learning.
- The notion of situated learning goes beyond an emphasis on learning as a process of knowledge building. It recognizes that part of being seen as 'knowledgeable' is being competent in activities that are culturally valued.
- One of the key features of a situated approach is the recognition that thinking and identity formation go hand in hand.
- It is important to note that the concerns of developmental psychologists are shaped by unarticulated cultural preconceptions about the context, goals and processes of learning and development in their society and at that point in time.

6 | Conclusion

In this chapter you have been introduced to some different psychological traditions, each of which has something to say about the processes by which children develop and learn. Some of the salient characteristics of the approaches presented and their relevance to education are summarized in Table 1.

Table 1 **Approaches to teaching and learning: a summary**

Aspect	Behaviourist	Constructivist	Socio-cultural and situational
View of the learning practice	Changes behaviour	Process in the head of the learner (including insight, information processing, memory perception)	Interaction/observation in a group context, akin to an apprenticeship
Site of learning	External resources and tasks are what matters	Making connections in learner's head is what really matters	Learning needs a relationship between people and environment
Purposes in education	Produce behavioural change in desired direction	Develop capacity and skills to learn better	Full participation in communities of practice, i.e. you graduate from apprentice to craftsman

Source: adapted from Kirriemuir and McFarlane, 2004, p. 13.

The preceding discussions of the psychological accounts of teaching and learning point to learning as being the result of multiple, embedded and interwoven influences. The complexity of teaching and learning is such that any single approach gives only a partial account of the nature of educational processes, as we conceived of them in Section 1. As a result, it is potentially problematic to rely on any one of these approaches to capture the full extent of teaching and learning processes.

So, we return to the secondary school children's descriptions of learning that we presented at the outset of the chapter. You should now be able to see, and understand the reasons, why Extract 1 represents a limited view of learning that none of the approaches outlined in this chapter would advocate. Extract 2, in presenting a more self-motivated account of learning, is closer to an ideal, although it says little about the actual processes by which the student would go about gaining the knowledge they desire. In this way psychological theories go beyond such simple descriptions to attempt to capture and understand the processes of teaching and learning. What this chapter has shown is that each psychological perspective complements and extends our understanding of the various dimensions of educational experience, although no single theory offers a complete account. However, each line of empirical work adds more detail to a picture that is necessarily complex and multifaceted.

References

Berry, J. and Sahlberg, P. (1996) 'Investigating pupils' idea of learning', *Learning and Instruction*, vol. 6, pp. 19–36.

Bigge, M. L. and Shermis, S. S. (1999, 6th edn) *Learning Theories for Teachers*, New York, NY, Addison Wesley Longman.

Bird, L. (1994) 'Creating the capable body: discourses about ability and effort in primary and secondary school studies', in Maynall, B (ed.) *Children's childhoods: observed and experienced*, London, Falmer Press.

Bliss, J., Askew, M. and Macrae, S. (1996) 'Effective teaching and learning: scaffolding revisited', *Oxford Review of Education*, vol. 22, pp. 37–61.

Burman, E. (1999) 'Morality and the goals of development', in Woodhead, M., Faulkner, D. and Littleton, K. (eds), *Making Sense of Social Development*, London, Routledge/in association with the Open University.

Crain, W. (2005, 5th edn) *Theories of Development: concepts and applications*, New Jersey, Prentice Hall.

Crocker, T. and Cheesman, R. (1998) 'The ability of young children to rank themselves for academic ability', *Educational Studies*, vol. 14, pp. 105–10.

Davis, A. (1991) 'Piaget, teachers and education: into the 1990s', in Light, P., Sheldon, S. and Woodhead, M. (eds), *Learning to Think*, London, Routledge.

Dawes, L., Mercer, N. and Wegerif, R. (2000) *Thinking Together*, Birmingham, Questions Publishing.

Doise, W. and Mugny, G. (1984) *The Social Development of the Intellect*, Oxford, Pergamon Press.

Dunn, J. (1988) *The Beginnings of Social Understanding*, Oxford, Blackwell.

Edwards, D. and Mercer, N. (1987) *Common Knowledge: the development of understanding in the classroom*, London, Methuen.

Elkind, D. (1981) *The Hurried Child*, Reading, MA, Addison-Wesley.

Farnham-Diggory, S. (1981) 'But how do we shape up rigourous behavioral analysts?', *Developmental Review*, vol. 1, pp. 58–60.

Gee, J. (2000) 'Discourse and socio-cultural studies in reading', in Kamil, M. Mosenthal, B., Pearson, P. and Barr, R. (eds) *Handbook of Reading Research, Volume III*, London, Lawrence Erlbaum Associates.

Greenfield, P. and Lave, J. (1982) 'Cognitive aspects of informal education' in Wagner, D. and Stephenson, H. (eds) *Cultural Perspectives on Child Development*, San Francisco, CA, Freeman.

Hoogsteder, M., Maier, R. and Elbers, E. (1998) 'Adult-child interaction, joint problem solving and the structure of cooperation', in Woodhead, M., Faulkner, D. and Littleton, K. (eds), *Cultural Worlds of Early Childhood*, London, Routledge.

Jackson, M. (1987) 'Making sense of school', in Pollard, A. (ed.) *Children and their Primary Schools: a new perspective*, London, The Falmer Press.

Jamieson, D., Suppes, P. and Wells, S. (1974) 'The effectiveness of alternative instructional media: a survey', *Review of Educational Research*, vol. 44, pp. 1–68.

Kamii, C. (1985) *Young Children Reinvent Arithmetic*, New York, NY, Teacher's College Press.

Kamii, C. (1994) *Young Children Continue to Reinvent Arithmetic: 3rd Grade*, New York, NY, Teacher's College Press.

Kamii, C. (2004, 2nd edn) *Young Children Continue to Reinvent Arithmetic: 2nd Grade*, New York, NY, Teacher's College Press.

Kennedy, M. (1978) 'Findings from the follow through planned evaluation study', *Educational Researcher*, vol. 7, pp. 3–11.

Kincheloe, J. L. and Steinberg, S. R. (1993) 'A tentative description of post-formal thinking: the critical confrontation with cognitive theory', *Harvard Educational Review*, vol. 63, pp. 296–320.

Kirriemuir, J. and McFarlane, A. (2004) *Literature Review in Games and Learning*, Bristol, NESTA Futurelab. Available at: http://www.nestafuturelab.org/research/reviews/08_01.htm (last accessed 16 March 2005)

Kohlberg, L. and Gilligan, C. (1971) 'The adolescent as philosopher', *Daedalus*, vol. 100, pp. 1051–86.

Lave, J. and Wenger, E. (1991) *Situated Learning: legitimate peripheral participation*, Cambridge, Cambridge University Press.

Lemke, J. (1997) 'Cognition, context and learning: a social semiotic perspective', in Kirshner, D. (ed.) *Situated Cognition Theory: social, neurological and semiotic perspectives*, New York, NY, Lawrence Erlbaum.

Lepper, M. and Greene, D. (1978) *The Hidden Costs of Reward*, Hillsdale, NJ, Lawrence Erlbaum.

Light, P., Sheldon, S. and Woodhead, M. (1991) *Learning to Think*, London, Routledge/in association with the Open University.

Littleton, K. and Hoyles, C. (2002) 'Gendering IT', in Yelland, N. and Rubin, A. (eds) *Ghosts in the Machine – feminist perspectives on computing*, pp. 3–32, New York, NY, Peter Lang.

Littleton, K., Mercer, N., Dawes, L., Wegerif, R., Rowe, D. and Sams, C. (in press) 'Thinking together at Key Stage 1', *Early Years: An International Journal of Research and Development*.

Mercer, N. (1995) *The Guided Construction of Knowledge*, Clevedon, Multilingual Matters.

Mercer, N. (2000) *Words & Minds*, London, Routledge.

Mugny, G., Perret-Clermont and Doise, A-N. (1981) 'Interpersonal co-ordinations and sociological differences in the construction of the intellect', in Stevenson, G. and Davis, G. (eds) *Applied Social Psychology, vol. 1.*, Chichester, Wiley.

Newman, D., Griffin, P. and Cole, M. (1989) *The Construction Zone: working for cognitive change in schools*, Cambridge, Cambridge University Press.

Open University, The (2002) *Child Development in Families, Schools and Society*, ED840 fOCUS CD-ROM, Milton Keynes, The Open University.

Piaget, J. (1926) *The Language and Thought of the Child*, London, Routledge.

Piaget, J. (1932) *The Moral Judgement of the Child*, London, Routledge/Kegan Paul.

Resnick, L., Pontecorvo, C. and Säljö, R. (1997) 'Discourse, tools and reasoning', in Resnick, L., Säljö, R., Pontecorvo, C. and Burge, B. (eds) *Discourse, Tools and Reasoning: essays on situated cognition*, Berlin and New York, NY, Springer-Verlag.

Rogoff, B. (1990) *Apprenticeship in Thinking: cognitive development in social Context*, Oxford, Oxford University Press.

Rogoff, B. and Gardner, W. P. (1984) 'Guidance in cognitive development: an examination of mother-child instruction', in Rogoff, B. and Lave, J. (eds) *Everyday Cognition: its development in social context*, Cambridge, MA, Harvard University Press.

Rose, N. (1990) 'Psychology as a "social" science', in Parker, I. and Shotter, J. (eds) *Deconstructing Social Psychology*, London, Routledge.

Skinner, B. F. (1938) *The Behavior of Organisms*, New York, NY, Appleton Century Crofts.

Skinner, B. F. (1954) 'The science of learning and the art of teaching', *Harvard Educational Review*, vol. 24, pp. 86–97.

Skinner, B. F. (1968) *The Technology of Teaching*, New York, NY, Appleton Century Crofts.

Tharp, R. and Gallimore, R. (1998) 'A theory of teaching as assisted performance', in Faulkner, D., Littleton, K. and Woodhead, M. (eds) *Learning Relationships in the Classroom*, London, Routledge.

Travers, R. M. W. (1983) *How Research has Changed American Schools*, Kalamazoo, MI, Mython Press.

Underwood, J. and Underwood, G. (1999) 'Task effects on co-operative and collaborative learning with computers', in Littleton, K. and Light, P. (eds) *Learning with Computers: analysing productive interaction*, London, Routledge.

Wells, G. and Claxton, G. (2002) 'Introduction: sociocultural perspectives on the future of education', in Wells, G. and Claxton, G. (eds) *Learning for Life in the 21st Century*, Oxford, Blackwell.

Wenger, E. (1998) *Communities of Practice: learning meaning and identity*, Cambridge, Cambridge University Press.

Wheldall, K., Merrett, F. and Glynn, T. (1986) *Behaviour Analysis in Educational Psychology*, London, Croom Helm.

Wirtanen, S. and Littleton, K. (2004) 'Collaboration, conflict and the musical identity work of solo-piano students: the significance of the student-teacher relationship', in Miell, D. and Littleton, K. (eds) *Collaborative Creativity: contemporary perspectives*, London, Free Association Books.

Wood, D. (1998) 'Aspects of teaching and learning', in Woodhead, M., Faulkner, D. and Littleton, K. (eds) *Cultural Worlds of Early Childhood*, London, Routledge.

Wood, D. and Middleton, D. (1975) 'A study of assisted problem solving', *British Journal of Psychology,* vol. 66, pp. 181–91.

Wood, D., Bruner, J. and Ross, G. (1976) 'The role of tutoring in problem solving', *Journal of Child Psychology and Psychiatry*, vol. 17, pp. 89–100.

Wood, D., Underwood, J. and Avis, P. (1999) 'Integrated learning systems in the classroom', *Computers and Education*, vol. 33, pp. 91–108.

Wood, D., Wood, H. and Middleton, D. (1978) 'An experimental evaluation of our face-to-face teaching strategies', *International Journal of Behavioural Development*, vol. 1, pp. 131–47.

Woodhead, M., Faulkner, F. and Littleton, K. (1999) (eds) *Making Sense of Social Development*, London, Routledge.

Acknowledgements

Grateful acknowledgement is made to the following sources for permission to reproduce material within this book. Every effort has been made to contact copyright holders. If any have been inadvertently overlooked the publishers will be pleased to make the necessary arrangements at the first opportunity.

Chapter 2

Tables

Table 1: Dent, H. R. and Stephenson, G. M. (1979) 'Experimental study of the effectiveness of different techniques of questioning child witnesses', *British Journal of Social and Clinical Psychology*, vol. 18, pp. 41–51, Cambridge University Press; *Table 2*: Talwar, V. and Lee, K. (2002) 'Development of lying to conceal a transgression: children's control of expressive behaviour during verbal deception', *International Journal of Behavioural Development*, vol. 26, pp. 436–44.

Figures

Figure 1: DCA (2001) Judicial Appointments Annual Report 2001–2002. Crown copyright material is reproduced under Class Licence Number C01W0000065 with the permission of the Controller of HMSO and the Queen's Printer for Scotland; *Figure 4*: Lyon, T. D. and Saywitz, K. J. (1999) 'Young maltreated children's competence to take the oath', *Applied Developmental Science*, p. 21, Lawrence Erlbaum Associates Inc.

Chapter 3

Figures

Figure 2: Photofusion Picture Library/Alamy; *Figure 3*: Dynamics Graphics Group/i2i Alamy; *Figure 4*: Adapted from Sheridan, C. L. and Radmacher, S. A. (1992) *Health Psychology: challenging the biomedical model*, New York, Wiley; *Figure 5*: Reprinted, with permission, from the *Annual Review of Psychology*, vol. 47 © 1996 by Annual Reviews, www.annualreviews.org; *Figure 7*: RubberBall/Alamy.

Chapter 4

Text

Reading: Reprinted by permission of Sage Publications Ltd from Lorna Wing, *Autism*, Copyright © NAS: The National Autistic Society and SAGE Publications Ltd, 1997.

Figures

Figure 1: Frith, U. (1989) 'Figure 3: The false belief paradigm', *Autism: Explaining the Enigma*, Blackwell Publishers Ltd; *Figure 5*: Karp and Konstadt (1971) Consulting Psychologists Press, Inc., Palo Alto, CA.

Cover photographs

© Getty Images.

Name index

Abraham, C. 112, 113
Adams, R. J. 103
Ajzen, I. 121
Albano, A. M. 127
Allen, G. 158
Anand, K. J. S. 126
Anderson, H. I. 36
Anthony, J. 185
Armitage, C. J. 122
Asher, S. R. 116
Asperger, H. 151, 159, 183, 185, 187–8

Baird, G. 156
Bala, N. 75
Baldwin, S. 43
Bandura, A. 83, 89, 109, 110
Baranek, G. T. 159
Baron-Cohen, S. 161, 162, 163, 164, 173, 188
Barrett, M. D. 125
Barrett, S. 171
Bauman, M. 158, 159, 188
Bearison, D. J. 128
Beck, A. T. 38
Becker, M. H. 105
Bedingfield, D. 80
Bender, W. N. 37
Bentovim, A. 61–2
Berman, S. M. 112
Berry, J. 195
Bettelheim, B. 157
Bibace, R. 124–5
Bigge, M. L. 199
Biklen, D. 156
Binet, A. 59
Bird, J. E. 125
Bird, L. 223
Bishop, M. 158
Blackburn, R. 149, 152, 153, 165
Bliss, J. 215
Blount, R. L. 131
Bolton, P. 188
Bolton, S. 31
Bond, G. G. 134
Bonnie, R. 57
Boote, R. 44, 45
Borland, R. 120
Bottoms, B. L. 69, 70
Boucher, J. 160
Bovee, J. -P. 177
Bowens, A. 32

Bowers, P. 51
Bowlby, J. 129
Brauner, A. 183
Brauner, F. 183
Brennan, M. 66
Brennan, R. 66
Brooks, L. 62, 63
Brophy, J. E. 39
Bruck, M. 59, 60
Bruvold, W. H. 111
Bryan, T. 40, 42
Buchanan-Barrow, E. A. 125
Buffing, F. 69
Burman, E. 224
Bussey, K. 76

Campbell, S. 126
Caplan, G. 119, 120, 128
Cardinal, D. N. 156
Carr, D. B. 126
Carrey, N. J. 184
Carson, D. 81
Carson, D. K. 131
Cass, H. D. 158
Cassidy, T. 114, 115, 129
Cates, W. 112
Ceci, S. J. 59, 60, 72, 86, 90
Cesaroni, L. 149, 152
Chambers, C. T. 127, 131
Charman, T. 171
Cheeseman, R. 223
Chen, E. 103, 104, 173
Christiano, B. 129
Claxton, G. 220
Cohen, S. 115, 116, 127
Coie, J. D. 116
Connor, M. T. 122
Conte, P. 117, 129, 130, 131
Cooper, P. 43
Coscia, J. M. 103
Courchesne, E. 158
Crain, W. 202
Creak, M. 187
Critchley, M. 186
Crocker, T. 223
Cross, P. 164
Cummings, E. 116–17

David, H. 69
Davies, G. M. 70, 74, 88
Davis, A. 202
Dawes, L. 218

Dawson, G. 171
Dein, S. 132
DeMeyer, M. K. 152, 187
Dent, H. R. 71, 72, 73
De Sanctis, S. 184
DeSimone Leichtman, M. 86
Diepgen, T. L. 109
DiMatteo, M. R. 131–2, 134
Ditto, P. H. 128
Doise, W. 206, 207, 208
Donnellan, A. M. 160
Donnelly, J. 177
Dorado, J. S. 78
Down, L. 184
Drotar, D. 132, 133
Dunne, E. A. 125
Dunn, J. 218

Earl, C. J. C. 184, 186
Ebbeling, C. B. 107
Edwards, D. 215
Ehlers, S. 188
Eisenberg, L. 187
Eiser, C. 119, 124, 128, 129
Elkind, D. 202
Engel, G. L. 105
Esam, B. 66
Evans, R. I. 112
Eveleth, P. B. 107
Everatt, J. 14

Fabbro, F. 20
Farnham-Diggory, S. 199
Farrington, D. P. 80
Fawcett, A. J. 13, 21
Felce, D. 126
Fincham, F. D. 116
Fishbein, M. 121
Fletcher, B. 117
Flin, R. 60, 66, 67, 68, 69, 88
Flynn, E. 170
Folkman, S. 116
Fonagy, P. 118
Forrest, J. D. 112
Freud, S. 83, 84, 89, 185
Frith, U. 156, 157, 162, 168, 169, 170, 183, 185, 188

Gafney, A. 125
Gage, M. 106, 135
Gallimore, R. 213–15
Garber, M. 149, 153

Gardner, W. P. 215
Garmezy, N. 118
Gee, J. 219
Geuze, R. H. 32
Gillan, A. 62
Gillberg, C. 156, 188
Gilligan, C. 202
Ginsberg, M. 202
Glanz, K. 109, 110, 111
Goin, R. P. 159–60
Goldstein, P. 38
Gollwitzer, P. M. 120
Goodhart, F. 163
Goodley, D. 173
Goodman, G. S. 59, 69, 70
Good, T. L. 39
Goreczny, A. J. 106, 135
Gould, J. 175, 187
Grandin, T. 149–50
Grayson, A. 156
Greene, D. 199
Greenfield, P. 215
Grigorenko, E. L. 19, 20
Grimbeek, E. J. 76
Grych, J. H. 116

Hagger, M. S. 122
Hamilton, C. 57, 91
Hanley, M. 114, 115
Happé, F. G. E. 168, 170
Harbeck, C. 125
Hargreaves, D. H. 39
Haslam, J. 184
Hayes, M. L. 38
Heller 184
Henderson, E. 66
Herbert, T. B. 116
Hergenrather, J. R. 126
Hermann, C. 129
Hermelin, B. 167
Heydon, J. 60
Hill, D. 121
Hobson, P. 158, 171
Hofferth, S. 112
Hollin, C. R. 80, 86
Hoogsteder, M. 219
Howells, K. 80
Howlin, P. 188, 189
Hoyles, C. 199
Huffman, M. L. 78–9
Hughes, C. 166–7
Hulse, W. C. 184
Hunt, A. 186
Huntingdon, D. D. 37

Ievers, C. E. 134
Itard, J. M. G. 184

Jackson, M. 218
Jacobsen, B. 38
Jacobson, L. 39
Jamieson, D. 199
Janz, N. K. 105
Jarrold, C. 175, 176
Jenney, M. E. M. 126
Jervis, G. A. 186
Johnson, K. 146
Jones, V. 160
Jones, J. 74, 90
Jordan, P. 156, 188

Kamii, C. 199, 202–5
Kanazawa 173
Kanner, L. 151, 157, 177, 183, 184–5, 185–6, 187, 188, 189
Kaplan, B. J. 19
Katz, E. R. 127
Kemper, T. 188
Kennedy, M. 199
Kibby, M. Y. 128
Kim-Cohen, J. 118
Kincheloe, J. L. 209
Kirby, A. 15
Kirk, K. 36–7
Kirriemuir, J. 225
Kistner, J. A. 38
Klonoff, E. A. 120
Kobasa, S. C. 118
Kohlberg, L. 82, 83, 84, 85, 89, 202
Köhnken, G. 68, 69
Kolvin, I. 187
Kost, K. 112
Kuipers, C. 185
Kynan, S. 74, 78, 91

Lamb, M. E. 72
Lamers-Winkelman, F. 69
Landrine, H. 120
Lane, H. 184
Lave, J. 215, 220, 221, 222
Lawson, W. 148–9, 165
Lazarus, R. S. 115, 116
Leary, M. R. 160
Lemke, J. 222
Lepper, M. 199
Leslie, A. M. 162
Lewis, M. 85
Lewis, V. 175
Ley, P. 133

Light, P. 201
Littleton, K. 75, 91, 199, 218, 222, 223
Lotter, V. 187
Lundy-Ekman, L. 21
Lyon, T. D. 67, 75, 76, 77, 78, 86

McAlpine, L. 127
McCabe, M. P. 108
McCaron, A. L. 78
McFarlane, A. 225
McGrath, P. J. 127
McGuire, W. J. 120
Macintyre, C. 15, 16
McMurran, M. 120
Mahler, M. S. 184
Mahler, V. 109
Manjiviona, J. 159
Mannino, D. M. 103
Maudsley, H. 184
Memon, A. 91
Mercer, N. 215–18, 220, 221
Middleton, D. 212–13
Miles, E. 14
Miles, T. R. 14
Miller, L. T. 43
Mody, M. 13
Montgomery, M. S. 37
Mori, L. 130
Morrison, B. 60, 63, 84
Mottron, L. 172
Mugny, G. 206, 207, 208
Müller, R. A. 159
Mullins, R. 120
Myers, B. J. 159–60
Myers, J. E. B. 59, 60

Newman, D. 201, 209
Nicholson, R. I. 13, 45, 46, 47
Nicklas, T. A. 106
Noon, E. 70, 88

Oates, R. K. 88
O'Connor, N. 167
Olsson, C. A. 119
Opper, S. 202
Orford, J. 119
Ozonoff, S. 167

Page, J. 160
Palmer, E. J. 86
Park, C. C. 150, 157, 168
Peer, L. 15
Peeters, T. 156
Pennington, B. F. 167

Perner, J. 75, 78, 163
Perret-Clermont, A. -N. 206
Peterson, L. 117, 125, 130
Phipps, S. 117
Piaget, J. 81–2, 84, 89, 124, 125, 201–2, 205–6, 208, 209, 212
Piek, J. P. 37, 38, 39
Pierce, K. 159
Plotnikoff, J. 67
Podmore, V. N. 125
Poole, D. 67
Portwood, M. 33, 34–5, 38, 39
Potter, H. W. 184
Powell, S. 188
Premack, D. 173
Preston, D. S. 109
Prior, M. 159, 160
Pry, R. 171

Rabinowitz, M. 126
Radmacher, S. A. 115
Rae, C. 21
Rand, C. S. 132, 134
Rapoff, M. A. 134
Reason, R. 44, 45
Regan, T. 14, 30
Reid, G. 36–7
Resnick, L. 223
Rhodes, R. E. 132
Ricciardelli, L. A. 108
Rice, M. 36
Riddick, B. 35–6, 37, 38, 39
Riekert, K. A. 132, 133
Riley, J. L. 127
Rivlin, G. 61
Robertson, J. 129
Robinson, M. E. 127
Rogers, S. J. 159
Rogoff, B. 215
Rose, N. 224
Rosenthal, R. 39
Ross, D. M. 125
Ross, M. W. 112
Ross, S. H. 125
Roth, I. 153
Rothman, A. 135
Ruble, L. A. 167
Ruck, M. D. 85–6
Rundall, T. G. 111
Russell, J. 166–7
Russ, S. W. 129
Rutter, M. 14, 118, 187, 188

Sahinler, B. E. 127
Sahlberg, P. 195
Saywitz, K. J. 76, 77
Scariano, M. M. 150
Scarlett, Stephen 80–1
Scott, M. M. 167
Selikowitz, M. 13
Sereny, G. 56
Shah, A. 168
Shepherd, C. 186
Sheridan, C. L. 115
Shermis, S. S. 199
Siegel, L. J. 117, 129, 130, 131
Sigman, M. D. 171
Sinclair, J. 152
Skinner, B. F. 197, 198, 199, 209
Skinner, R. A. 37, 38, 39
Sloat, R. S. 38
Smith, I. 32
Smyth, M. M. 36
Snowling, M. 170
Spencer, J. R. 60, 66, 68, 69, 70, 88
Stahl, L. 171
Steinberg, S. R. 209
Stein, J. 13
Steller, M. 69
Stephenson, G. M. 71, 72, 73
Stern, R. S. 109
Sternberg, K. J. 72, 74
Stern, C. 90
Stern, W. 59, 90
Stevenson, J. 19, 20
Stokols, D. 111
Stone, M. A. 133
Straub, R. O. 130
Suls, J. 117, 135
Szatmari, P. 156

Taddio, A. 126
Tager-Flusberg, H. 164, 165
Talwar, V. 78, 86–7
Tanner, J. M. 107
Tantam, D. 185
Tapert 119, 120
Tapper, K. 109
Tecchio, F. 159
Tharp, R. 213–15
Torgesen, J. K. 44, 46
Travers, R. M. W. 199
Treffert, D. 184
Trevarthen, C. 170
Tucker, C. M. 103

Underwood, G. 220
Underwood, J. 220
Undeutsch, U. 69
Urbas, G. 80

Van Krevelen, D. A. 185
Varendonck, J. 59
Varni, J. W. 126, 127, 128
Vogt, C. J. 107
Volkmar 156, 170, 172
Vrij, A. 69, 85, 87, 88, 90
Vygotsky, L. 210–12, 213, 215

Walmsley, J. 146
Walsh, M. E. 124–5
Wang, Y. 107
Warren-Leubecker, A. 67
Waterhouse, S. W. 151
Wells, G. 220
Wenger, E. 215, 220, 221, 222
Westcott, H. L. 70, 74, 75, 78, 90, 91
Wheldall, K. 198
Whitaker, R. C. 107
Whitehouse, S. 130
White, L. 67
Wight, D. 112, 113
Wilson, J. C. 84
Wing, L. 155, 175, 176–7, 183, 185, 187, 188
Wirtanen, S. 222, 223
Wolff, S. 188
Wolf, M. 13
Wood, D. 198, 199, 212–13
Woodhead, M. 223, 224
Woodruff, G. 173
Woods, W. 14, 30
Woolard, J. 57, 58
Woolfson, R. 67
Woolston, J. L. 107

Yule, W. 14

Zabell, C. 14

Subject index

ABD (atypical brain development)
19
academic attainment
  and operant conditioning 198
  and SpLDs 16, 35
    and depression 38
    and low self-esteem 37–8
    and motivation 39–41
accuracy, and children in the legal
  system 60, 89–90
*Achieving Best Evidence in
  Criminal Proceedings* 70, 74–5
active coping 117
ADHD (attention deficit
  hyperactivity disorder) 13, 32, 43
adolescents
  with dyslexia 38
  and the SHARE programme
    112–13
adversarial system of justice, and
  children in the legal system 66–9,
  88, 90
age of children
  and criminal responsibility 57–8,
    80–9
    and the Thompson and
      Venables case 62
  and legally constructed
    competencies 57
  and understanding of illness
    124–6
  and understanding of truth and
    lies 76–7
American Psychiatric Association
  155
ASDs (autism spectrum disorders)
  155–6, 174, 187–8, 189
Asperger Syndrome 13, 32, 159,
  174, 183
  and the autistic spectrum 187–8,
    189
  diagnosis of 155, 185
asthma
  hospitalization in childhood for
    103, 104
  risk factors in 103–4
attention deficit hyperactivity
  disorder (ADHD) 13, 32, 43
atypical brain development (ABD)
  19

Australia, children and criminal
  responsibility in 80–1
autism 8, 145–89
  autism spectrum disorders
    (ASDs) 155–6, 174, 187–8, 189
  and brain mechanisms 158–9
  causes of 156–8
  change and growth in 152–3
  and communication difficulties
    150, 151
  diagnosis of 154–6
  and Down Syndrome 164–5,
    173, 174, 184
  and dyslexia 170
  and dyspraxia 160, 184
  first-hand accounts of 145,
    146–54, 160
    incorrigibility of 153–4
    and published authors 154
    and science 153
  and high-functioning people
    173–4
  history of ideas on 155, 183–9
    legends and history 183–4
  and inflexibility in thought and
    behaviour 151–2
  integrating insider and outsider
    accounts of 160, 175–7
  'outsider' accounts of 145,
    154–60
  personal perceptions of 146
  prevalence of 156
  and psychoanalysis 185–6
  and psychological research 145
  psychological theories of
    161–74, 177
    central coherence 168–70,
      172
    and early transactions 170–1
    evaluating 172–3
    executive dysfunction 165–8,
      172, 176
    theory of mind 161–5, 166–7,
      170, 171, 172, 173, 174
  and psychology 171–2
  screening for 188
  self-help and advocacy
    organizations 146
  and sensation and movement
    152, 159–60

and social exclusion 150
spectrum of disorders associated
  with 155–6
and stereotypies 152, 153
triad of impairments 155, 159,
  175, 177
see also Asperger Syndrome
Autistic Network International 146

balance, tests of 21, *22*
behavioural difficulties, and
  dyslexia 14
behaviourism
  and eating behaviour in children
    109
  and learning 8, 197–200, 219,
    225
biofeedback, and pain
  management 128–9
biopsychosocial model
  of children's problematic eating
    behaviours 108–9
  of health and illness 105–6, 134
  and preventive intervention 119
blind children, and autism 158
blunting, reducing emotional stress
  by 117
body image, and dieting in
  childhood 108
Body Mass Index (BMI), and
  obesity 107
boys
  and body image 108
  circumcision and experiences of
    pain 126–7
  and sexual identities 113
  and SpLDs 14, 15, 18, 20
brain development, and SpLDs 19,
  20–2, *21*
brain plasticity, and pain 126
brain structure and function, and
  autism 158–9, 172, 174, 186, 188
British Dyslexia Association,
  definition of dyslexia 14–15
British Psychological Society (BPS)
  30, 102
British Society for Autistic Children
  186–7

cancer, and adherence to
  medication 134
central coherence, and autism
  168–70, 172
cerebellum, and SpLDs 20–2, 21
child defendants 7, 55, 56, 91
  and Children's Hearings 68
  and criminal responsibility 57–8,
    80–9
  and *doli incapax* 61, 80–1
  and trial in the Crown Court 61
  and Youth Courts 67
  see also Thompson and
    Venables case; young
    offenders
Children's Depression Inventory 38
Children's Hearings 68
child sexual abuse
  and child witnesses 60, 72
  and deception 87–8, 90
  and different legal systems 69
  and the legal system 55, 56
child witnesses 7, 55, 58, 65–6
  and accuracy 60, 89–90, 91
  and CBCA (criteria-based
    content analysis) 69
  and Children's Hearings 68
  and competency 59–60, 70–9
    children's understanding of
      truth and lies 6, 60, 75–9
    questioning 71–5, 90
  credibility of 90–1
  cross-examination of 66
  and the Crown Court 67
  and deception 85–8, 90
  in Germany 68
  and live (CCTV) links 70
  research on different
    questioning techniques 71–2
  and stress 67
  and SVA (statement validity
    analysis) 69
  and videotaped evidence-in-
    chief 70, 88
chronic illness, and adherence to
  medical treatment 132–3
civil proceedings, and children in
  the legal system 55, 65
classical conditioning 197
cognitive development, and
  children's understanding of illness
  124–6

Cognitive Orientation to daily
  Occupational Performance
  (CO-OP) 43
cognitive processing, and
  assessment for dyslexia 29
cognitive style, and autism 169–70
colour-blindness 20
communication difficulties, and
  autism 150, 151, 160
communities, learning 220–4
communities of practice, and
  situated learning 221–2
competence 7
  and children in the legal system
    8, 56–8, 90–1
    child witnesses 59–60, 70–9
    and the Thompson and
      Venables case 62–3
    and Youth Courts 67
  and children with SpLDs 11–12,
    38
  and psychological accounts of
    learning 224
competency requirement of
  witnesses 58
compliance, and adherence to
  medication 133
computer-based intervention, for
  children with SpLDs 46–7
computers, educational software
  198
condom use, and sex education
  programmes 113
conflict, styles of coping with
  parental conflict 116–17
constructivism 8, 201–9, 219, 225
  evaluating 208–9
  and mathematics teaching 202–5
  and peer interaction in learning
    205–8, 208
Contemporary Treatment Approach
  (CTA), to children with motor
  difficulties 43
contingent instruction 212–13
CO-OP (Cognitive Orientation to
  daily Occupational Performance)
  43
coping strategies
  and adherence to medication
    134
  and children in hospital 131

  and children's responses to
    illness 128
  and stress in childhood 128
comorbidity, and SpLDs 18, 19
CPS *see* Crown Prosecution Service
  (CPS)
criminal proceedings
  and children in the legal system
    55–6, 65–6
  see also child witnesses
criminal psychologists 55–6
criminal responsibility and children
  57–8, 80–9, 91
  and deception 84–8
  and *doli incapax* 80–1
  and psychological theories of
    moral development 81–4
cross-examination
  and adversarial systems of
    justice 66, 67
  of child witnesses 66
Crown Court 61, 64, 66, 67, 91
  and the Thompson and
    Venables case 61, 63, 67, 68
Crown Prosecution Service (CPS)
  62
  and the Thompson and
    Venables case 62–3
culpability 7, 8
  and children in the legal system
    7, 8, 56–8, 90–1
  and the Thompson and
    Venables case 62–3
cultures of learning 220–4
cumulative talk, and learning
  217–18
cystic fibrosis 134

DCD (development co-ordination
  disorder) 38
death
  children's fear of 127
  children's understanding of 124
deception in children, and the legal
  system 84–8, 90–1
deceptive box task, and autism
  163, 163–4
depression
  and children with SpLDs 38–9
  children's understanding of 125
  and hospitalization 129

developmental co-ordination
  disorder (DCD) *see* dyspraxia
'developmental lag', and dyslexia
  24
Developmental Test of Visual–
  Motor Integration (DVMI) 32
diabetes, and adherence to
  medication 134
dieting
    and body image 108
    and the theory of planned
      behaviour 123
discourse, and learning
  communities 221
disputational talk, and learning
  217–18
distal world, and autism 152
doli incapax
    and criminal responsibility 80–1
    and the Thompson and
      Venables case 61
Down Syndrome, and autism
  164–5, 173, 174, 184
drug misuse
    in adolescence 119–20
    in parents 132
drug treatments, for children with
  SpLDs 43
DVMI (Developmental Test of
  Visual–Motor Integration) 32
dyscalculia 13
dysgraphia 13
    assessing young offenders 36–7
dyslexia 7, 12, 13–15
    assessing 23, 24–31
        alternative approach to 30–1
        on the Wechsler Intelligence
          Scale for Children 25–9, *26,
          27*
    and autism 170
    case study 11
    consequences of experiencing
        academic achievement and
          motivation 40–1
        depression 38–9
        low self-esteem 37–8
        social exclusion 35, 36–7
    and comorbidity 18, 19
    definitions of
        British Dyslexia Association
          14–15
        discrepancy 14, 24, 30
        exclusionary 14, 24
    and 'developmental lag' 24

and dyspraxia 31, 32
and heritability 19–20
interventions 42, 44–7
key behavioural characteristics
  of 13–14
prevalence of 14
dyspraxia 7, 12, 13, 15–18
    assessing 23, 31–3
    and autism 160, 184
    case study 16
    consequences of experiencing
        depression 38
        low self-esteem 37
        social exclusion 36
    and comorbidity 18, 19
    effects on academic attainment
      16
    and heritability 19–20
    intervention 42
    key behavioural characteristics
      of 15
    prevalence of 15
    and visual feedback in
      handwriting 16–17

eating behaviour
    dieting and rational behaviour
      123
    influences on eating behaviour
      in childhood 106–9, *107*
ecological model, of health
  psychology 111
ecological validity 72
education 8, 195–225
    and behaviourism 8, 197–200,
      219, 225
    and constructivism 8, 201–9,
      219, 225
    and notions of teaching and
      learning 195–7
    outcomes of 195, 196
    socio-cultural approaches to 8,
      210–20, 225
    see also learning
educational psychologists
    and assessment of dyspraxia 32
    and assessments of dyslexia 24
egocentrism 205
    and Asperger Syndrome 188
    and socio-cognitive conflict
      206–7, 206–8
    and socio-cultural approaches
      to education 210
Electra complex, and moral

development 83
electromyograph (EMG) machines
  128
embedded figures task, and autism
  168–9, *169*
Embedded Phonics program 46
EMG (electromyograph) machines
  128
emotional dimensions of learning
  223
environmental factors, and autism
  157–8
equilibration, and constructivism
  201
ethical concerns in research
    and questioning of child
      witnesses 72
    use of deception 39–40
European Commission of Human
  Rights (ECHR), and the
  Thompson and Venables case 61,
  63
examination-in-chief 66
exclusion *see* social exclusion
executive dysfunction, and autism
  165–8, 172, 176
exercise behaviour in children, and
  the theory of planned behaviour
  122
expert witnesses 55, 56, 59, 60
    in Germany 68
    and the Thompson and
      Venables case 61
exploratory talk, and learning
  217–18
eye contact, and autism 151

facilitators, questioning child
  witnesses 73
false belief tasks, and autism 161–3,
  162, 163, 172
families
    and adherence to medical
      treatment 132
    and the prevention of illness 119
fear, and children's experiences of
  pain 127
focused questions, and child
  witnesses 73
Food Dudes scheme 109
forensic psychology 55–6, 91
free narrative, questioning child
  witnesses 74, 75

galvanic skin response (GSR) biofeedback machines 128
games, and mathematics teaching 204
gender
  and body image 108
  and sexual identities 113
  and SpLDs 14, 18, 20
  see also boys; girls
genetic epistemology 201–2
genetics
  and autism 156–7, 185, 188, 189
  and SpLDs 19–20
    assessing for dyslexia 24, 29
Germany, inquisitorial system of justice in 68
girls
  and body image 108
  and sexual identities 113
  and SpLDs 14, 20
GSR (galvanic skin response) biofeedback machines 128
guided construction of knowledge 215–16, 220

handwriting, visual feedback in 16–17
health belief model of health and illness 105
  and adherence to treatment 132
health professionals
  and adherence to medication 132
  and collaboration 135
health promotion 106–14
  influences on childhood eating behaviour 106–9, 107
  preventing skin cancer 109–11, 110
  sexual health and the social influence approach 111–13
health psychology 8, 101–35
  applications 102
  biopsychosocial model of 105–6, 119, 134
  defining 102
  and drug misuse in adolescence 119–20
  ecological model of 111
  and health advice in childhood 101–2
  health belief model of 105, 132
  and health promotion 106–14

  and health-related behaviour 103–6
    preventive interventions 119–24
  holistic approach to 135
  stress in childhood 114–18
  see also illness
Health Select Committee Report on Obesity 107
heritability, and SpLDs 19–20
high-functioning people, and autism 173–4
homographs, disambiguation of 170
homosocial learning, and sex education 113
hospitalization in childhood 102
  for asthma 103, 104
  improving experience of 129–31
  and stress 118

IA&T (Interactive Assessment and Teaching) reading programme 44–6, 47
identity, and learning 222–3
illness
  biopsychosocial model of 105–6
  and childhood obesity 107
  children's adherence to treatment 131–4
  children's experiences of pain and illness 126–9, 130
    and biofeedback 128–9
    and hospitalization 102, 103, 104, 118, 129–31
    and information about treatments 129
    and social support 127–8
  children's understanding of 123–31
    and cognitive development 124–6
  experiences of childhood 101, 102
  health belief model of 105
  prevention of 119–24
    and social inoculation theory 120–1
    and the theory of planned behaviour 121–3
  and preventive intervention 119
  and stress 115–16
ILS (integrated learning systems) 198

imagination, and autism 176–7
incorrigible accounts of autism 153–4
individual development
  and constructivism 208–9
  socio-cultural approaches to 210–20
infants, in hospital 130–1
inquisitorial system of justice 68–9
integrated learning systems (ILS) 198
intellectual development, and constructivism 209
intelligence
  and autism 156, 189
  and constructivism 201
intelligence quotient (IQ) 12
  and academic achievement and motivation 39–40
  and dyslexia 14
    assessment of 25, 30
Interactive Assessment and Teaching (IA&T) reading programme 44–6, 47
intersubjectivity, and psychological accounts of learning 224
introverted children, and deception 88
Israel, 'youth interrogators' 69

joint attention, and autism 167–8, 170–1, 172, 188
journals, and forensic psychology 56
juries 55, 56
  and the Thompson and Venables case 62, 63, 84
justice, adversarial and inquisitorial systems 66–9

knowledge, guided construction of 215–16, 220

language
  and autism 171
    and cognitive style 170
    mean length of utterance research 164–5
    and pretend play 175
  and learning communities 221
  socio-cultural approaches to learning 210–11

learning
  cultures of 220–4
  and identity 222–3
  nature of 195–7
  psychological accounts of 224
  self-motivated 225
  situated 220, 221–2
  see also education
learning communities 220–4
learning difficulties 146
  and autism 156, 173, 174, 186
  and SpLDs 12
legal cases
  R. versus Turner 55
  R. versus Wallwork 59–60
legal psychologists, and court
  proceedings 55, 56
legal system and children 7–8,
  55–91
  accuracy and honesty of
    children 87–90
  and adversarial and inquisitorial
    systems of law 66–9, 88, 89
  and civil proceedings 55, 65
  and competence 8, 56–8, 90–1
  and the court structure in
    England and Wales 63–4
  and criminal proceedings 55–6,
    65–6
  and criminal responsibility 57–8,
    80–9, 91
  and culpability 7, 8, 56–8, 90–1
  examination-in-chief 66
  and forensic psychology 55–6
  see also child witnesses;
    Thompson and Venables case
legislation
  Children and Young Persons Act
    (1933) 80
  Crime and Disorder Act (1998)
    80
  Criminal Justice Act (1991) 58,
    70
  Criminal Justice and Public
    Order Act (1994) 58
  Sexual Offences Act (1993) 80
  Youth Justice and Criminal
    Evidence Act (1999) 70
lies
  and child witnesses 75–9
  deception in children and
    children responsibility 84–8
  research on children's lie-telling
    behaviour 86–7

lifestyle choices, and health 106
Lindamood Phoneme Sequencing
  Program for Reading, Spelling
  and Speech (LIPS) 46

magistrates' court 64, 65, *68*
magnetic resonance imaging (MRI)
  158
magneto-encephalographic
  measurements (MEG) 159
mathematics teaching, and
  constructivism 202–5
mean length of utterance research,
  and autism 164–5
MEG (magneto-encephalographic
  measurements) 159
*Memorandum of Good Practice on
  Video Recorded Interviews with
  Child Witnesses for Criminal
  Proceedings* 70, 74–5
memory
  and child witnesses 59, 60, 69,
    73, 90
  and SpLDs 18
mental illness, children's
  understanding of 125
microgenetic development, and
  learning 215
migraine, and biofeedback 128–9
moral development
  and children in the legal system
    80–4
    and deception 84–5
    and the Thompson and
      Venables case 63, 80, 84
  psychological theories of 81–4
motivation, and children with
  SpLDs 39–41
motor impairment, and autism
  159–60
motor skills
  assessment of 21, *22*, 32, 33
  cognitive treatment for children
    with motor difficulties 43
movement, and autism 152
Movement Assessment Battery for
  Children (Movement ABC) 32
MRI (magnetic resonance imaging)
  158
Multidimensional Self Concept
  Scale 37–8
multidisciplinary teams, and
  assessment of SpLDs 33

National Autistic Society 187
National Literary Strategy, and
  assessment of dyslexia 30
Netherlands, child protection cases
  69
neuroimaging, and autism 158–9
neuroplasticity 21
neuropsychology, and SpLDs 20–2
neutral coping strategies 117
Nuffield Mathematics Project 202

obesity, and eating behaviour in
  childhood 106–8
occupational therapists, and
  assessment of dyspraxia 32, 33
Oedipus complex, and moral
  development 83
ontogenetic development, and
  learning 215
open questions, and child
  witnesses 73, 79
operant conditioning, and
  education 197–8
operational thinking, and
  education 205–6
option-posing questions, and child
  witnesses 73
organic disorders, and autism 156,
  158

pain
  biofeedback and pain
    management 128–9
  children's experiences of pain
    and illness 126–9
  children's understanding of 125
parents
  and adherence to medication
    134
  and autistic children 157–8,
    185–6, 186–7
  and childhood illnesses 102
  and children in hospital 130–1
  and children with SpLDs
    assessment of 24, 31, 32
    and self-esteem 38
    and social exclusion 35
  and deception in children 88
  and drug misuse in adolescence
    120
  and eating behaviour in children
    107–8
  and the Pool Cool programme
    111

styles of coping with parental conflict 116–17
PCQL (Pediatric Cancer Quality of Life Inventory) 126
PDD *see* pervasive developmental disorders (PDDs)
Pediatric Cancer Quality of Life Inventory (PCQL) 126
peer interaction in learning
    constructivist approaches to 205–8, *208*, 216–18
    and learning communities 220
    socio-cultural approaches to 210
peer pressure, and health-related behaviours 119–20, 121
peer relations, and stress 116
People First 173
perceived behavioural control, and the theory of planned behaviour 121–2
perinatal damage, and autism 156
perseveration, and executive dysfunction 165
pervasive developmental disorders (PDDs), and autism 153, 154–5
phenotypes, and diagnosis of autism 155
phenylketonuria 186
Pool Cool Programme *110*, 110–11
positive relationships, and stress 116
prepotent stimulus, and autism 166, 172
pretend play, and autism 167, 175–7, 188
primary prevention, and health-related behaviours 119, 120
privacy issues, and hospitalization 129–30
proactive coping strategies 117
professional collaboration, and criminal psychologists 56
programmed instruction/learning, and behaviourism 198, 199
proximal world, and autism 152
psychoanalysis, and autism 185–6
psychodynamic theory, of moral development 83
psychogenic disorders, and autism 157–8
psychologists
    as 'agents' of society 7
    and competence 7
    and court proceedings 55

punishment, and deception in children 85

QoL measures, and children's experiences of pain and illness 126
quasi-experiments, and autism 173
questioning child witnesses 71–5, 90
    research on 71–2
    typology of questions 73, 75
Quickscan test for dyslexia 36–7

rapport phase, questioning child witnesses 74, 75
rationality, and the theory of planned behaviour 122, 123
Reader's Interactive Teaching Assistant (RITA) 46, 47
reading
    and dyslexia
        assessment of 25, 29, 30
        case study 11, 40–1
        school-based interventions 44–6
repressive coping 117
resilience
    coping with childhood stress 118
    and hospitalization 131
    and the prevention of drug misuse 120
rewards, and eating behaviour in children 109
Ritalin 43
RITA (Reader's Interactive Teaching Assistant) 46, 47

Sally/Anne task, and autism 161–2, *162*
scaffolding 212, 214
    and classroom practice 215, 219
schizophrenia, and autism 184, 186, 187
school-based interventions, for children with SpLDs 44–7
schools, as communities of practice 221–2
scientific understanding, of autism 153
Scotland, Children's Hearings 68
secondary prevention, and health-related behaviours 119, 120
seeing-leads-to-knowing task, and autism 163–4

self-efficacy, and adherence to medication 133
self-esteem
    and children with SpLDs 35, 37–8
    and SpLDs 35, 37–8
    and stress 116
self-report studies, of children with SpLDs 36
semantic pragmatic disorder 13
sensation, and autism 152, 159
separation anxiety, and hospitalization 129
sexual abuse *see* child sexual abuse
sexual health, social influence approach to 111–13
sexually transmitted diseases, and health promotion 112
SHARE programme (Sexual Health and Relationships) 112–13
Sibelius Academy, Finland, study of learning and identity 222–3
situated learning 220, 221–2, 225
skin cancer, preventing 109–11, *110*
smoking
    and the theory of planned behaviour 121–2
    under-age 120
social cognition models
    and adherence to medical treatment 132, 133–4
    and health-related behaviour 121–2
social exclusion
    and autism 150
    and children with SpLDs 35–7
social inoculation theory, and health-related behaviours 120–1
social learning theory
    and eating behaviour in children 109
    of moral development 83, 84
    and the Pool Cool Programme *110*, 110–11
social support, and children's experience of pain and illness 127–8
social theory of learning 222
socio-cognitive conflict, and egocentrism *206–7*, 206–8
socio-cultural approaches to education 8, 210–20, 225
    and classroom practice 215–19

and contingent instruction 212–13

and scaffolding 212, 214, 215, 219

and teaching as assisted performance 213–15

spelling, and assessment of dyslexia 25, 29, 30

SpLDs (specific learning difficulties) 7, 11–48

  assessment 7, 23–33

  biological bases of 18–23

    and comorbidity 18, 19

    and heritability 19–20

    and neuropsychology 20–2

  and competence 11–12

  consequences of experiencing 34–41

    academic achievement and motivation 39–41

    case study 34–5, 37, 38, 39

    depression 38–9

    and self-esteem 35, 37–8

    social exclusion 35–6

  and individual differences 7

  intervention 42–8

    cognitive training 42–3

    drug treatments 43

    school-based 44–7

    when to intervene 43–4

  intervention programmes 7

  and learning difficulties 12

  range of conditions associated with 12–13

  testing 22

  see also dyslexia; dyspraxia

stage theories

  of moral development 81–2

  of understanding illness 124–6

stereotypies, and autism 152, 153

strategic deception task, and autism 166–7

stress 114–18

  and coping styles 116–18

  and drug misuse in adolescence 120

  sources of 115–16

  stress management programmes 118

  transactional model of 114–15

subjective norms, and the theory of planned behaviour 121, 122, 123

subjectivity, and psychological accounts of learning 224

suggestibility research, and deception 88

suicide

  and children with SpLDs 38

  and drug misuse 119

summary trial 65, 66

superego, and moral development 83

susceptibility, and adherence to medication 133–4

SVA (statement validity analysis) 69

synaptic pruning of brain cells, and autism 158

talk in the classroom, classifying 217–18

teachers

  and children with SpLDs 39–40

    assessments of dyslexia 24

    school-based interventions 44, 47

  and situated learning 222

  and the socio-cultural approach to learning 216, 218–19

teaching 196–7

  as assisted performance 213–15

  and behaviourism 199, 200

  and constructivism 202–5

  and the guided construction of knowledge 215–16

teaching machines, and operant conditioning 198

tertiary prevention, and health-related behaviours 119, 120

theory of mind, and autism 151, 161–5, 166–7, 170, 171, 172, 173, 174

theory of planned behaviour (TPB)

  and adherence to medication 132, 133–4

  and the prevention of illness 121–3

Thinking Together approach

  and learning communities 220

  to classroom intervention work 218–19

Thompson and Venables case 56, 60, 61–3, 67

  and competency and culpability 62–3

  and the Crown Court 61, 63, 67, 68

  and doli incapax 61, 80

  and moral development in children 63, 80, 84

Tower of Hanoi task, and autism 167

TPB see theory of planned behaviour (TPB)

transactional model, of stress 114–15

triangulation

  and research on children with SpLDs 36

  and research on autism 156

truth, and child witnesses 6, 60, 75–9

twin studies

  and autism 156–7

  and SpLDs 20

unexpected transfer task, and autism 161–2, 162

visual feedback in handwriting, and dyspraxia 16–17

Wechsler Intelligence Scale for Children (WISC)

  block design test and autism 168, 168

  and dyslexia 25–9, 26, 27

  and dyspraxia 33

'which one is thinking?' test, and autism 164, 164

Williams Syndrome 174

'windows task', and autism 166

WISC see Wechsler Intelligence Scale for Children (WISC)

Wisconsin Card Sort Test, and autism 167

witnesses

  competency requirement 58

  see also child witnesses; expert witnesses

young offenders

  and criminal psychologists 55, 56

  and moral reasoning 86

  testing for dyslexia 36–7

  see also child defendants

Youth Courts 61, 65, 67–8, 90, 91

ZPD (zone of proximal development) 212, 214–15